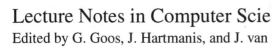

Lecture Notes in Computer Scie

Edited by G. Goos, J. Hartmanis, and J. van

T0237738

Springer
Berlin
Heidelberg
New York
Barcelona
Hong Kong
London
Milan
Paris
Tokyo

Chris Johnson (Ed.)

Interactive Systems

Design, Specification, and Verification

8th International Workshop, DSV-IS 2001
Glasgow, Scotland, UK, June 13-15, 2001
Revised Papers

 Springer

Series Editors

Gerhard Goos, Karlsruhe University, Germany
Juris Hartmanis, Cornell University, NY, USA
Jan van Leeuwen, Utrecht University, The Netherlands

Volume Editor

Chris Johnson
University of Glasgow
Department of Computing Science
Glasgow G12 8QQ, Scotland, UK
E-mail: johnson@dcs.gla.ac.uk

Cataloging-in-Publication Data applied for

Die Deutsche Bibliothek - CIP-Einheitsaufnahme

Interactive systems : design, specification, and verification ; 8th
international workshop ; revised papers / DSV-IS 2001, Glasgow, Scotland,
UK, June 13 - 15, 2001. Chris Johnson (ed.). - Berlin ; Heidelberg ; New
York ; Barcelona ; Hong Kong ; London ; Milan ; Paris ; Tokyo : Springer, 2001
   (Lecture notes in computer science ; Vol. 2220)
   ISBN 3-540-42807-0

CR Subject Classification (1998): H.5.2, H.5, I.3, D.2, F.3

ISSN 0302-9743
ISBN 3-540-42807-0 Springer-Verlag Berlin Heidelberg New York

Springer-Verlag Berlin Heidelberg New York
a member of BertelsmannSpringer Science+Business Media GmbH

http://www.springer.de

© Springer-Verlag Berlin Heidelberg 2001

Typesetting: Camera-ready by author, data conversion by PTP-Berlin, Stefan Sossna
Printed on acid-free paper   SPIN: 10840915   06/3142   5 4 3 2 1 0

Preface
Interface Design in a Period of
Consensus or Chaos?

The relative longevity of the Design, Specification and Verification of Interactive Systems (DSV-IS) workshop series raises a number of questions. After eight meetings, it is important to ask whether our previous work has established any degree of consensus about the core topics and techniques that should be the focus of research in formal and semi-formal aspects of interface design? The reviewing process revealed considerable debate and disagreement about particular papers. Such conflicts were, as usual, resolved by additional reviewing. These disagreements can be interpreted in a number of ways:

1. We have failed to achieve any general agreement about the formal and semi-formal tools and techniques that might support interface design. There may be consensus within specific areas of the DSV-IS community, for example over the benefits of particular temporal modeling notations or constraint-based techniques. However, individuals whose work lies outside those particular areas may still have fundamental concerns about the utility of these approaches.
2. Alternatively, we have achieved some agreement about approaches that support the design of previous generations of interactive systems. However, the changing nature of human computer interaction, including the development of mobile and context aware applications, poses new challenges that these existing techniques cannot easily address.
3. Finally, it can be argued that the lack of concensus is symptomatic of a vibrant research area. Academics continue to question the most basic assumptions of the field in which they work. This spirit of enquiry helps to reveal new insights from future workshops.

The final interpretation in this list could equally be rephrased as 'disagreements reflect the natural tendency of academics to argue at every available opportunity'. Rather than accept this cynical perspective, the following pages provide a brief critical review of the papers in this volume. The intention is to provide the reader with an introduction to some of the themes that will be re-iterated in several papers. The intention is also to determine whether or not this workshop series is creating a consensus or whether disagreements stem from the challenges posed by new forms of human-computer interaction.

There is certainly evidence that this workshop series has helped to build consensus. Many papers explicitly use tools and techniques that were proposed at previous meetings in the DSV-IS series. For instance, de Turnell, Scaico, de Sousa, and Perkusich's paper builds on the work of Palanque and Bastide. The paper in this volume shows how coloured Petri Nets can be used to analyze the navigation facilities that are provided by an industrial control system. The use of coloured nets enables de Turnell et al. to model the undo facilities that have proven to be problematic to previous attempts to use Petri Nets in this area. It is ironic, however, that the concept of 'undo' has only a limited application in the industrial context that they describe. It can be difficult to reverse the chemical reactions that lie at the heart of the process control system they have studied.

Navarre, Palanque, Paternó, Santoro, and Bastide provide further evidence of consensus through the development of techniques that have been proposed in previous workshops. Like de Turnell et al., this work exploits a variant of the Petri Net notation. However, Navarre et al. also use the ConcurTaskTree (CTT) notation to guide the analysis of their interface. This task analysis technique can be used to derive scenarios or sequences of interaction that can help to validate the system model. If a task sequence is not supported then the system model must be refined. Many of the ideas in this paper have been presented at previous meetings. The innovative element here is that Navarre et al. present them in an integrated way and apply them to a range of complex Air Traffic Management case studies.

The issue of consensus is most explicitly addressed in the work of Limbourg, Pribeanu, and Vanderdonckt. They describe the development of the DOLPHIN software architecture that provides a bridge between a vast array of task models. The diversity of these models together with the difficulty of anticipating their potential utility and the problems of moving between different notations can all dissuade designers from exploiting these, typically, semi-formal techniques. Limbourg et al. develop a meta-level model of particular task analytic concepts. This helps to explicitly represent key differences between alternative techniques. It also provides a means of translating between the products of these different approaches. We may not be able to achieve consensus over which task analysis techniques should be used for a particular system. It may, however, be possible to demonstrate consistency between task models developed using rival notations.

Du and England address the weaknesses of previous task analysis techniques in a slightly different manner. They extend the work of Hix and Hartson and of Gray and Johnson that focuses on temporal properties of interaction. Du and England argue that the application of techniques such as XUAN has been hindered by the way in which designers must exhaustively re-specify common interface solutions to similar problems. Du and England, therefore, introduce PUAN, Pattern-based User Action Notation, to capture similar temporal features across many different forms of user interface. The ultimate aim is to "cut down user interface bureaucracy". Of course, it could be argued that Du and England reflect a lack of coherence in the field by deliberately addressing an area that has not been explicitly considered by previous papers in the workshop series. Such an interpretation would, however, contradict the authors' expressed intention to extend rather than contradict previous work in this area.

Du and England's use of 'patterns' reflects the way in which several authors have sought to increase links between work in Human Computer Interaction

(HCI) and Software Engineering. Garrido and Gea provide a further example in their use of UML to describe features of CSCW and cooperative work. UML state diagrams are used to model how actors dynamically change their behavior and influence the behavior of groups of other actors. Doherty, Massink, and Faconti also show how techniques from other areas of Software Engineering can be recruited to represent and reason about particular aspects of interaction. They focus on the use of stochastic process algebras to model the non-determinism that characterizes human interaction with complex systems. There is, however, a strong contract between the work of Garrido and Gea and that of Doherty, Massink, and Faconti. These differences arguably illustrate some of the doubts that arise when attempting to argue for any consensus. For instance, Garrido and Gea aim to model interaction at an extremely high level of abstraction. They focus on the role of individuals and groups within particular working environments. In contrast, Doherty, Massink, and Faconti focus on the motor skill component of particular tracking tasks. It is difficult to envisage how the results from one paper might be used to inform the future work of the other research group. There are also deeper philosophical differences that exist between the use of stochastic and deterministic models to represent and reason about human behavior. It is interesting to note that by modeling low-level tracking behaviors, Doherty, Massink, and Faconti avoid raising many of the more fundamental differences that might have been exposed if they had argued for non-determinism at higher-levels of abstraction.

Philosophical differences about the use of stochastic or deterministic methods is one of several areas in which this year's DSV-IS has raised new challenges to any consensus that may have existed in this area of research. Technological innovation and market change are creating new problems for interface designers. New mobile and context aware devices are creating challenges for task modeling techniques that previously might have assumed a single context of use within an office or home. Luyten and Coninx's paper opens the collection with a proposal for an XML-based runtime user interface description language. The look and feel of an application can be updated using wireless communications. Designers can tailor the interface so that it responds to changes in the user's context or working environment. Mueller, Forbrig, and Cap propose a similar approach. In this case, XML is used to support interface design for mobile applications. The scope of this paper is slightly broader. It presents the TADEUS approach which integrates user, task, and business object models. These models provide important contextual information that can be used to tailor the presentation of information as a user moves within an environment. In contrast, Luytens and Coninx focus more narrowly on user profiling for the layout management of downloadable interfaces.

The impact of technological change can also be seen in Schneider and Cook's Abstract User Interface model and notation. These are intended to help designers improve the plasticity of an interface. The term 'plasticity' refers to the ease with which a particular system might be ported between a range of different devices. This does not simply relate to different renderings for particular widgets on a PC,

Apple Macintosh, or other desktop environment. A highly-plastic interface will adapt to the particular device that a user is operating by actively substituting *different* interface components. On a mobile device, there is often insufficient screen area for a pull-down menu and so an implementation will substitute a scrollable list etc.

The first DSV-IS workshop was held in 1994. At that time, it was difficult to conceive that users might download novel interfaces from remote servers as they move between different locations. Given such technological innovation, it is hardly surprising that the tools and techniques which were proposed in previous meetings might now have to be substantially revised to reflect new and changing technological possibilities. Pribeanu, Limbourg, and Vanderdonckt provide a good illustration of the impact of technological change on previous tools and techniques. They look beyond some of the implementation ideas of Schneider and Cook to explore the problems that arise when attempting to model user tasks for context sensitive applications. This is important because device and communication constraints may prevent users from performing particular tasks in certain environments. They show how the ConcurTaskTree notation might be used to represent different contexts as separate branches of a single, larger task model. Alternatively, separate graphs might be used to model the possible tasks that are available in different contexts. Complexity arises when higher-level tasks are composed of both context sensitive and non-context sensitive sub-tasks. This is an important paper not simply for its technical contribution. It, arguably, provides the best example of how new generations of interactive applications are testing the previous consensus over the utility of particular techniques such as the ConcurTaskTree notation.

Technological innovation is not the only factor that challenges the consensus of previous DSV-IS workshops. There is an increasing awareness of particular social aspects of computing that have, arguably, not been adequately addressed in previous research. Sutcliffe investigates the characteristics that users/customers perceive to influence the success or failure of web pages. His motivation is to derive a set of heuristics that might inform the formative evaluation of a potential design. His analysis is driven not simply by usability but also by elements of marketing and of affective computing. Many of his proposed heuristics, therefore, focus on aspects of the design that arguably affect the subjective experience offered by a particular interface. This is an entirely novel area for DSV-IS. It also challenges some of the traditional attributes, such as consistency, that have been the center for much of the previous work in this series. Aesthetic heuristics, such as the use of 'people and personality' to project a particular image, cannot easily be represented in any of the formal or semi-formal techniques that have been presented at previous workshops. Thimbleby's paper shows how elements of Sutcliffe's analysis might be related to fundamental psychological properties. Rather than simply assessing the surface appeal of an interface, Thimbleby examines whether subjective judgements might be derived from universal concepts such as symmetry. His analysis also suggests that the notion of affordance can be defined in terms of the symmetries that apply under actions that are relevant to the particular tasks that are performed by an object. In this sense, symmetry is not simply related to subjective appeal but also to more basic properties that relate to the context in which the artifact is used. It is a difficult and challenging paper. It only provides an initial sketch of the relationship between generic concepts and their realization within particular interfaces. In contrast to Pribeanu, Limbourg, and Vanderdonckt's paper, relatively little is said about constructive ways of using information about particular tasks in particular contexts. It remains to be seen whether future workshops will be able to forge more coherent links between such diverse contributions.

August 2001   Chris Johnson

Review Committee

Howard Bowman, University of Kent, UK.

Steve Brewster, University of Glasgow, Scotland.

David Duce, Oxford Brookes University, UK.

David Duke, University of Bath, UK.

Nick Graham, Queens University, Canada.

Phil Gray, University of Glasgow, Scotland.

Michael Harrison, University of York, UK.

C. Michael Holloway, NASA Langley Research Centre, USA.

Denis Javaux, Université de Liége, Belgium.

Chris Johnson, University of Glasgow, Scotland.

Peter Johnson, University of Bath, UK.

Dan Olsen, Brigham Young University, USA.

Philippe Palanque, University of Toulouse I, France.

Fabio Paternó, CNUCE-CNR, Italy.

Helen Purchase, University of Queensland, Australia.

Alistair Sutcliffe, UMIST, UK.

Harold Thimbleby, Middlesex Univ., UK.

Jean Vanderdonckt, Université de Louvain, Belgium.

Table of Contents

An XML-Based Runtime User Interface Description Language for Mobile Computing Devices

Kris Luyten and Karin Coninx

Expertise Centre for Digital Media
Limburgs Universitair Centrum
Wetenschapspark 2
B-3590 Diepenbeek-Belgium
{kris.luyten, karin.coninx}@luc.ac.be

Abstract. In a time where mobile computing devices and embedded systems gain importance, too much time is spent to reinventing user interfaces for each new device. To enhance future extensibility and reusability of systems and their user interfaces we propose a runtime user interface description language, which can cope with constraints found in embedded systems and mobile computing devices. XML seems to be a suitable tool to do this, when combined with Java. Following the evolution of Java towards XML, it is logical to introduce the concept applied to mobile computing devices and embedded systems.

1 Introduction

There is a clear evolution from desktop computing towards embedded and mobile computing devices. Users of these devices are not always experts in their usage, and these users must be taken into account as much as possible. This is not an easy task for user interface designers: while facing diverse environments they have to make user interfaces in the same family of products as consistent as possible. A second challenge is to delegate the user interface design for embedded systems to people who have expertise in designing a user interface as opposed to the people who know how to program an embedded system. Most of the time programming for embedded systems requires very specific technical knowledge, e.g. real-time systems. Finally we will have to take into account very heterogeneous user groups who want to use their device in their own specific way. We will explore the possibility of profiling the users to solve this problem.

Consider the following scenario to give an outline of the problem. A university decides to install projectors on the ceiling of every classroom. They will be using the system described in this paper to make the projectors accessible to different members of the teaching staff and maintenance personnel. All of the employees of the university have a PDA device (e.g. a Palm device), which can receive data over an infrared connection. Alternatively, a radio-based Bluetooth link between the PDA and the projector can be used. The PDA will be used as a

C. Johnson (Ed.): DSV-IS 2001, LNCS 2220, pp. 1–15, 2001.
© Springer-Verlag Berlin Heidelberg 2001

remote control for the projector. During the first class of Thursday, professor Wasaname will have to use the projector for her lectures in HCI. She walks into the classroom and transmits her slides, stored on the PDA, to the projector using the infrared connection. Let us assume the projector knows the slide format and can store and project these. After she has finished transmitting the slides she indicates on her PDA she wants to control the projector. Because her user profile is stored on the PDA, it infers she only wants to cruise through the slides, maybe zoom in on some details and make some annotations, but nothing more. She is not interested in configuring the projector settings like changing the resolution or the color settings. Using this knowledge the PDA "asks" the projector to transmit only those parts of its user interface professor Wasaname is interested in. The projector serializes that part of the user interface and passes it to the PDA device, using the infrared connection. The professor can now project the slides using the PDA as a remote control.

During her first class, professor Wasaname notices the bad resolution and brightness of the projector. After her lesson, a member of the maintenance personnel is asked to fix the problem. The diligent responsible man gets right to the classroom and indicates he wants to use the projector. Looking at his profile, the PDA notices this person is mainly interested in the configuration possibilities of the projector, and asks the projector to only transmit that part of the user interface dedicated to that task. Using his PDA the maintenance man adjusts the brightness and resolution of the projector to a satisfying level.

The previous scenario emphasizes how a user interface should be downloadable and adapted to the users' preferences. We can consider this also as a person entering in an environment in which he or she can use several services offered by a networked computing environment, and use it according to the personal interests of this user. This requires a dynamically downloadable interface for interacting with the desired interface. This can be obtained by serializing a user interface for interacting with a particular service, and migrating the parts of interest of that serialized user interface to the user. For serialization of the user interface an appropriate user interface description language can be used. XML is proposed as a user interface description language for the described problem.

Up to now we are not aware of any project combining mobile computing devices and embedded systems with XML and Java in a similar way. Especially the runtime user interface migration provides the user with powerful means to dynamically take advantage from available services. [19] introduced XWeb, for cross-modal interaction. This work proposes a similar approach, but also includes more interactivity possibilities in the user interfaces that are migrated. Other related work on highlighted aspects will be mentioned in the appropriate sections.

The next section takes a look into what a user interface description language containing constraints should support. Then we choose a description language to develop our example. Next, we consider our proposal for converting a user interface *at runtime* to its description in the chosen description language. We continue our description by investigating the possibilities of the opposite conversion: an automatic conversion of the user interface description to a user interface for a particular device taking the defined constraints into account. Finally we propose the usage of profiling to reduce the complexity of the problem.

2 Describing User Interfaces Subject to Constraints

As mentioned above, an embedded system or mobile computing device is subject to several constraints, which we generally are not facing with desktop computers. We can divide these constraints in two categories:

Static constraints : these are constraints which are not likely to change over time, mostly dependent on our bodily functions. E.g. a very small screen may have a very high resolution, but our eyes will only allow a certain maximal visual capacity. Another example is the number of buttons a device contains: a certain minimal area for the buttons is required if we want to be able to manipulate them with our fingers.

Evolving constraints : these are constraints on memory usage, bandwidth, processor speed, etc. Constraints of this kind are likely to change over time and may possibly disappear. To come to a practical proposition for the envisioned systems they should also be included in this discussion.

Our goal is to use a user interface description language which is suitable for a wide range of embedded and mobile computing devices, working in heterogeneous environments, and utilize it at runtime. The example in the introduction shows what kind of problems can be solved using such a description language. Certainly in the case of extensibility of a networked system, integrating new kinds of devices, it will be easier to control the evolution of the system. This can be done without having to cope with inconsistencies in the user interface and interaction methods. We find it also important for the user interface description language to be suitable for design-time usage, providing the designer with a powerful tool to build platform independent and even device independent user interfaces taking constraints in account. Designing a user interface, while taking into account different user groups, is already an extensively explored research domain [24]. Unfortunately, current approaches are either not general enough for embedded systems, do not take the resource limitations of embedded systems into account or do not care about changing environments. Without providing details, we mention some approaches in UIDLs (User Interface Description Languages) [4,20,24]: language-based, grammar-based e.g. BNF, based on state transition diagrams, declarative (e.g. declarative descriptions of application data types), event-based, constraint-based, UAN (User Action Notation, in particular for direct manipulation) and widget-based. Because of the evolving market towards mobile computing devices and embedded systems, a more general approach for describing a user interface for an embedded system or mobile computing device is necessary. In search of a notation for describing such a user interface it should satisfy the following requirements:

Platform independent : because of the heterogeneity of embedded systems, a user interface designer should be allowed to design without having to worry about the system on which the interface will be used. Of course there are certain restrictions to this, which we will discuss further on in this text

Declarative : describing a user interface asks for a certain level of expressiveness for describing human-computer interaction

Consistent : the notation should offer consistency of the user interface among different environments and systems [22]

Unconventional I/O : embedded and mobile computing devices are less conservative in input and output devices. For example: while "normal" desktop computers have a mouse and a keyboard, this is not a requirement for a mobile device, which could very well have a touch-screen and speech recognition

Rapid prototyping : in a highly competitive market, such as mobile devices, developers and designers want to tailor the software towards the users or user groups. A user interface notation should allow rapid prototyping to get the users involved in the development process sooner

Constraint sensitive : because of the constraints embedded systems are coping with, the designers must be able to specify the constraints, or have the system automatically generate them

Easily extensible : we want to extend our user interface with extra functionality, without starting from scratch

Reusability : when a family of products is evolving, we want to reuse the design for the old devices in an optimal way

Notice these are not style guidelines, but rather structure guidelines. It is the designer's responsibility to follow style guidelines as defined in [17] for example.

The demand for a notation enabling the designer to describe constraints for a computing system is an important part of our user interface description language. A constraint can be described as a cost function in which the cost must be limited or kept within an interval for example. Existing specification languages designed for embedded systems use finite-state machines or message sequence charts to represent constraints like this.

3   Choosing a Descriptive Language for UI Design

The previous section listed several properties the user interface description language should have. Instead of creating a new kind of description language, we propose the usage of the eXtensible Markup Language (XML) for describing a user interface. This description language can offer us the properties we want:

Platform independent : XML is platform independent in the same sense that Java is platform independent: if there is an XML parser available on the system, the XML description can be used. If there is no suitable XML parser available for your target platform, XML is so simple that writing your own parser is fairly easy

Declarative : through the usage of XSL[1] [7] XML can be declarative. XSL specifies a stylesheet which is applied to an XML document, and offers powerful transformations on the XML document

Consistent : through the usage of DTD[2] XML can be consistent. A DTD specifies a set of rules for the XML file to follow

Unconventional I/O : XML can describe unconventional I/O: there are plenty of examples to provide evidence: WML [7], SpeechML [5], VoxML [6], etc.

Rapid prototyping : using a stylesheet you can see the results immediately in a browser

Constraint definitions : XML can contain constraint definitions; as well for the form of the XML itself, as for external resources we can add constraint definitions

Easily extensible : because XML is a metalanguage it is by nature an extensible language

Reusability : it is relatively easy to fit an existing piece of XML into another

There is another advantage not addressed in the previous paragraph: because of the simple grammar and structure of XML it is an intuitive markup language. User interface designers do not need a firm technical background to work with XML. Also, it is easy to convert an XML description to different kinds of output presentation using XSLT[3]. Using XSLT, XML can be converted into HTML+CSS[4] for desktop browsers, VoxML for speech driven input or into WML for mobile phones [16]. However, we have to realize that XSLT is no silver bullet for transforming an XML user interface description into different shapes.

This is not the first time XML is proposed to be used as a user interface description language [1,9,11,15]. [9] is aimed for mobile computing devices, while [1,11] are implementations for the desktop computer using Java user interfaces. While most of these description languages only work at design time, we would like to propose an architecture for *runtime* serialization of Java user interfaces into an XML description, inspired by migratory applications [3] and remote user interface software environments [12]. This would enable us to "download" a user interface together with constraints and necessary transformations, which will be discussed in section 4.2. Our description language should serve two purposes: adaptation and plasticity of user interfaces like introduced in [27]. While enabling us to tailor the user interface for particular devices and particular users (adaptation) it should take the defined constraints into account while preserving usability (plasticity). Our proposition will focus on dynamic plasticity.

Having summarized the benefits of using XML as a user interface description language, it remains an open issue how the user interface will be presented in the XML file, including the constraint definitions. Looking at figure 1, we see that a user interface can be structured as a tree, which is the basic structure of an XML file. We have a main window in which the user interface building blocks like

---

[1] eXtensible Stylesheet Language
[2] Document Type Definition
[3] eXtensible Stylesheet Language Transformations
[4] Cascading Stylesheets: a stylesheet for an HTML document

buttons, sliders, etc. are laid out. In the main window we can have other windows containing building blocks, which in turn can be windows. It is advisable to make an abstraction here, like the proposed distinction into abstract interaction objects (AIO) and concrete interaction objects (CIO) [28], presented in figure 1, or to use abstract widgets [10]. An AIO represents an abstract interface widget, independent of any platform. A CIO is a possible "implementation" for such an AIO. Using these concepts allows abstracting the user interface independent of the target platform. Abstract widgets represent practically the same thing: they are abstract platform independent representations of platform dependent widgets. If we want to add runtime layout management taking into account constraints defined by the environment, we will have to dynamically change the presentation of an AIO. This can happen due to screen size limitations for example. [9] tries to solve this problem at design time using an intelligent agent (a mediator) for laying out UI components. For mobile devices this seems too much focused on actual screen-output, because no unconventional output device is taken into account. There might be an embedded system or computing device that has no screen at all, and has only some buttons and speech interaction for example. Then the on-screen data could be converted into a spoken dialog either way. Assuming speech interaction can be stored in XML, we follow the same tree-structure for a speech-enabled dialog as we did for the windows. A full description of conversion to speech interaction is beyond the scope of this paper. We are aware that it is not reasonable to say we can construct complex speech driven dialogs using a runtime conversion technique at this time.

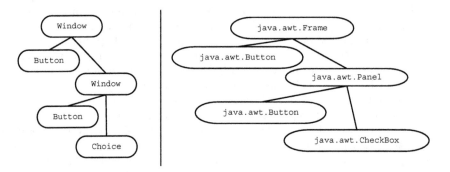

Fig. 1. On the left a contextual representation (AIO), on the right the java.awt classes used to represent the presentation (CIO)

4   Using XML at Runtime

4.1   Runtime User Interface Conversion

As opposed to most modeling approaches, this approach goes one step further: runtime conversion from user interfaces to a user interface description language,

XML in this case. In our current approach we have implemented a conversion mechanism for Java user interfaces. There are two well-known user interface toolkits in Java: the oldest one; AWT[5] and a newer and more consistent one: Swing; a subset of the Java Foundation Classes. Because Swing is still too big for most systems with low resources like limited storage capacity and RAM, our implementation is focused on AWT. Using the *Java Reflection Mechanism* all the inspector methods, starting with the prefix **get** are retrieved, and their return values are stored in the XML tree. An advantage of this approach is that not only a user interface can be serialized this way, but all kinds of objects where the state can be retrieved using their inspectors can be serialized. To work with AWT, some ad hoc solutions are required, avoiding unnecessary overhead and circular references. For example, not all inspector methods starting with the prefix **get** are relevant and give useful data. A collection of possible general CIOs is defined, and the matched AWT classes for these CIOs are mapped onto the defined CIO tag names. This process is presented in a simple manner in figure 2. This way the XML description of the user interface preserves the state and stays general enough for converting the XML description into another toolkit like Swing.

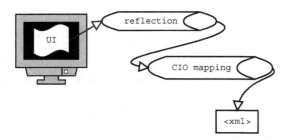

Fig. 2. Serializing a user interface into its XML description

The current implementation supports a serialization of the Java user interface (AWT or Swing) into XML, filtering out the unimportant properties. We presume a user interface can always be hierarchically structured. Our implementation takes advantage of this tree-based structure to recursively descend into the tree, adding widgets to the user interface corresponding to the nodes in the tree and pruning the unwanted branches. A parent node is a widget container for its children this way. For now, we limit the user interface being composed out of JavaBeans, because these have a consistent structure.

Our general approach lacks an important issue: optimizing bandwidth. To optimize the dataflow from source to target, it is a good idea to reduce the size of the XML description. There is a trade-off between several aspects like energy, functionality and time constraints (or performance) [8]. This is why we need to

---

[5] *Abstract Windowing Toolkit*

avoid storing redundant or unnecessary data in the user interface description. The method of serializing a Java user interface as presented in the previous paragraph is not smart enough. It needs to make a decision of which data is relevant for the user interface serialization, and which data is not. We have to keep in mind that besides state information and CIOs, constraints must be inserted in the description as well as additional information for layout management, (remote) event handling and type information.

A description of constraints is related to the device it describes. This description should be readable by our system, so it can take decisions how to adapt the transported user interface fulfilling the required constraints. We want the system to be as extensible as possible, so future devices can be easily "plugged in" the existing framework. To accomplish this the description should be as general as possible. It can be described using XML as follows:

```
<Device>
   <Out class="screen">
      <Constraint type="size" data="30*30"/>
      <Constraint type="color" data="8"/>
   </Out>
</Device>
```

This is just a simple example serving the purpose of illustrating the concept; the same can be done for other aspects of IO devices. There are other, more functional and algebraic methods for describing physical devices, but these methods are not further investigated here. At the moment only screen size constraints are taken into account.

Another disadvantage of this approach is the lack of support for other programming languages. In one direction, conversion from XML to an actual user interface, this can be solved easily depending on the maturity of the user interface toolkit, which is targeted. Unlike Java, most other programming languages have no class reflection mechanism, and are much harder to interrogate for their structures at runtime. A conversion from a user interface to its XML description without dedicated data to ease this conversion is rather hard to accomplish. This may imply the need for a supporting framework for XML conversion, inserted into the toolkits built on these programming languages. An example of such a runtime XML conversion of the interface presented in figure 3 is given in the next listing:

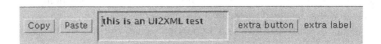

Fig. 3. A user interface example

```
<Application NAME="test.testUI">
<Property NAME="title">this is an UI2XMLtest</Property>
<Property NAME="name">main-window</Property>
<Properties>
 <Property NAME="copyButton">
   <AIO CLASS="Button">
      <Properties>
         <Property NAME="name">button0</Property>
         <Property NAME="actionCommand">Copy</Property>
         <Property NAME="label">Copy</Property>
      </Properties>
   </AIO>
 </Property>
 <Property NAME="pasteButton">
    <AIO CLASS="Button">
      <Properties>
        <Property NAME="name">button1</Property>
        <Property NAME="actionCommand">Paste</Property>
        <Property NAME="label">Paste</Property>
      </Properties>
    </AIO>
 </Property>
 <Property NAME="textField">
    <AIO CLASS="TextField">
      <Properties>
        <Property NAME="name">textfield0</Property>
        <Property NAME="selectionEnd">0</Property>
        <Property NAME="columns">20</Property>
        <Property NAME="selectionStart">0</Property>
        <Property NAME="selectedText"></Property>

...

      <Property NAME="extraLabel">
  <AIO CLASS="Label">
    <Properties>
       <Property NAME="name">label0</Property>
       <Property NAME="alignment">0</Property>
       <Property NAME="text">extra label</Property>
    </Properties>
  </AIO>
 </Property>
</Properties>
</Application>
```

The listing is kept simple for illustrating purposes. It illustrates how the user interface shown in figure 3 is converted into an XML description. For the buttons, the command to be used when they are pushed is also included in the XML description.

Besides just serializing the properties of the user interface, there must be an indication of which services can be accessed by the user interface, and how these services are connected to the user interface. In fact, we need to connect the services presented by the user interface into actions in the code. There are several ways for doing this: sending the corresponding classes to the remote virtual machine, but this occupies more bandwidth and memory space. A second solution is using a facade that accepts the events and transmits them using a socket connection. Finally, we can use remote method invocation, which connect the events immediately to the remote services. Currently we are investigating the third alternative: using Remote Method Invocation.

4.2   Downloading the User Interface

Now that the user interface is enabled to produce its XML description, we can move the description to another device, where it can be "deserialized" into a user interface for the target device, as presented in figure 4. This deserialization involves mapping the platform independent AIOs on platform specific CIOs. The subsystem responsible for the deserialization has to have sufficient knowledge of the user interface widgets available for the target platform. Notice the scenario in the introduction illustrated this: the persons could use their PDA to retrieve a user interface for operating the projector with. Notice that the structure of the user interface has to stay the same, because the XML file defines it. XML gives us another advantage; it describes the structure but not the look of the program. We can use a kind of stylesheet to adapt the look to a platform. For example, it should be possible to operate the projector by downloading its user interface and using a web browser on a web pad to interact with this user interface.

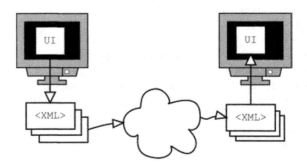

Fig. 4. Downloading a Remote User Interface

Once the user interface is set up on the target platform, it has to be fully functional. This requires a kind of remote event handling, like RPC. [12] already proposes a remote user-interface software environment (RUSE) using RPC and a Scheme interpreter. Nowadays there are more flexible architectures possible for this purpose. From a software developer point of view, Java is a perfectly suitable tool to overcome this problem. Java makes it possible to download the code (e.g. applets), make your own Classloaders and use Remote Method Invocation [13, 25,26]. The only requirements left are a Java Virtual Machine on the device and network capabilities.

5   User Profiling for Semi-automatic Layout Management

In the introductory story we have mentioned the use of profiling in function of the part of the user interface, which is downloaded. The scope of this paper is not to investigate profiling of users in depth, only to engage it as a possible tool for a better support for "downloadable" user interfaces and meeting the user's demands. To use profiling, the machine (embedded system, mobile computing device, desktop computer, airplane, cell phone, etc.) has to know who is operating it. This can be very clear, PDAs for example are usually limited to a single user, but in other situations (like a workstation) this requires an identification procedure.

Once the system knows who will be the user of the user interface, it knows which functionality the particular user is most interested in. This is an issue to handle with care: of course the system has to take into account changing preferences of the user. In our scenario, the maintenance man is mostly interested in configuring the projector, but possibly this person wants to test a new configuration by projecting some slides. This is functionality for which there was no indication in the profile, but still must be available to the user.

Making use of a profile can reduce the user interface to be migrated. When using an automatic layout agent this information can also be used to present the user interface in a way it is most suitable to the user. While dealing with certain constraints the profile can help making decisions about omitting a certain subset of the user interface. [9] proposes the generation of an appropriate presentation structure using Logical Windows and Presentation Units where Logical windows group AIOs and Presentation Units group Logical Windows. Using redesign strategies a particular presentation model is composed at design-time. Algorithms for automatic layout management are investigated in [19,14,2]. Combining the user profile with target platform specific constraints could ease the presentation modeling which has to be done at runtime. It certainly can reduce the complexity of possible presentation compositions. Besides this problem, the system should be enabled to switch from interaction modes at runtime. [10] proposes a designing interface toolkit using abstract widgets for dynamically selecting the interface modality for this purpose.

We propose XSL for describing the user profile. Using the XSLT it is possible to filter out the interested parts for the user. We can make an XSL, which describes the kind of functionality the user is interested in. Letting the XSLT work on a XML structure results in another XML structure only showing the contents of those parts the particular user is interested in. An important part of this conversion is only selecting the relevant paths in the XML user description. This can be done using XPath: an implementation to locate particular branches in the logical tree XML presents. Using an XSL structure we filter out the appropriate section out of the XML description of the user interface. Such an XSL structure can be made by hand, or by monitoring the user's action by an agent, which automatically generates a profile. XSL has declarative properties, which allows us to easily describe what we want, rather than how it has be done. The following simplified example gives an idea of how an XSL structure for the projector user interface introduced in the example in the introduction could look like. It simply specifies it is only interested in properties related to "configuration". When it encounters a configuration property it will call another template making the appropriate actions to preserve that part. We can extend the list of interested parts (by hand or automatically) and create a template for each of them, which will preserve the necessary parts. Notice an XSL structure is also an XML structure [16].

```
<xsl:template match="/">

  <xsl:for-each select="./Property">
    <xsl:if test="contains(Property/@NAME,'configuration')"
      <xsl:apply-template select="./Property"/>
    </xsl:if>
  </xsl:for-each>
</xsl:template>

<xsl:template match="Property">
  ...
</xsl:template>
```

6   Connections

The eight Workshop of *Design, Specification and Verification of Interactive Systems* (DSVIS 2001) provided an excellent opportunity to situate this work in the current research for the specification of user interfaces. [18] indicates the usage of markup languages and provides a sufficient level of abstraction to describe user interfaces in a device independent way. Besides the usage of a model-based approach, it also defines a framework for describing user interfaces in an model-based way. We like to think this works complements the work presented in this paper as it lays out a framework for user interface descriptions using XML.

We also mentioned plasticity in this paper as one of the important properties of a runtime user interface description language. [23] provides a detailed description of how to reach a certain level of plasticity by providing an abstraction of the user interface. Unfortunately the approach taken here is not very suitable for embedded systems and mobile computing devices, but the idea of abstracting the user interface with rich semantic feedback is certainly one of the ideas we also want to introduce in our work for improving the plasticity.

While this work focuses on the runtime serialization and deserialization of user interfaces to make it migratable between different devices and platforms, it does not consider the context in which it will be provided. Whereas there is a distinction between the abstraction of the user interface and the concrete interactors presenting the abstract user interface, the task model is not considered. [21] gives a solution for this: the design of context-sensitive user interfaces. Our work is situated in the last stage; a working user interface, and [21] "extends" the first stage: the creation of a context sensitive model. Our work could be easily combined with the topic presented in [21] because both use a Markup Language (XML) to describe the resulting user interface in a generic way.

7   Conclusions and Future Work

In this paper we have presented a runtime user interface description language, which can cope with constraints found in embedded systems and mobile computing devices. XML seems to be a suitable tool to do this, certainly when it is combined with Java. The usage of XML to generate a user interface description at runtime implies an automatic conversion. Using abstract widgets this can be done in a generic way. To target mobile devices and embedded systems the user interface description has to take the constraints of those particular systems into account. This means the conversion from the user interface description in XML to a system dependent user interface results in a consistent user interface subject to the constraints of the current platform. Users indicate their particular interest in some functionality of a service, by providing a profile (possibly automatically generated).

Future implementations should allow storing more information in the user interface description language (XML in this case). To avoid overhead and waste of bandwidth the description should eliminate redundancy, keeping the user interface description as consistent as possible. Care has to be taken to allow the designer to generate the XML code for the User Interface, without having to build the user interface (as opposed to the runtime method), and choose to generate a specific implementation for it. For getting the actual functionality to migrate with the user interface, a framework for remote event handling has to be provided using RMI[6] or sockets for example.

Acknowledgements. Our research is partly funded by the Flemish government and EFRO (European Fund for Regional Development). The SEESCOA[7] project IWT 980374 is directly funded by the IWT (Flemish subsidy organization).

---

[6] Remote Method Invocation

[7] *Software Engineering for Embedded Systems using a Component-Oriented Approach*;
http://www.cs.kuleuven.ac.be/cwis/research/distrinet/projects/SEESCOA/

References

1. Marc Abrams, Constantinos Phanouriou, Alan L. Batongbacal, Stephen M. Williams, and Jonathan E. Shuster. *UIML: An Appliance-Independent XML User Interface Language.* World Wide Web,
   `http://www8.org/w8-papers/5b-hypertext-media/uiml/uiml.html`, 1998.
2. Blaine A. Bell and Steven K. Feiner. Dynamic space management for user interfaces. In *Proceedings of the 13th Annual Symposium on User Interface Software and Technology (UIST-00)*, pages 239–248, N.Y., November 5–8 2000. ACM Press.
3. K. Bharat and L. Cardelli. Migratory applications. In *Eighth ACM Symposium on User Interface Software and Technology*, pages 133–42, 1995.
4. Keith A. Butler, Robert J.K. Jacob, and Jennifer Preece. *CHI 2000 tutorial notes: HCI: Introduction and overview.* ACM, 2000.
5. Robin Cover. *SpeechML.* World Wide Web,
   `http://www.oasis-open.org/cover/speechML.html`, 1999.
6. Robin Cover. *VoxML Markup Language.* World Wide Web,
   `http://www.oasis-open.org/cover/voxML.html`, 2001.
7. Robin Cover. *WAP Wireless Markup Language Specification (WML).* World Wide Web, `http://www.oasis-open.org/cover/wap-wml.html`, 2001.
8. Maria R. Ebling and M. Satyanarayanan. On the Importance of Translucence for Mobile Computing. In C.W. Johnson (ed.), *Proceedings of First Workshop on Human-Computer Interaction for Mobile Devices*, Technical report, University of Glasgow, Scotland, pages 69–72, 1998.
9. Jacob Eisenstein, Jean Vanderdonckt, and Angel Puerta. Applying Model-Based Techniques to the Development of UIs for Mobile Computers. In *IUI 2001 International Conference on Intelligent User Interfaces*, pages 69–76, 2001.
10. Shiro Kawai, Hitoshi Adai, and Tadao Saito. Designing Interface Toolkit with Dynamic Selectable Modality. In *Proceedings of the second annual ACM conference on Assistive technologies*, pages 72–79, 1996.
11. Thierry Kormann. *The Koala User Interface Language.* World Wide Web,
    `http://www-sop.inria.fr/koala/kuil/`, 2000.
12. J. Landay and T. Kaufmann. User Interface Issues in Mobile Computing. In *Fourth Workshop on Workstation Operating Systems, Napa, CA*, 1993.
13. Sheng Liang and Gilad Bracha. Dynamic class loading in the Java virtual machine. In *ACM SIGPLAN Conference on Object-Oriented Programming, Systems, Languages and Applications (OOPSLA'98)*, pages 36–44, 1998.
14. Mark A. Linton, John M. Vlissides, and Paul R. Calder. Composing User Interfaces With InterViews. *IEEE Computer*, 22(2), Febuary 1989.
15. Kris Luyten, Karin Coninx, Jan Van den Bergh, and Jos Segers. Software engineering for embedded systems using a component oriented approach; deliverable 4.2: Implementation of a component based user interface, seescoa confidential. Technical report, Expertisecentrum Digitale Media; Limburgs Universitair Centrum, 2001.
16. Didier Martin, Mark Birbeck, Michael Kay, Brian Loesgen, Jon Pinnock, Steven Livingstone, Peter Stark, Kevin Williams, Richard Anderson, Stephen Mohr, David Baliles, Bruce Peat, and Nikola Ozu. *Professional XML.* Wrox Press, 2000.
17. Sun Microsystems. From desktop to consumer devices; the applet writer's style guide. Technical Report 408-343-1400, Sun Microsystems, JavaSoft, 2550 Garcia Avenue, Mountain View, CA 94043 U.S.A., December 1997.

18. Andreas Müller, Peter Forbrig, and Clemens Cap. Model-Based User Interface Design Using Markup Concepts. In C.W. Johnson (ed.) *Proceedings of the Eight Workshop of Design, Specification and Verification of Interactive Systems*, pages 30–39, June 2001.

19. Dan R. Olsen, Sean Jefferies, Travis Nielsen, William Moyes, and Paul Fredrickson. Cross-modal interaction using XWeb. In *Proceedings of the 13th Annual Symposium on User Interface Software and Technology (UIST-00)*, pages 191–200, N.Y., November 5–8 2000. ACM Press.

20. Fabio Paterno. *Model-Based Design and Evaluation of Interactive Applications.* Springer, 2000.

21. Costin Pribeanu, Quentin Limbourg, and Jean Vanderdonckt. Task Modelling for Context-Sensitive User Interfaces. In C.W. Johnson (ed.) *Proceedings of the Eight Workshop of Design, Specification and Verification of Interactive Systems*, pages 60–76, June 2001.

22. Pekka Savolainen and Hannu Konttinen. A Framework for management of sophisticated User Interface's Variants in Design Proces. In Jean Vanderdonckt and Angel Puerta, editors, *Computer-Aided Design of User Interfaces II*, pages 205–215. Kluwer Academic Publishers, 1999.

23. Kevin A. Schneider and James R. Cordy. Abstract User Interfaces: A Model and Notation to support plasticity in Interactive Systems. In C.W. Johnson (ed.) *Proceedings of the Eight Workshop of Design, Specification and Verification of Interactive Systems*, pages 40–58, June 2001.

24. Ben Schneiderman. *Designing the User Interface, third edition.* Addison Wesley, 1998.

25. Frank Sommers. *Object mobility in the Jini environment.* World Wide Web, http://www.javaworld.com/javaworld/jw-01-2001/jw-0105-jiniology.html, january 2001.

26. Sun Microsystems. *Java Remote Method Invocation.* World Wide Web, http://java.sun.com/products/jdk/rmi/, 1997.

27. David Thevenin and Joelle Coutaz. Adaptation and Plasticity of User Interfaces. In *Workshop on Adaptive Design of Interactive Multimedia Presentations for Mobile Users*, 1999.

28. J. Vanderdonckt and F. Bodart. Encapsulating knowledge for intelligent automatic interaction objects selection. In *ACM Conference on Human Aspects in Computing Systems InterCHI'93*, pages 424–429. Addison Wesley, 1993.

Model-Based User Interface Design Using Markup Concepts

Andreas Mueller, Peter Forbrig, and Clemens Cap

University of Rostock
Department of Computer Science
Albert-Einstein-Str. 21, 18051 Rostock, Germany
xray@informatik.uni-rostock.de

Abstract. In the field of model-based development of interactive systems, several approaches have been proposed to integrate task and object knowledge into the development process and its underlying representations. This paper follows such an approach with a special focus on mobile devices. It presents a concept of device independent user interface design based on the XML-technology. The concept is applied to an e-commerce example.

1 Motivation

Modern information and communication systems have to present their application logic on different devices with different capabilities. A banking software should for instance provide a HTML[1]-based user interface for a web-based usage of the service as well as WAP[2]-based mobile communication service. It should also be possible to use the system by special automata (bancomat) usually installed in the buildings of a bank.

Our model-based approach TADEUS [ElSc95] is based on user, task and business-object models. It allows the computer based development of interactive systems. The three models are the basis for the development of the application logic and the user interface design. Figure1 represents the main relations between different models.

This approach allows a reuse of the designed models apart from final representations. To have a flexible development process from an abstract interaction model to a specific representation there was the idea to use the XML[3] technology [Gold99] for representation and transformation features.

---

[1] **HTML** - Hypertext Markup Language
[2] **WAP** - Wireless Application Protocol – http://www.wapforum.org/
[3] **XML** - Extensible Markup Language – http://www.w3.org/XML

C. Johnson (Ed.): DSV-IS 2001, LNCS 2220, pp. 16–27, 2001.

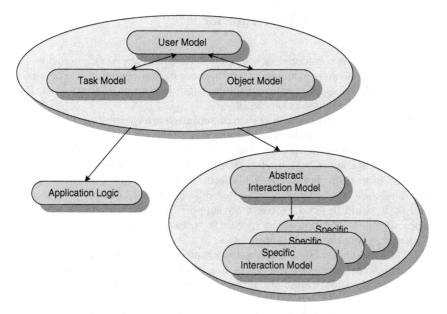

Fig. 1. Model-based User Interface Design

2   Related Work in Specifying User Interfaces by XML

There are already some approaches to specify user interfaces by markup languages. There is for instance UIML[4][Abra99] a XML-based language for describing user interfaces. It comes with different rendering programs allowing the generation of user interfaces on different platforms. Up to now the generation for WML, Java.AWT and swing is available.

A special renderer for each target-device is needed. This is an important disadvantage. The flexibility for selecting target-device features is limited because of a lack of a mapping concept.

XUL[5] has its focus on window-based graphical user interfaces by XML. Its disadvantage is the limitation to such graphical user interfaces. It is not applicable to interfaces of small mobile devices.

There is no abstraction of interaction functionality available. The device-independent specification of user interfaces was not planned.

---

[4] **UIML** - User Interface Markup Language – http://www.uiml.org
[5] **XUL** - XML-based User Interface Language – http://www3.sympatico.ca/ndeakin/ mozilla/xultu/

3   Specification of User Interfaces

A user interface is considered as a simplified version of the MVC[6] model and is separated into a model component and a presentation component. The model component describes the feature of the user interface on an abstract level. It is also called abstract interaction model.

The user-interface objects with their representation are specified in the presentation component. During the development a mapping transforming the abstract interaction model to the specific interaction model is necessary. TADEUS uses a term representation of both models. The transformation process is described by attribute grammars. For different platforms different grammars are necessary. The development of such grammars for different mobile devices is time consuming. It would be good to have more support for the transformation process. Especially the integration of the specific features of different devices is difficult. A general support would be appreciated.

The XML technology offers such an opportunity. It allows the description of the abstract interaction model, the description of specific characteristics of different devices and the specification of the transformation process, which will be shown later.

User, tasks and object models are a good starting point for developing a user interface but it is not necessary to specify them explicitly.

Let us first have a look at a model of the transformation process forming an abstract interaction model to a specific user interface:

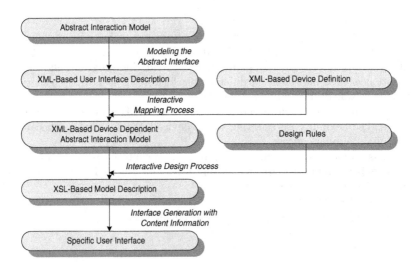

Fig. 2. Creation of a User Interface

---

[6] **MVC** - Model View Controller

Following requirements should be fulfilled by a markup language for specifying user interfaces:

- device independence,
- flexibility on representing user interfaces depending on the contexts,
- ability to specify virtual and physical [Muel01] user interfaces,
- localisation,
- extensibility of abstractions (abstract UIO's describing interaction behaviour),
- extensibility of concrete UIO's (UIO's of specific representations).

The following paragraphs will show a specific way of using XML in the proposed manner. The example of an e-shop will be used to demonstrate the principles of this approach. The transformation from an abstract specification to a concrete user interfaces will be shown. If the reader wants to get a visual impression of the shop he may have a look at the example in figure 3.

3.1   XML-Based Abstract Interaction Model

The abstract interaction model is transformed into a notation which is based on a language of the XML family. The document type definition (DTD[7]) of our approach has the following form:

```
<?xml version="1.0" encoding="ISO-8859-1"?>
          <!--MARK 1 -->
<!ELEMENT ui (uio+, context*)>
   <!ATTLIST ui
   ui_name CDATA #REQUIRED>
<!ELEMENT uio (uio | ((output+, context*)* , (input+, context*)*))>
   <!ATTLIST uio
   name CDATA #REQUIRED>
          <!--MARK 2 -->
<!ELEMENT context (context_value+)>
<!ELEMENT context_value (#PCDATA)>
<!ELEMENT output ((output_string | output_1-n | output_m-n | output_table), context*,
          optional?)>
   <!ATTLIST output
   name CDATA #REQUIRED> .   .   .   .
<!ELEMENT output_table (#PCDATA)>
   <!ATTLIST output_table
   num_x CDATA #IMPLIED
   num_y CDATA #IMPLIED>
<!ELEMENT input ((input_1-n | input_m-n | input_trigger | input_string | input_table),
          context*, optional?)>
   <!ATTLIST input
   name CDATA #REQUIRED>
          <!--MARK 3 -->
<!ELEMENT input_1-n (#PCDATA)>
   <!ATTLIST input_1-n
   range_min CDATA #IMPLIED
   range_max CDATA #IMPLIED
   range_interval CDATA #IMPLIED
   list_n CDATA #IMPLIED>
          <!--MARK 4 -->  .   .   .   .
<!ELEMENT input_table (#PCDATA)>
   <!ATTLIST input_table
```

---

[7] **DTD** - Document Type Definition

```
num_x CDATA #IMPLIED
num_y CDATA #IMPLIED>
<!ELEMENT optional (optional_value+)>  .  .  .  .
```

Example 1: DTD for user interface description

This example includes some marks (e.g. `<!-- MARK 1 -->`) to support the explanation in the following text. A user interface is at this stage composed of one or more user interface objects (UIO). A UIO can be composed of other UIOs or one or more input-/output values (Mark 1-2). These values are in an abstract form and describe interaction features of the user interface in an abstract way. Later there will be a mapping process of these abstract UIOs to concrete ones. Between Mark 2-3 you can see different types of these abstract UIOs. They have different attributes to specify their behaviour. An example to explain this is the input_1-n type (Mark 3-4). Here we have some attributes to specify this abstract UIO. The input_1-n type for instance can be mapped to a slider as a concrete UIO. The `range_min` attribute specifies the minimum-value of input possibilities, the `range_max` attribute specifies the maximum-value. The `range_interval` attribute is for fixing the interval within the range. Also we can specify a list of input values.

Now lets have a look at an example of a simple user interface of a little e-shop system:

```
<?xml version="1.0" encoding="ISO-8859-1"?>  .  .  .  .
<ui ui_name="e-shop">
    <uio name="title"> .   .   .   .
        <output name="title">
            <output_string/>
        </output>
    </uio> .   .   .   .
    <uio name="Art_group">
        <input name="Art_group">
            <input_1-n/>
        </input>
    </uio> .   .   .   .
    <uio name="Article">
        <output name="Art_Name">
            <output_string/>
        </output> .   .   .   .
        <input name="Order">
            <input_trigger/>
        </input>
    </uio> .   .   .   .
</ui>
```

Example 2: Description of a simple user interface of an e-shop system

Because of a lack of space only a few attributes are mentioned here. But it seems to be clear how such a specification looks like.

3.2   XML-Based Device Definition

A universal description language for describing properties of various target devices in abstract and comparable manner is necessary to support the transformation process from an abstract interaction model to a device dependent specific interaction model. Based on [Mund00] such a language was developed. Specifications written in this language are XML documents describing the specific features of devices. Let us have a look at the corresponded DTD.

```
<?xml version="1.0" encoding="ISO-8859-1"?>
<!ELEMENT device (device*, service*, vendor, version)>
   <!ATTLIST device
    id ID #REQUIRED>
<!ELEMENT service (name+, feature+, service*)>
   <!ATTLIST service
    kind CDATA #REQUIRED>
<!ELEMENT name (#PCDATA)>
   <!ATTLIST name
    language CDATA #REQUIRED>
<!ELEMENT feature (description)>
   <!ATTLIST feature
    id ID #IMPLIED>
<!ELEMENT description (text+, value, property)>
<!ELEMENT property (#PCDATA)>
<!ELEMENT value (#PCDATA)>
<!ELEMENT vendor (url*, text)>
<!ELEMENT url EMPTY>
   <!ATTLIST url
    ref NMTOKEN #REQUIRED>
<!ELEMENT version (#PCDATA)>
<!ELEMENT text (#PCDATA)>
```

Example 3: DTD for Device Definition

The specifications are not only necessary for this transformation they influence the specification of formatting rules as well.

Following example shows a very short fragment of a device definition for java.AWT:

```
<?xml version="1.0" encoding="ISO-8859-1"?>
<device id="Advanced Windowing Toolkit">
   <device id="java.awt.Button">
      <service id="?" kind="input_trigger">
         <name>Location</name>
         <feature>java.awt.Button.setLocation</feature>
      </service>
   </device>
   <vendor>SUN Microsystems</vendor>
   <version>2.0</vendor>
</device>
```

Example 4: Device definition for java.AWT

3.3   XML-Based Device Dependent Abstract Interaction Model

This model is still on an abstract level but it fulfills already some constraints coming from the device specification. It uses available features and omits not available services. The result of the mapping process is a file in which all abstract UIOs are mapped to concrete UIOs of a specific representation. The structure of this file is based on a XML-DTD which was introduced as follows:

```
<?xml version="1.0" encoding="ISO-8859-1"?>
<!ELEMENT ui_map (class, device*, uio+, context?)>
   <!ATTLIST ui_map
     uim_name CDATA #REQUIRED>
<!ELEMENT class (UID, target)>
<!ELEMENT UID (#PCDATA)>
<!ELEMENT target (#PCDATA)>
   <!ATTLIST target
     version CDATA #IMPLIED>
<!ELEMENT device (device | (type, parameter+))>
<!ELEMENT type (#PCDATA)>
<!ELEMENT parameter (text?, option, value)>
<!ELEMENT text (#PCDATA)>
<!ELEMENT option (#PCDATA)>
<!ELEMENT value (#PCDATA)>
<!ELEMENT uio (uio | ((output*), (input*)))>
   <!ATTLIST uio
     name CDATA #REQUIRED>
<!ELEMENT output ((output_string | output_1-n | output_m-n |
        output_table), device+, optional?)>
   <!ATTLIST output    name CDATA #REQUIRED . . . . .>
<!ELEMENT output_string (#PCDATA)>  . . . .
<!ELEMENT input ((input_1-n | input_m-n | input_trigger |
        input_string | input_table), device+, optional?)>
   <!ATTLIST input    name CDATA #REQUIRED . . . .>
<!ELEMENT input_string (#PCDATA)> . . . .
<!ELEMENT context (context_value+)>
<!ELEMENT context_value (#PCDATA)>
<!ELEMENT optional (optional_value+)>
<!ELEMENT optional_value (#PCDATA)>
   <!ATTLIST optional_value
     name CDATA #REQUIRED
     value CDATA #REQUIRED>
```

Example 5: DTD for UIO-Mapping

This file is specific according to a target device and includes all typical design properties of concrete UIOs like colour, position, size etc. It is a collection of option-value pairs where the content of the values is specified later on in the design process and describes a "skeleton" of a representation of a specific user interface. The user interface is designed on the basis of this skeleton during the following design process by designers or ergonomics.

Our simple example of an e-shop system mapped as a HTML-representation looks like the following specification:

```
<?xml version="1.0" encoding="ISO-8859-1"?>
<ui_map uim_name="e-shop-html">
   <uio name="Title">
      <output name="Title">
         <output_string/>
         <device>
            <type>H3</type>
            <parameter>
               <option></option>
               <value></value>
               </parameter> . . . .
            </device>
         </output>
      </uio> . . . .
   <uio name="Art_Group">
      <input name="Group">
         <input_1-n/>
```

```
    <device>
       <type>SELECT</type>
       <parameter>
          <option>SIZE</option>
          <value>1</value>
       </parameter>
       <parameter>
          <option>OPTION</option>
          <value></value>
       </parameter>.  .  .  .
    </device>
 </input>
</uio> .  .  .  .
<uio name="Ok">
   <input name="Ok">
      <input_trigger/>
      <device>
         <type>BUTTON</type>
         <parameter>
            <option>TYPE</option>
            <value>submit</value>
         </parameter> .  .  .  .
      </device> .  .  .  .
   </uio> .  .  .  .  .
</ui_map>
```

Example 6: E-shop abstract UI mapped to abstract device dependent (HTML) interaction model

The same user interface mapped as a java.AWT looks like introduced in the next example:

```
<?xml version="1.0" encoding="ISO-8859-1"?>
<ui_map uim_name="e-shop-awt">
   <uio name="Title">
      <output name="Title">
         <output_string/>
         <device>
            <type>java.awt.Label</type>
            <parameter>
               <option>java.awt.Label.setLocation</option>
               <value></value>
            </parameter>
            <parameter>
               <option>java.awt.Label.setSize</option>
               <value></value>
            </parameter>  .  .  .  .
         </device>
      </output>
   </uio> .  .  .  .
   <uio name="Art_Group">
      <input name="Group">
         <input_1-n/>
         <device>
            <type>java.awt.Choice</type>
            <parameter>
               <option>java.awt.Choice.setLocation</option>
               <value></value>
            </parameter> .  .  .  .
         </device>
      </input>
   </uio> .  .  .  .
   <uio name="Ok">
      <input name="Ok">
         <input_trigger/>
```

```
        <device>
           <type>java.awt.Button</type>
           <parameter>
              <option>java.awt.Button.setLocation</option>
              <value></value>
           </parameter> .  .  .  .
        </device> .  .  .  .
    </uio> .  .  .  .
</ui_map>
```

Example 7: E-shop abstract user interface mapped to abstract device dependent (java.AWT) interaction model

We demonstrate the HTML and java.AWT dependent generation. The wml-example is omitted because of its similarity to the HTML document.

3.4   XSL-Based Model Description

The creation of the XSL[8]-based model description is based on the knowledge of available UIOs for specific representations. It is necessary to know which values of properties of a UIO are available in the given context. The XML-based device dependent specific interaction model (skeleton) and available values of properties are used to create a XSL-based model description specifying a complete user interface.

The HTML-based e-shop example looks like the following specification:

```
<?xml version="1.0"?>
<xsl:stylesheet xmlns:xsl="http://www.w3.org/XSL/Transform/1.0">
<xsl:output method= "html"
    xml-declaration="yes"/>
    <html> .  .  .  .
       <h3> E-Shop-System </h3>
       <br/>
       <SELECT size=1>
          <option>"content-input" </option>
          <option>"content-input" </option> .  .  .  .
       </SELECT>
       <br/>    .  .  .  .
       <BUTTON type=submit>Ok</BUTTON>
       <br/> .  .  .  .
          <TABLE>
          <CAPTION>purchase list</CAPTION>
          <TR>
             <TD>"content-input"</TD>
             <TD>"content-input"</TD>
          </TR> .  .  .  .
       </TABLE>
    </html>
</xsl:stylesheet>
```

Example 8: XSL-file for generation of a HTML user interface of the e-shop

The wildcard "content-input" shall symbolise a content handling from applications or databases in a later step of the development.

---

[8] **XSL** - Extensible Style Language – http://www.w3.org/TR/xsl

3.5   Specific User Interface

By XSL transformation a file describing a specific user interface will be generated. Examples for java.AWT and HTML are given in [Muel01]. Unpublished WML examples were developed as well. The XSL transformation process consists of two sub-processes:

1. Creation of a specific file representing the user interface (WML, VoiceXML[9], HTML, Java...) and
2. Integration of content (database, application) into the interface.

The generated model is already a specification runable on the target platform. It is constructed by a transformation process which uses the device dependent specific interaction model as input, which is coded in XML.

There are two different cases. The user interface is generated once like for java.AWT or it has to be generated dynamically several times like for WML.

In the first case there is no need for a new generation of the user interface if the contents changes. The content is handled within the generated description file.

In the second case the content will be handled by instructions within the XSL-based model description. Each modification of the content results in a new generation of the description file.

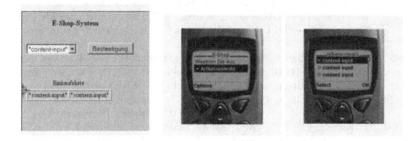

Fig. 3. Resulting user interfaces of the e-shop example

4   Results – Future Work

The current work includes the specification of XML-based languages describing different abstraction of a user interface for mobile devices. A concept for the mapping process from abstract UIOs to concrete UIOs was developed. A XML language was developed which allows the specification of the features of the user interface of mobile devices. The transformation process of user interfaces is based

---

[9] XML-based markup-language for voice – http://www.voicexml.org/

on specifications written in this language. In an interactive design process based on an abstract device dependent abstract interaction model and some design rules a more refined XSL-description of user interfaces is developed, which allows the generation of specific user interfaces.

This concept is already evaluated by several examples. A tool supporting the mapping and design process is under development. A first prototype is already available, which delivers already promising results. Up to now this tool is not integrated in previous phases of the design process. The abstract interaction model has to be edited manually. This will be omitted in the near future.

Our experiments show that XML is a promising technology for the platform independent generation of user interfaces. Further studies will demonstrate whether dialogue sequences of already developed applications can be integrated into the design process. Such patterns of already developed user interfaces could extremely enhance the development process. The most important results of this research will be the way to find and to integrate such patterns.

References

[Abra99]   Marc Abrams u.a.: UIML Tutorial. http://www.harmonia.com

[Beny99]   D. Benyon, T. Green, D. Bental: Conceptual Modelling for User Interface Development. Springer (1999)

[ElSc95]   T. Elwert, E. Schlungbaum: Modelling and Generation of Graphical User Interfaces in the TADEUS Approach. In: P. Palanque, R. Bastide (Eds.): Designing, Specification, and Verification of Interactive Systems. Springer (1995)

[Fole99]   J.D. Foley: History, Results and Bibliography of the User Interface Design Environment (UIDE), an Early Model-based Systems for User Interface Design and Implementation. in Proc. of DSV-IS'94, Carrara (1994)

[Forb99]   P. Forbrig: Task- and Object-Oriented Development of Interactive Systems: How many models are necessary? DSVIS'99, Braga, Portugal (1999)

[FoSt98]   P. Forbrig, C. Stary: From Task to Dialog: How Many and What Kind of Models do Developers Need. CHI Workshop, Los Angeles, USA (1998)

[Gali97]   W. Galitz: Essential Guide to UI-Design. Wiley (1997)

[Gamm96] E. Gamma et al.: Design Patterns. Addison-Wesley (1996)

[Gold99]   C. F. Goldfarb, P. Prescod: XML-Handbook. Prentice Hall (1999)

[HaTo97]   M.D. Harrison, J.C. Torres (Eds.): Proceedings of the 4th Eurographics Workshop on Design, Specification and Verification of Interactive Systems University of Granada (1997)

[MaJo98]   P. Makopoulos, P. Johnson (Eds.): Design, Specification and Verification of Interactive Systems '98. Springer (1998)

[SzLu98]   P. Szekely, P. Luo, R. Neches: Beyond Interface Builders: Model-Based Interface Tools, in Proc. INTERCHI'93 Human Factors in Computing Systems. (1993)

[Mark95]   A. Markus, N. Smilonich, L. Thompson: The Cross-GUI-Handbook. Addison-Wesley (1995)

[Muel01]   A. Mueller: Spezifikation von Benutzungsschnittstellen durch eine XML-basierte Markup-Sprache. Rostocker Informatik-Berichte 25 (2001)

[MuFo01]   A. Mueller, P. Forbrig, C. Cap: Using XML for Model-based User Interface Design. Accepted for CHI-Workshop "Transforming the UI for *anyone anywhere*" Seattle (2001)

[Mund00]   T. Mundt: Geraetedefinitionssprache DEVDEF.
http://wwwtec.informatik. uni-rostock.de/IuK/gk/thm/devdef/

[Pate00]   F. Paternó: Model-Based Design and Evaluation of Interactive Applications. Springer (2000)

Abstract User Interfaces: A Model and Notation to Support Plasticity in Interactive Systems

Kevin A. Schneider[1] and James R. Cordy[2]

[1] Department of Computer Science, University of Saskatchewan, 57 Campus Drive,
Saskatoon, Saskatchewan S7N 5A9 Canada,
kas@cs.usask.ca,
[2] Department of Computing and Information Science, Queen's University, Kingston,
Ontario K7L 3N6 Canada,
cordy@cs.queensu.ca,

Abstract. This paper introduces the Abstract User Interface (AUI) model and notation for specifying abstract interaction in interactive software systems with graphical, direct manipulation user interfaces. The AUI model is aimed at improving the plasticity of an interactive system. An interactive system is considered to be plastic when it is easily adaptable to concrete user interface styles. To support plasticity, an AUI specification defines the interaction between input, output and computation in terms of the abstract elements of the user interface: a relation we refer to as *abstract interaction*. Concrete characteristics of the user interface, such as events, callbacks and rendering, are deliberately factored out so that the abstract interaction relation can be exposed. Clearly defining the abstract interaction ensures that consistent interaction semantics is maintained independent of changes to the concrete user interface. To demonstrate the AUI concept, a range of user interface styles are presented for a single AUI specification of a drawing tool, and examples of commercial applications are presented.

1   Introduction

In 1999, David Thevenin and Jolle Coutaz outlined a framework and research agenda that introduced the notion of user interface *plasticity* [16]. Plasticity addresses the requirement that an interactive system be accessed from a variety of physical devices including 'dumb' terminals, personal computers and handheld computers. The desire is to specify the interactive system once while preserving its usability across the various physical environments, and at the same time minimizing development and maintenance costs. A plastic interactive system is one that adapts to a wide range of user interface styles. The abstract user interface (AUI) model and notation described in this paper, has been developed to help improve the plasticity of interactive systems. The approach is intended to be used not only in the development of new interactive systems, but also in adding plasticity to existing legacy applications. It is often the case that existing interactive systems were developed with little or no notion of plasticity.

C. Johnson (Ed.): DSV-IS 2001, LNCS 2220, pp. 28–49, 2001.

The AUI model separates a user interface into concrete and abstract components so that a number of concrete user interface styles may be specified for a single abstract user interface. The AUI notation is an executable specification language used to define the abstract user interface. By only specifying abstract interaction once, it is hoped that development and maintenance costs will be reduced and that interaction semantics of an interactive system will remain consistent across multiple concrete user interfaces. The primary goal of this paper is to introduce the AUI model and notation, showing how the notation is used to define abstract interaction. A secondary goal is to show how the model has been used to introduce plasticity into existing interactive systems. The choice of a functional notation is important for a number of reasons. First, it provides a means to explicitly state abstract interaction and its semantics. Second, a notation is conducive to automated evaluation in both designing and verifying an interactive system. Third, using a functional language approach helps ensure that various optimizations may be made when integrating the application and the user interface. Fourth, the side-effect free nature of functional programming allows synchronization and communication to be handled implicitly. The paper is organized into seven sections. Section 2describes the AUI model and shows how multiple concrete user interface styles may be specified for a single abstract user interface specification. Section 2 also points out differences between the AUI model and other user interface models. The AUI language is presented in Section 3 with examples of how it was used to specifying the abstract user interface of using an example of a graphical drawing editor. Section 4 describes a prototype of an AUI language compiler and how it was used to implement the graphical drawing editor, complete with a concrete user interface based on a commercial drawing tool. Section 5 describes the application of the AUI model to existing large-scale legacy systems. Two examples of using the AUI model for adding plasticity to legacy applications in a commercial setting are described. Section 6 relates the AUIwork to other research presented in this volume and Section 7 concludes the paper, describing future research.

2   The AUI Model

The AUI model considers an interactive system to be composed of three components, the functional core of the application (or computation), the abstract user interface (AUI) and the concrete user interface (CUI). Together, the AUI and CUI form the user interface of the interactive system. To support plasticity of the user interface, multiple CUI's maybe defined for one AUI specification (cf. Figure 1). By maintaining the distinction between abstract interaction and concrete interaction, it is hoped that a large portion of an interactive system can be designed, developed and evolved as a single entity and yet be usable across a wide range of platforms and concrete interaction styles.

The AUI model is a synthesis of ideas from existing user interface architectural models, such as the Seeheim model [15], Arch[18], ALV [11], Interactors

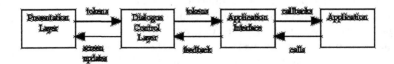

Fig. 1. AUI model. A number of concrete user interfaces (CUI's) may be defined for a single AUI. The combination of Computation, AUI and one of the CUI's forms an interactive system.

[14], Clock[8], TRIDENT [3] and PAC [5]. Traditionally the Seeheim model, shown in Figure 2, is used to compare user interface architectures and models.

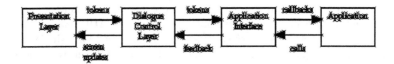

Fig. 2. The Seeheim model of user interface management systems.

The Seeheim model separates a user interface into Presentation Layer, Dialogue Control Layer and Application Interface. The Abstract User Interface (AUI) model presented here differs in that it abstracts elements from each one of these components (cf.Figure 3). Therefore, the AUI specification is not limited to describing a single Seeheim component, and can be used to describe the relation between presentation, dialogue and application interface. That is, the AUI specification defines the abstract interaction between input, output and computation.

The AUI model is not a replacement for the Seeheim model, but rather an orthogonal refinement of the Seeheim components into their abstract, environment independent aspects and their concrete, environment dependent ones. The refinement is explicitly aimed at improving the plasticity of interactive systems. The AUI approach is similar to research that separates the interactor portion of a user interface into abstract and concrete components [6]. With such separation, different concrete input and output mechanisms can be used depending on user preferences, available resources or the context of the interactor. TRIDENT[3] separates presentation into abstract interaction objects and concrete interaction objects and uses matching tables to automatically transform the abstract interaction objects to concrete interaction objects depending on the specific physical target environment. The AUI research focuses on the specification of the abstract user interface. Approaches, such as that used in TRIDENT, may integrate well

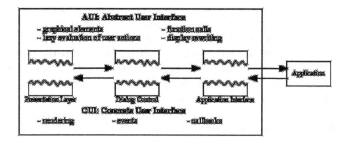

Fig. 3. Separating Seeheim components into CUI and AUI components.

with the AUI model for automatically generating the concrete user interface
and addressing ergonomic issues. The AUI approach is also related to markup
languages that are used to describe hypertext documents, such as XML [4],
WML[10] and UIML [1]. These markup languages separate the concrete presentation of a document from its logical description. XML is intended for the
communication of structured documents, WML is intended to describe documents for wireless appliances, and UIML is intended to describe documents for
a wide range of appliances including personal computers with web browsers, hand
held computers and cellphones. Each style of user interface is often document
and forms oriented. A wider range of user interface styles is supported by the
AUI approach, including user interfaces with direct manipulation of application
objects as exemplified by a graphical drawing editor.

2.1   Abstract User Interface Component

The abstract user interface (AUI) component, models output as a sequence of
display values and input as a sequence of user actions. The AUI specification
provides pattern matching rules that recursively transform the current display
value and user action into a new display value (cf.Figure 4).

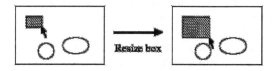

Fig. 4. Display change resulting from a user action to resize a box.

The AUI considers a display to be composed of a set of graphical and interactive elements. The graphical elements, *gels*, are specified with a set of built in constructor functions in the AUI language. Primitive *gels* have a shape, a size and an optional set of attributes for specifying characteristics, such as, pen width, fillcolour and font. Some primitive *gel* shapes include *box*, *oval*, *line*, *label* and *point*. The composite graphical element *canvas*, is used to provide position to the graphical elements. A *canvas* has a size, an optional set of attributes, and a set of <*gel,position*> tuples. A < *gel, position*> tuple is referred to as a *pin*. An example display value is shown in Figure 5.

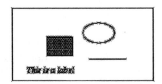

```
canvas <200,100> {
    < box <35,25> (Fill Shaded),<50,40>>,
    < oval <45,28> (Fill Clear),<100,20>>,
    <line <50,0> (Arrows None),<110,70>>,
    <label <Font Times)(FontSize 14) (Style Italic),<20,80>>}
```

Fig. 5. Example AUI display value and its possible rendering. The display consists of a **canvas** and four pins. The **canvas**, **box**, **oval**, and **line** gels each have their size specified by a <width,height> tuple. For example, the **box** has a size of <35,25>, is shaded and is positioned on the **canvas** at <x,y> location <50,40>.

Input is abstracted as a sequence of choices. It could be expressed as
canvas <300,200> {<**box** <35,25> (Fill shading),<50,40>}
    where
        shading = **choose** {Shaded,Clear,Black}
    end where

Output is abstracted as a sequence of user interface expressions, each to be rendered by the concrete user interface. Evaluating the previous equations may result in one of the following values:

canvas <300,200> {<**box** <35,25> (Fill Black),<50,40>}
canvas <300,200> {<**box** <35,25> (Fill Clear),<50,40>}
Instead of having the location predefined to be <50,40>, the location of the rectangle may be chosen by the user. The function, *location*, is added to the specification to denote choosing an <x,y> coordinate from a set of points. Each

time the user chooses a new location or shading for the rectangle a new canvas expression will be passed to the CUI for rendering.

canvas size {<**box** <35,25> (Fill shading),location}
    where
        location = **choose** points
        shading = **choose** {Shaded,Clear,Black}
   end where Abstract interaction is defined by AUI functions that transform one user interface value to another. For example, when a user presses the CLEAR button the graphical elements on the canvas may be removed. The following equation captures this notion:

    aui <**canvas size** pins,Clear> = **canvas size** {}

When the function *aui* is evaluated with a *canvas* and a *Clear* action as arguments, a *canvas* is returned with an empty set of *pins*.

Fig. 6. Possible CUI elements for the AUI expression **choose** {Red,Green,Blue}.

The binding of the CUI and AUI is modelled as sequences of user choices and sequences of expressions to be rendered (cf.Figure 7). For example, as the user makes menu choices over time, the choices are passed to the AUI as a sequence of menu choices. Based on the choices, a sequence of graphical expressions is passed back to the CUI. The CUI renders the graphical expressions.

Fig. 7. Abstract user interface/Concrete user interface communication.

2.2 Computation Component

Computation is modelled as external functions in the AUI. The computation functions are used where needed in the AUI specification, and so the arguments the computation depends on are clearly expressed. The signature of the computation functions are part of the AUI specification to ensure correct typing, but the implementation of the functions is external. Similar to the CUI binding, the binding of the AUI and computation is modelled as streams of arguments and results (cf.Figure 8). Although computation is modelled as function application, in practice the binding may update a variable or be used to bring computation in-line. The definition of the computation may not correspond to a function in the application language but may be a procedure, a message or may correspond to the execution of a statement.

Fig. 8. Abstract user interface/Computation communication.

3   AUI Language

This section introduces the AUI notation for specifying abstract interaction using an example of a graphical drawing editor. The complete syntax of the language is provided in the appendix. The next section will describe an implementation of a concrete user interface and an AUI interpreter for the drawing editor. The basic framework of the simple drawing editor includes a menu bar, a tool palette, a pointer and a canvas. The AUI specification for the basic framework of the drawing editor is

```
drawingEditor = choose {tool,menuBar}
    where
        tool = choose {pointerTool,boxTool,ovalTool,lineTool}
        menuBar = choose {file,edit,fill,arrows}
        file = choose {new,open,close,save,saveAs,print,quit}
        edit = choose {undo,cut,copy,paste}
        fill = fillAttr (choose {None,White,Shaded,Black})
        arrows = arrowAttr (choose * {AtStart,AtEnd})
    end where
```

Example concrete user interfaces for the AUI specification of the drawing editor are shown in Figure 9.

Each *choose* in the AUI specification is modelled in the concrete user interface as an interaction technique. Figure 10 shows an example of using a pull down menu to represent choosing a fill attribute.

The AUI language is similar to non-strict, pure functional languages like Haskell[12] and Miranda [17]. The AUI language is non-strict; that is, it uses lazy

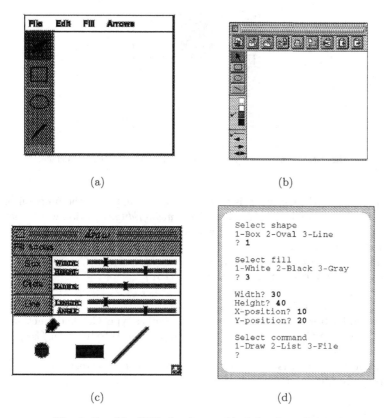

(a)

(b)

(c)

(d)

Fig. 9. Possible CUI's for the graphical drawing editor.

evaluation to evaluate function arguments. Arguments to the *choose* function are only evaluated when a value is required (lazy evaluation). When the value is required, the AUI will wait for the concrete user interface to return a value. The CUI may do one of three things:

1. A choice has already been made in the CUI and that choice is returned.
2. Although a choice has not yet been made in the CUI, the CUI returns a default choice.
3. The interaction blocks, waiting for the user to make a choice using an interaction technique. The resulting choice is returned.

3.1   Modelling Canvas Interaction

To model the interaction with the drawing canvas, a function, say *draw*, is recursively applied to a canvas expression. Function *draw* is defined as a choice

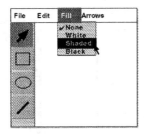

Fig. 10. Choosing a fill attribute in the concrete user interface.

between leaving the canvas as is (the base case) or applying the function recursively to the *drawingEditor* function. The *drawingEditor* function will be defined in terms of the original canvas and will return a new canvas. The functions are defined as follows:

```
main = f (canvas <300,200> {})
draw c = choose {c,draw drawingEditor}
    where
        drawingEditor = ...c ...
```

end where The function *drawingEditor* has type 'Gel' and function *draw* has type 'Gel -> Gel'. Passing an initially empty canvas to function *f* is specified as

```
    main = f (canvas <300,200> {})
```
As the canvas is recursively changed, the concrete user interface renders the new canvas.

3.2   Computation

Computation, or application specific functionality, is added to the AUI specification as external functions. By convention, the names of the external functions are preceded with an underscore (_). In the AUI specification only the signatures of the external functions are specified. For example, the following signatures may be defined:

```
_new :: -> Gel
_open :: String -> Gel
_save :: Gel -> Gel
_print :: Gel -> Gel
```

The external functions may then be used where appropriate in the AUI specification as long as their function signatures are respected. External functions do not necessarily correspond to procedures or functions in traditional languages but may correspond to changing a data value or transmitting a message. In the simple drawing editor a number of the file menu functions are expanded to use external functions. Examples, include:

```
new = _new
open = _open (openDialog)
save = _save c
print = _print c
```

3.3   Modelling the Pointer

To model drawing using a pointer requires a CUI interaction technique to accept a sequence of pointer positions, such as

[<100,150>,<100,155>,<100,160>,<100,170>]

The first point in the sequence corresponds to a point on the drawing canvas where the user first pressed the mouse button. The last point in the sequence corresponds to a point on the drawing canvas where the user released the mouse button. The intermediate points in the sequence correspond to the pointer position on the drawing canvas while the mouse button is being held and moved. In the CUI, a cursor will track the mouse movement. In the AUI, pointer interaction is defined as choosing from a set of points:

```
pts = choose * points
points = {<x,y> | x<-[0..(width c)];y<-[0..(height c)]}
    where
        width (canvas <w,h> pins) = w
        height (canvas <w,h> pins) = h
    end where
```

For example, if the canvas is defined as 'canvas <200,300> {}' then the results of the function *width* will be 200 and the results of the function *height* will be 300. *Points* will have the value '{<0,0>,<0,1>,...,<200,299>,<200,300>}'. following value:

{<0,0>,<0,1>,...,<200,299>,<200,300>}

Choosing from the *points* set may result in the following value which represents moving the mouse pointer from position <30,30> to position <130,130>.

[<30,30>,<30,31>,...,<130,129>,<130,130>]

If the concrete user interface is text based, only the first and last points will need to be typed in. Alternatively, a text based concrete user interface may generate a list of coordinates from an <x,y> position, a width and a height.

3.4   Drawing

To create an object the user selects a tool from the tool bar, positions the pointer on the canvas, presses the mouse button to specify the starting point of the object and while holding the mouse button down, moves the pointer until the object is the appropriate size and then releases the button. In this way objects are specified with a list of <x,y> points. The following functions construct a box shaped graphical element given two points from the canvas. From these two points, the size and position of the box is calculated. In a typical drawing editor, the first point,*pt1*, corresponds to where the pointer was when the mouse button was pressed and the second point, *pt2*, corresponds to where the pointer was when the mouse button was released.

```
boxPin pt1 pt2 = <gel,pos>
    where
        gel = box (gelSize pt1 pt2) attr
        pos = gelPos pt1 pt2
        gelSize <x1,y1> <x2,y2> = <abs (x1-x2),abs (y1- y2)>
        gelPos <x1,y1> <x2,y2> = <min [x1,x2],min [y1,y2]>
    end where
```

The function *min* returns the minimum value from a list of values. The function *max* returns the maximum value from a list of values. The function *abs* returns the absolute value of its operand. Figure 11 shows an example of pressing and holding the mouse button at position <30,30> and releasing the mouse button at <130,130>. The result box will have a width of 100 and a height of 100.

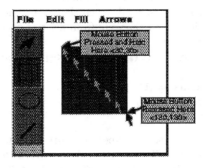

Fig. 11. Drawing a box.

Normally, graphical elements are placed on the composite graphical element *canvas*. Adding a *pin* to a *canvas* is accomplished with function,*place*.

```
place pin (canvas size pins) = canvas size (pin:pins)
```

The operator ':' inserts its left operand into the set that is its right operand. To provide rubber band feedback to the user, the following definitions are applied to the *place* function:

```
boxTool = foldc (rubberBox (first pts)) c pts
rubberBox pt1 c pt2 = place (boxPin pt1 pt2) c
```

The function *foldc* reduces a list in the following way

```
foldc f c [x1,x2,...,xn] = (...((c $f$ x1) $f$ x2)...) $f$ xn
```

Applying *foldc* to the canvas 'canvas <192,192> {}' and the pointer sequence

```
[<30,30>,<31,31>,<31,32>,<31,31>,...,<130,129>,<130,130>]
```

results in the sequence of canvases:

```
(1) canvas <192,192> {<box <0,0> attr,<30,30>>}
```

(2) **canvas** <192,192> {<**box** <1,1> attr,<30,30>>}
(3) **canvas** <192,192> {<**box** <1,2> attr,<30,30>>}
(4) **canvas** <192,192> {<**box** <1,1> attr,<30,30>>}
. . .
(n-1) **canvas** <192,192> {<**box** <100,99> attr,<30,30>>}
(n) **canvas** <192,192> {<**box** <100,100> attr,<30,30>>}

Rendering the sequence of canvases will provide the rubber band feedback effect (cf. Figure 11).

3.5 Selecting

In typical graphical drawing editors, a pointer tool is provided to select one or more graphical elements for the purpose of repositioning, deleting or changing their attributes. The user selects an element by clicking on it. When a previously selected element is clicked on, the element becomes *deselected*. By holding the mouse button down while moving the pointer, the selected graphical elements are repositioned. When a *fill* or *arrows* attribute is chosen and there are selected elements, the corresponding attribute of those elements is changed appropriately. The *pointerTool* is defined as follows:

```
pointerTool = foldc (repositionGels (first pts))
                     (selectGels (first pts) c) pts
```

The function *selectGels* selects (or deselects) the graphical element(s)that the pointer is within. The function *repositionGels* computes a newposition for each of the selected graphical elements, relative to the position of the pointer. The functions *selectGels* and *repositionGels* are defined as follows:

```
selectGels xy (canvas size pins) = c'
     where
        c' = canvas size (map (selectWithin xy) pins)
        selectWithin xy pin = select pin, if within xy pin
        selectWithin c pin = pin   otherwise
     end where
```

```
repositionGels xy1 (canvas size pins) xy2 = c'
     where
        c' = canvas size (map (reposition xy1 xy2) pins)
        reposition xy1 xy2 <gel Sel,pos> = <gel Sel,pos'>
        reposition xy1 xy2 pin = pin
        pos' = newpos xy1 xy2 pos
        newpos <x1,y1> <x2,y2> <x,y> = <x+x2-x1,y+y2-y1>
     end where
```

```
select :: PIN -> PIN   select - turns on or off the selected gel's attribute
select <gel Sel,pos> = <gel,pos>   deselect
select <gel,pos> = <gel Sel,pos>   select
```

```
within :: XY-POSITION - > PIN -> BOOLEAN
```

```
within <x1,y1> <shape <w,h> attrs,<x2,y2>> = True,
        if x1 >= x2 and x1 <= (x2+w) and y1 >= y2 and y1 <=
(y2+h)
    within xy pin = False
```

This section provided examples of using the AUI notation for modelling interactive systems with graphical user interfaces. The next section discusses a prototype implementation.

4   Implementation

The graphical drawing editor specified in the previous section has been implemented on the Apple Macintosh platform. A concrete user interface was developed similar to the drawing component of the commercial software package AppleWorks [2]. An AUI language interpreter was developed based on the Gofer runtime engine [13]. Gofer is functional language environment for a dialect of the functional programming language Haskell [12]. The *choose* expressions are bound to common Apple Macintosh interaction technique routines written in C/C++ that access the Apple Macintosh toolbox. The graphical elements are rendered using the Apple Macintosh imaging language, Quickdraw. Computation functions are also written inC/C++. This section discusses the implementation of the graphical drawing editor by first discussing its runtime architecture. The AUI evaluation, CUI interaction techniques and the rendering facility are subsequently discussed.

4.1   Runtime Architecture

The communication between the CUI and the AUI, and the AUI and the computation is through the input and output streams of the functional language and the input and output features of C/C++. Input to the CUI runtime is a stream of built-in functions to be evaluated (rendered) and the output from the CUI runtime is a stream of *choose* values and computation function results. The input/output mechanism of the AUI runtime was modified to use monitored queues, and these queues were also accessed by the CUI runtime instead of using input and output routines (cf. Figure 12). The queues can be thought of as channels, input/output streams or message passing facilities.

The next sections discuss the AUI to functional language translation, the CUI interaction techniques and the CUI graphical element rendering.

4.2   AUI Evaluation

Since the AUI notation is based on pure functional languages, it is relatively easy to translate most of the language features directly into previously implemented functional language, such as Haskell and Miranda. As with those languages, the AUI language has structured types, pattern matching, function application, and higher order functions. And like both Haskell and Miranda, the AUI notation

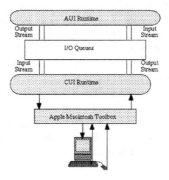

Fig. 12. Runtime Architecture.

has a non-strict semantics(lazy evaluation) and is strongly typed. The communication between the AUI and the CUI is modelled as a stream of values. For example the AUI expression

    fill = **choose** {None,White,25 Gray,50 Gray,75 Gray,Black}

may have '[Black,White,None,75 Gray]' as a stream of values. the following stream of values

    [Black,White,None,75 Gray]

In general, a *choose* is bound to a stream of values where the following holds.

    choose min..max S = [s| s in powerset(S) and min $\leq$ |s| $\leq$ max]

The CUI also needs to render the canvas values. As with choose the canvas value over time is a stream of canvas values. That is,

    [**canvas** <300,200> {},
    canvas <300,200> {<oval (Radius 30) fill,<120,30>>},
    canvas <500,200> {<oval (Radius 30) fill,<120,30>>}]

Communication to the computation functions is also modelled with streams. Each element of a stream of arguments is passed to the computation function and its result is packaged into a stream of results. The streams of choices, canvases, arguments and results are communicated between the CUI, AUI and computation through the input and output mechanisms of the implementation languages. In this way, the semantics of each implementation language does not need to be altered. To enhance responsiveness separate threads of control are used for the user interaction and computation, and the input and output mechanisms are replaced with reads and writes to monitored queues (cf. Figure 12).A functional language runtime engine based on Gofer [13] is provided to interpret the AUI specification. The runtime engine has been modified to communicate input and output through the monitored queues instead of through the file system. The AUI model defers the specification of temporal constraints to the interpretation of the AUI specification and its connection to the CUI. At this time temporal constraints are implicit. Three interpretations could be taken: sequential, parallel, or a combination of both. In the case of the prototype a sequential interpretation is used. That is, the order a user chooses a value, dictates the evaluation. Once the AUI specification is transformed into its functional language counterpart, each choice is bound to an interaction technique in the CUI, each canvas is bound to a render routine in the CUI, and each computation function is bound to the appropriate functionality. Connecting the CUI, AUI and computation involves simply connecting the streams of choices and canvases to *enqueue* and *dequeue* routines. The interaction techniques, rendering routines and computation functions access the queues as necessary. Associating a *choose* in the AUI with an interaction technique in the CUI is done by simply using the same queue.

4.3   CUI Interaction Techniques

To build the CUI, each of the *choose* expressions are associated with an interaction technique. In the prototype interactive elements commonly available in the Macintosh toolbox, such as menus, are used. On the Apple Macintosh, each file has a *data fork* and a *resource fork*. The resource fork may contain icon, window and menu definitions. An Apple supplied visual specification tool, ResEdit, is used to draw the icons and define the menus for the CUI. Figure 13 shows ResEdit windows for defining the icons in the application. Figure 14 shows images of the menu bar and pull down menus, also defined with ResEdit.

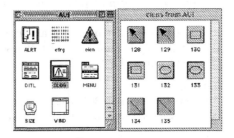

Fig. 13. The Macintosh ResEdit tool was used to define the CUI's visual resources.

The interaction technique in the concrete use interface enqueues the user's choice on the queue assigned it. For example, *chooseTool* will enqueue the tool choice made by the user. The AUI runtime will dequeue the choice when needed. The C/C++ code to handle a mouse event and place the point selection on a queue is:

```
GetMouse(&mouseLoc); /* Apple Toolbox Routine */
enqueue(ch9,mouseLoc.h); /* ch9 is the choose queue for pts */
enqueue(ch9,mouseLoc.v);
```

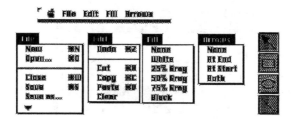

Fig. 14. Concrete interaction techniques of drawing editor.

4.4 CUI Rendering

The stream of canvas values is monitored by a *render* function in the CUI. The canvas value is translated into calls to Apple Quickdraw routines. For example, the following C/C++ code renders a *pin* of type *line*:

```
/* c1 is the queue assigned to the canvas */
if (dequeue(c1) == linePin) {
    pin.shape = linePin;
    pin.w = dequeue(c1);
    pin.h = dequeue(c1);
    pin.arrows = dequeue(c1);
    pin.x = dequeue(c1);
    pin.y = dequeue(q);
    pin.selected = dequeue(q);
    /* Apple Quickdraw routines to draw Line */
    PenMode(patCopy);
    RGBForeColor(&black);
    MoveTo(pin.x,pin.y);
    Line(pin.w,pin.h);
    if (pin.arrows>0) {.../* draw arrows */...}
    if pin.selected {.../* draw handles */...}
} An example screen image of the prototype is shown in Figure 15.
```

This section discussed a prototype implementation (cf. Figure 15) of an interactive system using the AUI specification of a graphical drawing editor, introduced in the previous section. A commercial graphical drawing editor was used as a template for the concrete user interface. The next section discusses commercial applications of the AUI concept.

5   Application to Legacy Systems

The AUI model has recently been used in a commercial setting for increasing the plasticity of legacy applications. In one example, the AUI model was used to separate business and user interface logic so that the business rules could be

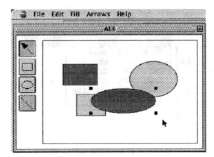

Fig. 15. Drawing editor prototype running on the Apple Macintosh.

adapted to a wide range of user interfaces through a multi-channel messaging architecture (cf. Figure 16). In a second example, the AUI model was used to migrate a legacy application from a single session to a multiple session web-based architecture (cf.Figure 17). In both cases, the AUI modelled the interface between application functionality (computation) and concrete user interface.

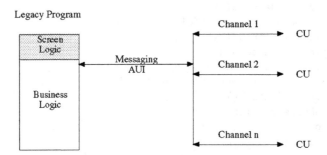

Fig. 16. Multi-channel messaging to add plasticity to a legacy system. The user interface is modelled with the AUI and the concrete user interface components communicate through a multi-channel messaging architecture. The concrete user interfaces may be automated teller machines, personal computers, telephones, etc. The abstract user interface is XML-like.

6 Connections

The abstract user interface notation provides a means of investigating and expressing abstract interaction. To further the research, the notation needs to be used to express a variety of interaction relations to determine common patterns

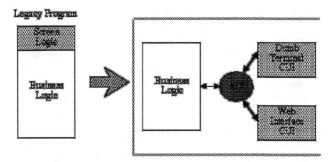

Fig. 17. Multi-session architecture for adding plasticity to a legacy system. The AUI models the interface between the user interface logic and the business logic. The AUI also manages the state necessary to achieve multi-session processing. The user interface logic is separated to handle terminal I/O. As well, a web interface was implemented using the same AUI.

and the usability of the notation. Research presented at this workshop into 'Temporal Patterns for Complex Interaction Design' will aid in identifying some of these common patterns. As well, the idea of 'Symmetry as a Connection Between Affordance and State Space' may help establish criteria for connecting CUI and AUI. To aid in practically exercising the AUI notation a supporting user interface builder should be designed and implemented. With an AUI development environment the AUI notation could be further exercised and accessible to a larger audience. The AUI development environment will need to integrate with other user interface tools. Ideas for such integration have been presented at this workshop in the chapter on 'Tool Suite for Integrating Task and System Models Through Scenarios'. Related to user interface plasticity is the notion that user interfaces may need to adapt to different contexts of use. The chapter on 'Task Modelling for Context-Sensitive User Interface' addresses this issue.

7   Conclusion

The abstract user interface (AUI) model and supporting notation provide a means of specifying abstract interaction to aid in the design and development of plastic interactive systems. The AUI model separates an interactive system into three components, the concrete user interface (CUI), the abstract user interface (AUI) and the computation. The CUI is concerned with issues of events and display updates, the computation is concerned with issues of application specific functionality, and the AUI relates the two. The AUI approach is conducive to producing alternative user interfaces for an application, since much of the interaction can be specified in the AUI. A textual CUI, a graphical CUI and CUI's for multiple platforms could be constructed for the same AUI. By having a clearer and more structured way of expressing application interaction using the AUI notation, iterative development of interactive systems may prove to be easier and less error prone. As well, having clearly stated the relation between user interface and application, an interactive system may be more robust since the dependencies are more easily accounted for. Temporal issues are not addressed in the AUI notation. The AUI notation can be used to specify some simple sequential dependencies but complex temporal dependencies must be managed either by the concrete user interface or by the computation component. Unfortunately there may be cases where it is desirable to express temporal constraints in the AUI in terms of AUI elements. For example, some temporal constraints may need to be maintained regardless of the given CUI or application bindings. It would be interesting to investigate an orthogonal notation based on ideas from Clock [7] for expressing temporal constraints. The AUI notation supplemented with temporal constraints would be conducive to demonstrational techniques, especially for specifying sequencing. As well, a notation based on UAN [9] for expressing the concrete user interface could provide a CUI complement to the AUI notation. Although the research has focused on single user, non-distributed user interfaces with a direct manipulation style, the techniques are not necessarily limited to that domain and may be found useful for distributed, multi-user, multi-media or network based software. The AUI notation could be expanded to model these non-WIMP user interfaces. Using the AUI model to improve the plasticity of existing legacy systems is an exciting area for future research. The techniques that have been used commercially need to be generalized so they may be easily applied to a range of legacy systems. The AUI model is hoped to be a preliminary step in expressing abstract interaction as a foundation for building more elaborate user interfaces with rich semantic feedback and for improving the plasticity of interactive systems.

Acknowledgements. The authors wish to thank the Natural Sciences and Engineering Research Council of Canada for their support. We also wish to thank T. C. N. Graham for his valuable comments and feedback.

References

1. M. Abrams, C. Phanouriou, A. L. Batongbacal, S. M. Williams and J. E. Shuster. UIML: An Appliance-Independent XML User Interface Language. WWW8, Toronto May 1999.
2. AppleWorks 6, Copyright ©2000 Apple Computer. Apple Computer, 2000.
3. F. Bodart, A.-M. Hennebert, J.- M. Leheureux, and J. Vanderdonckt. A Model-Based Approach to Presentation: A Continuum from Task Analysis to Prototype. In Proceedings of 1st Eurographics Workshop on Design, Specification and Verification of Interactive Systems DSVIS'94 (Bocca diMagra, Jun 8-10, 1994). F. Paternó (ed.). Eurographics Series, Berlin,1994, pp. 25-39.
4. T. Bray, J. Paoli, and C. M. Sperberg-McQueen, eds. Extensible Markup Language (XML) 1.0. W3C Recommendation, 1998.
5. J. Coutaz, L. Nigay and D. Salber. PAC: An Object Oriented Model for Implementing User Interfaces. ACM SIGCHI Bulletin, vol. 19, 1987, pages37-41.

6. M. Crease, P. Gray and S. Brewster. A Toolkit of Mechanism and Context Independent Widgets. In Design, Specification and Verification of Interactive Systems (Workshop 8, ICSE 2000), Limerick, Ireland, 2000, pp. 127-141.

7. T. C. N. Graham. Declarative Development of Interactive Systems. Volume 243 of Breichte der GMD. R. Oldenbourg Verlag, July 1995.

8. T. C. N. Graham and T. Urnes. Integrating Support for Temporal Media into an Architecture for Graphical User Interfaces. In Proceedings of the International Conference on Software Engineering (ICSE97). IEEE Computer Society Press, Boston, USA, May 1997.

9. H. R. Hartson, A. C. Siochi and D. Hix. The UAN: A User-Oriented Representation for Direct Manipulation Interface Designs. ACM Transactions on Information Systems, 1990, 8(3):181-203.

10. J. Herstad, D. Van Thanh and S. Kristoffersen. Wireless Markup Language as a Framework for Interaction with Mobile Computing and Communication Devices. In C.W. Johnson (ed.) Proceedings of the First Workshop on Human Computer Interaction with Mobile Devices, Glasgow, Scotland, 1998.

11. R. D. Hill. The Abstraction-Link-View Paradigm: Using Constraints to Connect User Interfaces to Applications. In Human Factors in Computing Systems (Monterey, California, USA), 1992, pages 335- 342.

12. P. Hudak, S. P. Jones, P. Wadler, B. Boutel, J. Fairbairn, J. Fasel, M.M. Guzman, K. Hammond, J. Hughes, T. Johnsson, D. Kieburtz, R. Nikhil, W. Partain and J. Peterson. Report on the Programming Language Haskell. Technical Report, Yale University, USA, 1988.

13. M. P. Jones. An Introduction to Gofer. Functional programming environment, Yale University, 1991.

14. B. A. Myers. A New Model for Handling Input. ACM Transactions on Information Systems, 1990, 8(3):289-320.

15. G. E. Pfaff, editor. User Interface Management Systems. Springer-Verlag, Berlin, November 1983.

16. D. Thevenin and J. Coutaz. Plasticity of User Interfaces: Framework and Research Agenda. In M.A. Sasse and C.W. Johnson (eds.) Proceedings of INTERACT'99. (IFIP TC.13 Conference on Human-Computer Interaction, 30th August-3rd September 1999, Edinburgh, UK), Technical Sessions, 1999, pages 110-117.

17. D. A. Turner. Miranda: A non-strict functional language with polymorphic types. In Proceedings IFIP International Conference on Functional Programming Languages and Computer Architecture (Nancy, France), 1985, pages 1-16.

18. The UIMS Tool Developers Workshop. A Metamodel for the Runtime Architecture of an Interactive System. SIGCHI Bulletin. Volume 24, Number 1, 1992, pages 32-37.

Appendix. AUI Syntax

auiSpecification ::= { equation }
equation ::= functionDef | functionSignature | typeDef | typeSynonyn | matchEqn
functionDef ::= functionName { pattern } = expression [whereClause]
whereClause ::= **where** { equation } **end where**
functionSignature ::= functionName **::** typeName1 { -> typeName2}

typeDef ::= typeName { typeVar } ::= constructorExpr { | constructorExpr }
constructorExpr ::= constructor { typeExpr }
typeSynonym ::= typeName == typeExpr
matchEqn ::= **match** identifier = pattern
expression ::= identifier | literal | functionName { expression } |
                unaryOperator expression |
                  expression binaryOperator expression | choose | gel |
                  expression , **if** expression | comprehension | (expression)
list ::= [[expression { , expression }]]
set ::= **{** [expression { , expression }] **}**
tuple ::= < [expression] { , expression } >
unaryOperator ::= - | **not** | **first** | **rest**
binaryOperator ::= arithmeticOps | logicOps | listOps | functionComposition
arithmeticOps ::= + | - | / | * | ^ | **div** | **rem**
logicOps ::= == | <= | >= | = | < | > | **and** | **or**
listOps ::= : | ++
functionComposition ::= .
comprehension ::= listComprehension | setComprehension
listComprehension ::= [expression | generator { , generator }]
setComprehension ::= { expression | generator { , generator } }
generator ::= name <- listOrSetExpression |
              < name , name > <- 2-tupleListOrSetExpression |
              < name , name , name > <- 3- tupleListOrSetExpression | ...
listOrSetExpression ::= listExpression | setExpression
listExpression ::= [number .. number] | [char .. char] | [type]
setExpression ::= { number .. number } | { char .. char } | { type }
pattern ::= identifier | literal | _ |
           < [pattern { , pattern }] > | [[pattern { , pattern }]] |
            { [pattern { , pattern }] } | ([pattern { , pattern }]) |
            pattern : pattern | constructor { pattern } | (pattern)
gel ::= **canvas** { attribute } { [pin { , pin }] } | shape { attribute }
shape ::= **circle** | **line** | **box** | **point** | **label**
pin ::= < gel , xy-offset > | gel xy-offset
xy-offset ::= < number , number > | **X** number **Y** number
attribute ::= < number , number > | (**Fill** fill) | (**Arrows** arrows) |
             (**Font** font) | ...
choose ::= **choose** [name] [cardinality] setOrList
cardinality ::= * | number | min .. max | min .. *
externalFunction   ::=   **external_**functionName | **ext_**functionName |
_functionName
Note: *functionName, typeName, typeVar, typeExpr* and *name* are all identifiers.

Task Modelling for Context-Sensitive User Interfaces

Costin Pribeanu[1,2], Quentin Limbourg[1], and Jean Vanderdonckt[1]

[1] Université catholique de Louvain, Institut d'Administration et de Gestion
Place des Doyens, 1 - B-1348 Louvain-la-Neuve, Belgium
`limbourg, vanderdonckt@isys.ucl.ac.be`
[2] National Institute for Research and Development in Informatics
Bd Averescu 8-10 - R-71316 Bucharest, Romania
`pribeanu@acm.org`

Abstract. With the explosion of devices, computing platforms, contextual conditions, user interfaces become more confronted to a need to be adapted to multiple configurations of the context of use. In the past, many techniques were developed to perform a task analysis for obtaining a single user interface that is adapted for a single context of use. As this user interface may become unusable for other contexts of use, there emerges a need for modelling tasks which can be supported in multiple contexts of use, considering multiple combinations of the contextual conditions. For this purpose, the concept of unit task is exploited to identify a point where traditional task models can break into two parts: a context-insensitive part and a context-sensitive part. A widespread task model notation is then used to examine, discuss, and criticise possible configurations for modelling a context-sensitive task as a whole. One particular form is selected that attempts to achieve a clear separation of concern between the context-insensitive part, the context-sensitive part, and a new decision tree which branches to context-sensitive tasks, depending on contextual conditions. The questions of factoring out possible elements that are common across multiple contexts of use and representation of the resulting task model are discussed.

1 Introduction

User interfaces (UIs) of today's applications seem no longer condemned to be executed in a single fixed context of use. Indeed, a multiplication of possible contexts of use is provoked by a new heterogeneity of computing platforms, each of them with its own device capabilities that are always posing new constraints. This heterogeneousness results in computing platforms exhibiting drastically different interaction capabilities. Coping with these differences implies reconfigurations of the UI that are beyond traditional UI change [6,7], such as widget resizing, reduction of a full widget to its scrollable version, graceful degradation of a sophisticated widget into a moderate one, or redistribution of widgets across windows. Beyond this classic problem of having cross-computing platform UIs is appearing a new collection of constraints that are no longer imposed by the

C. Johnson (Ed.): DSV-IS 2001, LNCS 2220, pp. 49–68, 2001.
© Springer-Verlag Berlin Heidelberg 2001

computing platforms themselves, but rather by other factors, such as the type of user, the external resources manipulated by the UI (e.g., the network, the ambient environment).

For instance, we studied a registration procedure which should be performed in two completely different contexts of use. In the first context, a secretary registers a child for a leisure activity on her personal computer in a quiet environment, with all accessible facilities. In the second context, she is equipped with a PalmPilot and should register many children (at least, 50) arriving with their parents in a very short amount of time (typically 20 minutes). This atmosphere is very tense because she cannot stop the children for a long time nor she want to catch the parents to collect all required information. Moreover, children are running everywhere in the entrance, making the context of use a very stressed one. For these reasons, the interactive task is reduced to its minimum vital. UIs are consequently expect to gracefully evolve in a rather changing environment where several changes of the context of use may occur. And these changes may endanger the predicted usability of a predefined UI [1,16,18].

The *context of use* is hereby defined as the complete environment in which the user is carrying out an interactive task to fulfill a given role played in a specific organisation. Two types of characteristics simultaneously determine the context of use:

1. Characteristics *internal* to the application and its UI (e.g., the computing platform, the software/hardware parameters, the interaction devices, the network bandwidth, the latency, the screen resolution).
2. Characteristics *external* to this technical system (e.g., the type of user, her skills and knowledge, her preferences, the sound and light conditions, her geographic position in a building, the stress level, the organisation structure, the information channels).

Any change of at least one of these characteristics may generate one possible change of the context of use. Of course, a combination of changes on multiple characteristics also impose a further complicated change of the context of use. The challenge for the UI and for the designer is to match the UI configuration (e.g., look and feel) with the set of constraints imposed by the new characteristics of the resulting context of use. *Context-sensitivity* is hereby referred to as the ability of a UI to execute reconfiguration after a context of use variation so as to stay adapted to the new context. The importance of designing UIs for multiple contexts of use has already been stressed and studied in some work, such as, but not limited to, [2,4,1,7]. In particular, it is underlined in [10] that a return to considering model-based approaches to address the issues of context-sensitivity might be expected, due to the wide variety of contexts of use. Indeed, it seems critical that models should allow an elegant way to segment different aspects of UI design that are relevant to different contexts of use and to isolate context-generic issues from context-specific ones.

In model-based approaches [3,8,11,16], the task model is typically used for a user-task elicitation process that results into a task model and a user model, possibly along with a domain model. At least, the task model is recognised as one fundamental point to initiate a UI design process which is user-centred.

In this paper, we would like to address the issues raised by task modelling for context-sensitive UIs. Section 2 reviews some efforts undertaken towards modelling context-sensitivity in task models and examines how these efforts can be situated on a four-steps method for designing context-sensitive UIs. To initiate this method, Section 3 analyses some possible approaches for modelling a task for context-sensitive UIs, based on a selected task model and associated notation. The resulting model is then exploited in Section 4 to highlight various model configurations for a varying amount of context-sensitive sub-tasks and for a single or multiple contexts of use. The problem of factoring out common elements in such models is then studied in Section 5. A case study is provided in Section 6. A conclusion explains the main benefits of this approach and how this model is currently being used for tool support and the rest of the method.

2   Designing Context-Sensitive User Interfaces

Based on [4,9,16], four major steps for producing a context-sensitive UI may be identified (Fig. 1):

1. Production of a context-sensitive task model: this task model should foresee all sub-tasks that might be considered in a single context of use or in multiple contexts of use. This activity may involve adding sub-tasks that are especially supported in a particular context of use and withdrawing of sub-tasks that are not supported in a particular context of use. This task model should obey to the separation of concern principle : the context-insensitive part should be clearly separated from the context-sensitive part, while showing relationship between them.
2. Production of a generic UI model: this generic UI model is supposed to model a UI independently of any context of use, thus considering the context-insensitive part of the context-sensitive task model.
3. Production of a specific UI model: this specific UI model is supposed to model a UI depending on the constraints of intended contexts of use, thus considering the context-sensitive part of the context-sensitive task model. Due to variation of these constraints, multiple UI models may be produced. In [4], one model covers as many contexts of use as possible, provided that the usability properties are preserved and that a same UI can hold the expected properties simultaneously.
4. Production of a final running UI: the previous model can then be exploited at design time to automatically generate code (e.g., in HTML with CSS cascading style sheets for Web-based contexts, WML for cellular phone contexts, in XML with XSL eXtensible Style Sheets for XML-compliant browsers), for a particular con-text of use or be interpreted at run-time to produce the expected UI.

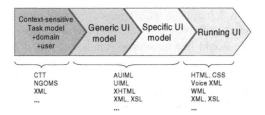

Fig. 1. Steps of the method for designing context-sensitive user interfaces

Fig. 1 highlights that some approaches or languages are more targeted at some steps of this method. For example, UIML [2] does not encompass any task model, but precisely supports a smooth transition from a platform-independent UI model to a platform-dependent UI model, which is in turn converted into code of a programming language of the target computing platform.

To locate points in the task model where a separation points between the context-insensitive part and the context-sensitive part of the task can be specified, we have to look back to the concept of basic task and unit task. The question is therefore: what is the most useful base unit for task decomposition between the two parts? We suggest to answer this question by relying upon the concept of *unit task*.

Although identification of the elementary task is an important concern for over a decade there is not a generally agreed definition yet. Card, Moran & Newell [5] defined the unit task as the lowest level task a user really wants to perform. Later on, Tauber [17] defined the basic task as a task for which the system provides with one single command or unit of delegation. According to van Welie, van der Veer and Eliens [19], a unit task should only be executed by performing one or more basic tasks. The relationship between unit tasks and basic tasks is important because it shows problems a user may experience when she tries to accomplish her goals with a given UI. However, they give no indication how this task decomposition should be done.

In the ConcurTaskTree (CTT) notation elaborated by Paternó [12,13,11], basic tasks are defined as tasks that could not be further decomposed. Basic tasks are classified in three types: user tasks, application tasks and interaction tasks. This classification extends the definition of Tauber to other tasks than those related to a single function provided by the system. In order to design the user interface he starts from the specification of the so-called User's Virtual Machine (UVM) which is the conceptual model of a "competent user", i.e. a user knowing how to delegate a task to the computer. The specification of basic tasks is done in terms of conceptual events (commands), objects, states, attributes, values and places, each being an entry in UVM.

This definition of Tauber relates basic tasks to UI objects but it leaves outside the specification of user tasks that are not related to UI objects. Basic tasks as defined by Tauber roughly correspond to interaction tasks in CTT. Basic task classification proposed by Paternó is more complete since it comprises also user tasks and application tasks that reflect cognitive activities of the user. We therefore consider that unit tasks are potential candidates to separate a task model between the context-insensitive part (which stops a unit tasks which are device- or context-independent) and the context-sensitive part (which ends up with basic tasks which are device- or context-dependent).

In [15], a method is developed to support task models that address multiple types of user, which is one form of multiple contexts of use. This method is based on polymorphic tasks. The main advantage of this method is its ability to incorporate style variations depending on user types into a single model, rather than having different models, possibly inconsistent.

In the next section, possible approaches for modelling a context-sensitive task that could initiate any instance of the above four-steps method are analysed.

3   Possible Approaches for Modelling Context-Sensitive Tasks

A *context-sensitive task* is hereby defined as any task that may require at least one context of use switching for its performance. After a user has performed a particular sub-task in a given context, some other sub-tasks, or possibly task units located deeper in the task hierarchy, may require that the user changes the current context of use in which the task is carried out to another one to complete the main task. Or the varying context of use itself imposes a change to the user. It is not necessary that all sub-tasks to be context-sensitive for a task to be context-sensitive itself. Rather, any task unit that require context of use switching implies that the encompassing task is context-sensitive. In addition, some task unit may be particular to only one context of use, some other, to multiple contexts of use, which are perhaps similar in nature. It could even be imagined that the context-sensitivity is intrinsically part of carrying out the global task.

To model a context-sensitive task, we can start from scratch and invent a totally new way of modelling tasks to take into account their context-sensitivity. We preferred to rely upon an existing task modelling technique that has received attention, theoretical soundness, and experimental studies enough to warrant its selection.

The ConcurTaskTree notation [12] has been selected for these reasons and because a ConcurTaskTree editor already exists [11]. Based on previous work [13] for expanding the original CTT notation to support co-operative tasks, there are at least three possible approaches to extend CTT to explicitly modelling context-sensitive tasks: a monolithic approach, a graph oriented approach, and an additional context-sensitive part.

The *monolithic approach* consists of drawing a global task model that directly encompass context insensitive parts and context-sensitive parts. In these parts, we can find every level of the task decomposition into sub-tasks and so forth. Indeed, for all classic task models represented as a tree decomposition, the parent-child relationship is exploited. The question is therefore where to cut the tree to show a clear separation between context-insensitive and context-sensitive task units. As the context of use may occur wherever in the task accomplishment, this separation may be located everywhere in the task tree. A distinction can be drawn on the tree itself: dotted lines surround context-sensitive parts to make them distinguishable from the rest in a task tree (Fig. 2). For the simplicity, only the parent-child relationship is drawn in this task model: temporal relationships have been omitted temporarily.

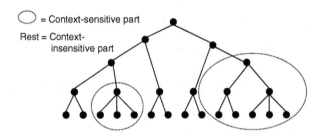

Fig. 2. The monolithic approach for modelling a context-sensitive task

The main advantage of this approach is the unicity of the task model as everything is modelled into a single model. However, within context-sensitive parts, it is hard to differentiate nodes branching to sub-trees to reflect possible changes of context from nodes indicating task units to carry out after the context of use changed. There are consequently no visual cue identifying changes of context. The *graph oriented approach* attempts to address this shortcoming by extracting sub-trees resulting from the context-sensitive part into separate trees that can be related where needed. It consists of establishing a relationship to all sub-trees describing task units resulting from changes of context (Fig. 3).

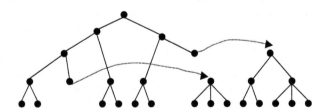

Fig. 3. The graph oriented approach for modelling a context-sensitive task

The biggest advantage of this approach relies in its distinction between non-context-sensitive and context-sensitive parts. However, the resulting model looses its hierarchical structure to become a directed graph. This approach is introducing additional relationships that may increase model cluttering. According to [13], this kind of graph is also harder to interpret and to manipulate by a tool. Conversely, no representation of how and when the context of use may change in the task model is given. The *context-sensitive separation approach* attempts to solve this problem by recognising that the context-sensitive part actually holds two types of arcs and nodes:

1. Traditional arcs and nodes as one can find in a classic task tree: these nodes represent the task units at their various levels of decomposition and the arcs express their parent-child relationship.
2. Decision arcs and nodes so as to select the particular sub-tasks to carry out, depending on conditions expressed on properties of the context of use. These properties are called *contextual properties*, such as, for example, the type of computing platform, the screen resolution, and the network bandwidth. Conditions on these contextual properties are called in turn *contextual conditions*. The chaining of contextual conditions form a decision tree that properly branches to the appropriate task units, depending on the context of use selected.

The context-sensitive separation approach therefore consists in drawing (Fig. 4):

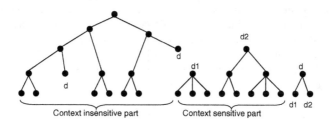

Fig. 4. The context-sensitive separation approach for modelling a context-sensitive task

- A context-insensitive tree containing the decomposition into tasks units that do not change if the context of use changes which ends up with decision points, where to branch to a decision tree for considering right context (*d* points in Fig. 4).
- A series of context-sensitive trees modelling task units for all supported contexts of use (middle in Fig. 4).
- A decision tree (right part of Fig. 4) summarising all contextual conditions. It is expected that each branch is labeled with one contextual condition at a time to avoid multiple logical formula and that all branches appearing at

a same level should form a partition of all possible values of a same contextual condition. For instance, a contextual condition could be "What is the currently used computing platform?", while the possible values could be "PC, Macintosh, WebTV". The decision tree could de detailed as needed with several levels of contextual conditions, and not only one, but one contextual condition is considered at a time. The leaves (d_1 and d_2 here) of this tree should branch to any context-sensitive tree (to the tree having d_1, respectively d_2, as root).

This approach makes more clear the distinction between the context-insensitive part, the context sensitive part, and the decision tree making the link between those parts. However, it is likely that different contexts of use may be considered similarly at different locations of the context-insensitive part. There is consequently no way to factor out the common parts of the context-sensitive part, depending on the selected context of use.

The *complete separation approach* is aimed at factoring out similar sub-trees which are possibly used at different locations in the global task tree, thus minimising duplication of these context-sensitive sub-trees. It consists of identifying (Fig. 5):

- A non-context sensitive part, which similarly produced by the context-sensitive separation approach.
- A series of separate decision trees representing branching to all the possible contexts of use with decision points as root (middle in Fig. 5).
- A series of sub-trees of factored task units to carry out when needed, one sub-tree for each considered value of the final contextual condition (dotted part right in Fig. 5). The difference with respect to the previous approach is that this context-sensitive part consists of a collection of sub-trees that may be called from different places in the decision tree. Therefore, each such sub-tree is unique.

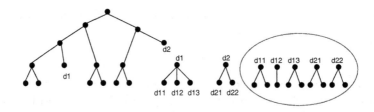

Fig. 5. The complete separation approach for modelling a context-sensitive task

The advantages of this complete separation approach are the following: everything is more obviously separated than in the context-sensitive separation approach (one context-insensitive part, one decision part, and one context-sensitive

part, all consisting of unique sub-trees); decision trees can be edited and maintained independently of each other, with their own logic (the context-sensitive
and context-insensitive parts are task oriented while the other is context-
detection oriented). The major inconvenience of this approach is that it dramatically suffers from a proliferation of trees, even if unique trees, with no direct
linking between them. Moreover, maintaining such series of trees in a repository
becomes quite complex, especially for future algorithms for UI derivation, and
the modelling becomes very different from the initial task model as noted in
CTT. For these reasons, we came to the conclusion that a better solution could
be set up by combining the unique representation of the monolithic approach
with decision tree and clear separation as discussed in the context-sensitive separation approach to produce a model that is closer to the initial CTT notation.
The final solution consists of (Fig. 6):

1. A context-insensitive part as typically modelled in a CTT task model.
2. A decision tree represented by three CTT notation elements: the different
   contexts of use are linked sequentially as optional sub-tasks at the first level
   with the sequencing operator, then the different contextual conditions are
   expressed as sub-sub-tasks with choice operator (mutual exclusion), and finally the leaves of the decision trees are the roots for the context-sensitive
   part
3. A context-sensitive part as a series of sub-trees as typically modelled in
   CTTE.

This final approach is more close to the traditional CTT notation, while re-
specting the identification of the three areas, especially the decision tree. However, to preserve the hierarchical structure, there is a risk of sub-tree reproduc-
tion if one sub-tree of the context-sensitive part is used at different locations,
which is not the case in the complete separation approach.

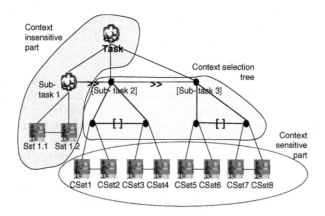

Fig. 6. The final approach for modelling a context-sensitive task

4   Configurations of Context-Sensitive Task Models

Adopting the formalism introduced in Fig. 6, we now may consider different configurations of this context-sensitive task model depending on the number of context-sensitive sub-tasks in the model and the number of possible contexts of use. Let us assume a single interactive task consisting of q sub-tasks at the first level of decomposition and at most m possible contexts of use. Depending on the values of q and m, different configurations can be examined as summarised in Table 1. To graphically depict and analyse possible configurations of context-sensitive task models, let us assume that a horizontal line represents any CTT operator and let us consider task tree with only one level of decomposition for all parts. A sub-task is said to be *context-sensitive* if at least one of its sub-sub-tasks or itself may change if the context of use changes.

Table 1. Possible configurations of context-sensitive task models

	Single context of use	Multiple contexts of use (m)
No context-sensitive sub-task	One context-insensitive tree (Fig. 7a)	One context-insensitive tree, one decision tree, no context-sensitive tree (Fig. 7b)
One context-sensitive sub-task	One context-insensitive tree, one decision tree with one branch, one context-sensitive tree (Fig. 8a)	One context-insensitive tree, one decision tree with m branches, m context-sensitive trees (Fig. 8b)
$p < q$ context-sensitive sub-tasks	One context-insensitive tree, p decision trees with one branch each, p context-sensitive trees (Fig. 9a)	One context-insensitive tree, p decision trees with m branches each, $p \times m$ context-sensitive trees (Fig. 9b)
q context-sensitive sub-tasks	One context-insensitive tree, q decision trees with one branch each, p context-sensitive trees (Fig. 10)	One context-insensitive tree, p decision trees with q branches each, $q \times m$ context-sensitive trees (Fig. 11b)

When there is no context-sensitive sub-task, the configuration is the same as traditionally found in a CTT-like model in a single context of use (Fig. 7a). The multiplicity of the contexts of use in this case does not affect anything since nothing is context-sensitive. Therefore, the decision tree gives rise to a void context-sensitive part (Fig. 7b) and is therefore unuseful.

When there is only one context-sensitive sub-task, the decision tree is reduced to considering only one branch (the one for the only context-sensitive sub-task) for a single context (Fig. 8a) or m branches for multiple contexts (Fig. 8b). In the first case, it means that the context-sensitive part is only conditionally performed if there is a change of context; in the second case, the occurrence of any new context of use may trigger a new decomposition of the context-sensitive part.

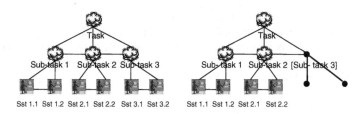

Fig. 7. Configurations with no context-sensitive sub-task: **(a)** single vs. **(b)**multiple contexts.

As discussed above, there is no guarantee that each of these context-sensitive sub-tasks remains unique.

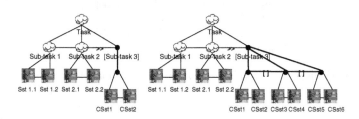

Fig. 8. Configurations with one context-sensitive sub-task: **(a)** single vs. **(b)** multiple contexts.

When there are numerous context-sensitive sub-tasks, let us say $p < q$, but not all of them, there are p possible decision trees in the decision tree part, one for each such sub-task. Each branch leads to one context-sensitive task, respectively p context-sensitive tasks, for a single context of use (Fig. 9a), respectively for multiple contexts of use (Fig. 9b). In the last case, we obtain a maximum of $p \times m$ context-sensitive trees. Indeed, it is likely that not all context-sensitive tasks should respond to all possible contexts of use. It is more likely that only a subset will appear.

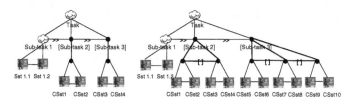

Fig. 9. Configurations with $p \times q$ context-sensitive sub-task: **(a)** single vs. **(b)** multiple contexts.

When all q sub-tasks are context-sensitive, of course there is no longer a need for keeping a context-insensitive part (thus, empty). In a single context of use, the task model is reduced to a decision tree with only one branch to test if we are in the right context of use and q context-sensitive trees related to the context-sensitive sub-tasks (Fig. 10).

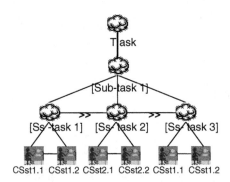

CSst1.1 CSst1.2 CSst2.1 CSst2.2 CSst1.1 CSst1.2

Fig. 10. Configurations with all context-sensitive sub-tasks in a single context.

In the case of m multiple contexts of use, the context-insensitive part is still empty, but leaves space for a potentially huge decision tree with m branches at the first level and at most $q \times m$ context-sensitive tasks at the subsequent level (Fig. 11). In these two last cases, the task model begins directly with the decision tree to branch to the context-sensitive sub-tasks which are appropriate to consider depending on the identified context of use resulting from parsing the decision tree.

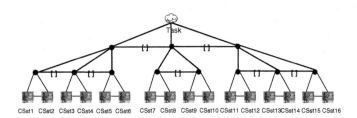

CSst1 CSst2 CSst3 CSst4 CSst5 CSst6   CSst7 CSst8 CSst9 CSst10 CSst11 CSst12 CSst13CSst14 CSst15 CSst16

Fig. 11. Configurations with all context-sensitive sub-tasks in multiple contexts.

5   Factoring Out Common Parts for Multiple Contexts of Use

As criticised above, the possible configurations of task models which have been examined in the previous section do not address the problem of factoring out identical elements in the tree. The worst consequence of this is that some similar elements in the task model (e.g., some task units) may be reproduced several times, actually as many times as the same part is used. This raises the question of whether to concentrate all contextual conditions for branching to the differ-ent context-sensitive tasks into one decision tree or to distribute them among the global task tree to maximise factoring out of common parts and to avoid duplication. To discuss this issue, let use assume a task model for inputting per-sonal information that needs to be carried out on three computing platforms (i.e. Personal Computer, cellular phone, and Web-based appliance with low or high resolution). This gives rise to four possible contexts of use. Let us also assume in this scenario that the task contains a sub-task displaying general information (i.e. company logo, date and time) whatever the context of use is. Let us also consider that any Web-based appliance should additionally display help links to provide guidance to visitors. A context-sensitive task model without any factor-ing out is represented in Fig. 12a. The model begins with a decision tree with two contextual conditions: one for identifying the computing platform, another for detecting the screen resolution. All sub-tasks are put as sub-trees of the leaves of the decision tree. In Fig. 12b, a hybrid factoring out is adopted. Observing that the sub-task "Display information" is carried out in all possible contexts of use, this sub-task is extracted from the rest to become the non-context-sensitive part. As all sub-tasks in the mobile phone case may be performed in a sequential and individual manner, this model prefers to leave this arrangement of sub-tasks as it is. A contextual condition states that if a Web appliance is detected, help links should be displayed. Since the arrangement of sub-tasks is unique for the Web case with low resolution, a context-sensitive decom-position is produced and maintained.

However, the arrangement of sub-tasks is identical in both the PC and Web with high resolution cases, thus leading to a last contextual condition gathering these two contexts of use. This factoring out is hybrid since, on the one hand, the "Display information" is correctly factored out, but on the other hand, the leaves of the tree are not unique (e.g., "Input first name" is duplicated two times). More regrettable is that the contextual conditions are no longer equiv-alent: they are no longer simple conditions with simple values as output and they are not necessarily mutually exclusive. To avoid complex contextual condi-tions and to avoid possible overlapping of their values, we suggest modelling a context-sensitive task with progressive factoring out. In Fig. 12c, the "Display information" sub-task is common to all possible contexts of use, thus it is kept in the context-insensitive part. The decision tree then begins with only one sim-ple contextual condition: what is the currently used computing platform? The nodes associated with the values of this condition give rise to other individual sub-trees, one for each computing platform. Observing that the sub-task "Dis-

Fig. 12. Task model without factoring out (**a**), with hybrid factoring out (**b**) with progressive factoring out (**c**).

play links" is common to all sub-cases of the Web appliance case, it is added as a context-sensitive sub-task that is local to the sub-tree. Next, the second contextual condition is asked: what is the resolution of the Web appliance's screen? The two possible values give rise to two individual sub-trees detailing what are the specific context-sensitive sub-tasks to perform in that case. Since the "Input person" sub-task is common to both cases with same decomposition beneath, it could also make sense to isolate it by analogy with the "Display links" sub-tasks. This progressive way of factoring out identical elements of the context-sensitive part ensure that only simple contextual conditions are preserved. But the price to pay to this is that a mixing of decision tree and context-sensitive part arcs and nodes is introduced, thus increasing the importance of the notation to see the difference. Otherwise, it may also be desirable not to factor out common parts.

6   A Case Study

To illustrate how this can be applied, let us introduce a case study described by a user scenario of the task "child registration for a leisure activity". A child must be registered in a leisure club for children where various activities are organised. Each time a child wants to participate into any activity, he or she must register not only for organisation issues, but also for producing an invoice to any person who is responsible for the child. This interactive task should be carried out in two contexts of use:

1. A non-stressing context where a written registration form is sent to the club secretariat. In this context, the task may be decomposed into three sub-tasks:
   - Identifying a child for an activity: this subtasks covers all signaletic information such as first name, last name, birth date, sex, computed age, phone number of the responsible person. This information may also include public and private information (e.g., a free text in case of need). A picture can be added. To identify a child, the secretary searches a data base by first name and/or last name. This action may be processed iteratively until a child can be selected in the current list.
   - Identifying a responsible person for the child: for each possible person, a personal identification number is provided, along with first name, last name, title, address, city, zip code, country, up to four phone numbers.
   - Registering the child: depending on the computed age and space availability for activities, a list of possible activities is displayed. Each activity is char-acterised by a name, a monitor, a place, a date, the hours, an age interval, the current attendance, the maximum attendance. Depending on this information, the cost of the registration is computed and added in an invoice. If the child is not a club member, an automated registration is added with cost.
2. A stressing context where a vocal registration is communicated from the responsible person to a secretary in a very noisy and confusing environment. The morning of the activity date, the secretary downloads on a PDA a list of current club members and the list of possible activities of the day. When a child suddenly arrives at the club entrance, often with a responsible person, the secretary asks her a first name and a last name and attempts to quickly locate her in the list. If the child is located, the secretary assumes that the rest can be found after without too much trouble. If not, in order not to stop the responsible person too long, the secretary input name and address. The remainder will be filled up afterwards. The secretary also takes a picture of the child with an ID. An activity is then selected, provided that constraints are met. The secretary works with pressure: many people arrive at the same time in a short amount of time and the running children prevent her to quickly grasp all information accurately. After this stressing period, the secretary comes back to her PC, transfers information, and completes the task by retrieving information from data bases as described above. Fig. 13 represents a possible task model for this task which is restructured depending on the context, but which holds the same sub-tasks.

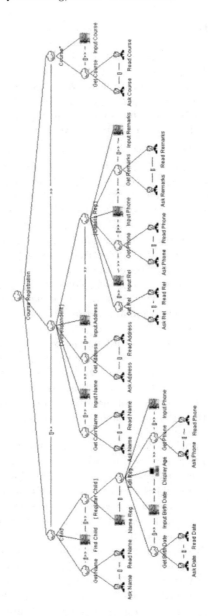

Fig. 13. A possible task model for the "Child registration for a leisure activity".

In the task modelling process, the child registration task was simplified as follows :

- In the stressing context, the operator is searching the name of the child in the list; if found, then desired courses are chosen, else the name of the child, the name of the correspondent and his address are recorded and then the then desired courses are chosen. Hence, the responsible person registration is optional, only if the child was not previously recorded.
- In the normal context, the full registration of the child and his correspondent (for a new child) are performed. The case when the correspondent has more then one child was not considered.

This task modelling is progressively illustrated in Fig. 14, 15, and 16.

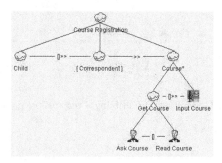

Fig. 14. Main task "Child registration for a leisure activity" partial modeling.

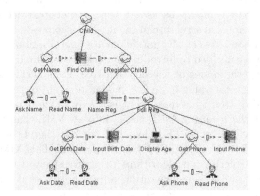

Fig. 15. Sub-Task "Identifying a child".

As it could be seen, there is another context of use, depending on the data source: written document or verbal. The second could be seen as co-operative (although the correspondent role is not so relevant). However it illustrates a second context of use. The first context of use was modelled as follows. For child registration, if not found, either input child name (stressing context) either full registration are performed ([ ] operator). For correspondent registration, in the stressing context only name and address are recorded. In the normal context, details are also recorded (optional task). The second context of use is modelled using [ ] operator.

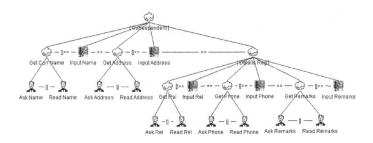

Fig. 16. Sub-Task "Identifying a responsible person".

7   Conclusion

This paper presented a method for modelling context-sensitive tasks with the aid of the ConcurTaskTree notation [12]. Several approaches were considered and analysed to come up with a final approach combining clear separation of context-sensitive part, context-insensitive part, and context decision tree, while preserving the hierarchical structure of the model, as expressed in CTT. In order to make a distinction between the normal choice operator and the ones used for the decision tree, we decided to introduce a marked structured annotation in the tasks representing the nodes of the decision tree. Each such task is then augmented with the current value (e.g., low/moderate/high) of the contextual condition considered at that time (e.g., what is the available bandwidth). We then choose to export the resulting CTT model into an XML-compliant file thanks to the facility provided by CTTE. This XML file can then transformed into an XIML-compliant file [14] using XSLT transformations. This XIML file can then be exploited by UI derivation algorithms to progressively derive a generic UI, then a specific UI, and a code generation/interpretation as described in Fig. 1. The study of this derivation process is another importance piece of research, where the context-sensitive task model, along with its domain model are separately or simultaneously considered to derive presentation and dialog models, that are in turn refined into a specific one after considering the user model. Today, some case studies of context-sensitive tasks have been performed with the above method, including the Map Annotation Assistant as described in [11] and the multi-context registration procedure (both in a stressed highly-constrained and in a quiet moderately-constrained environments). A limitation of this current model is relying in its inability to highlight change of context during task accomplishment. The extended model is able to show different sub-task trees depending on different contexts of use considered at a decision point. But it is unable to show how one of these sub-task trees can branch to another sub-task tree to denote a dynamic change of context, where the context is changing while the user is carrying out the task.

References

1. G.G. Abowd and A.D. Key. Towards a better understanding of context and context-awareness. Technical Report Research report 1999-22, Georgia University of Technology, 1999. Accessible at ftp://ftp.cc.gatech.edu/pub/gvu/tr/1999/99-22.pdf.
2. M. Abrams, C. Phanouriou, A.L. Batongbacal, S. Williams, and J. Shuster. UIML: An appliance-independent XML user interface language. In A. Mendelzon, editor, *Proceedings of 8th International World-Wide Web Conference WWW'8 (Toronto, May 11-14, 1999)*, Amsterdam, 1999. Elsevier Science Publishers. Accessible at http://www8.org/w8-papers/5b-hypertext-media/uiml/uiml.html.
3. B. Bomsdorf and G. Swillius. From task to dialogue: Task based user interface design. *SIGCHI Bulletin*, 30(4):40–42, 1998.
4. G. Calvary, J. Coutaz, and D. Thevenin. A unifying reference framework for the development of plastic user interfaces. In *Proceedings of IFIP WG 2.7 Conference on Engineering the User Interface EHCI'2001 (Toronto, May 11-13, 2001).*, London, 2001. Chapman & Hall.
5. S.K. Card, T.P. Moran, and A. Newell. *The Psychology of Human-Computer Interaction*. Lawrence Erlbaum Associates, New York, 1983.
6. J. Eisenstein, J. Vanderdonckt, and A. Puerta. Adapting to mobile contexts with user-interface modeling. In *Proceedings of IEEE Workshop on Mobile Computing Systems and Applications WCSMA'2000 (Monterey, December 7-8, 2000).*, pages 83–92, Los Alamitos, 2000. IEEE Press.
7. J. Eisenstein, J. Vanderdonckt, and A. Puerta. Applying model-based techniques to the development of user interfaces for mobile computers. In *Proceedings of ACM Conference on Intelligent User Interfaces IUI'2001 (Albuquerque, January 11-13, 2001)*, pages 69–76, New York, 2001. ACM Press.
8. P. Johnson. *Human-Computer Interaction: Psychology, Task Analysis and Software Engineering*. McGraw-Hill, Maidenhead, 1992.
9. V. Kaptelinin and B. Nardi. Activity theory: Basic concepts and applications. ACM Press (New York), 2000. CHI'2000 Tutorial Notes vol. 5.
10. B. Myers, S. Hudson, and R. Pausch. Past, present, future of user interface tools. *ACM Transactions on Computer-Human Interaction*, 7:3–28, 1. Accessible at www.acm.org/pubs/articles/journals/tochi/2000-7-1/p3-myers/p3-myers.pdf.
11. F. Paternò. *Model-Based-Design and Evaluation of Interactive Applications*. Springer-Verlag, Berlin, 2000.
12. F. Paternò, C. Mancini, and S. Meniconi. ConcurTaskTree: A diagrammatic notation for specifying task models. In S. Howard, J. Hammond, and G. Lindgaard, editors, *Proceedings of IFIP TC 13 International Conference on Human-Computer Interaction Interact'97 (Sydney, July 14-18, 1997)*, pages 362–369, Boston, 1997. Kluwer Academic Publishers.

13. F. Paternó, C. Santoro, and S. Tahmassebi. Formal model for cooperative tasks: Concepts and an application for en-route air traffic control. In P. Markopoulos and P. Johnson, editors, *Proc. Of 5th Int. Workshop on Design, Specification, and Verification of Intractive Systems DSV-IS '98 (Abingdon, June 3-5 1998)*, pages 71–86, Vienna, 1998. Springer-Verlag.

14. A. Puerta and J. Eisenstein. A representational basis for user interface transformations. In Ch. Wiecha and P. Szekely, editors, *Proceedings of CHI'2001 Workshop "Transforming the UI for Anyone, Anywhere - Enabling an Increased Variety of Users, Devices, and Tasks Through Interface Transformations" (Seattle, April 1-2, 2001)*, New York, 2001. ACM Press.

15. A. Savidis, D. Akoumianakis, and C. Stephanidis. *The Unified User Interface Design Method*, chapter 21, pages 417–440. Lawrence Erlbaum Associates, Mahwah, 2001.

16. P. Szekely, P. Sukaviriya, J. Castells, Muthukumarasamy, and E. Salcher. Declarative interface models for user interface construction tools : The MASTERMIND approach. In *Engineering for Human-Computer Interaction*, pages 120–150. Chapman & Hall, London, 1996.

17. M. J. Tauber. ETAG: Extended task action grammar. a language for the description of the user's task language. In D. Diaper, D. Gilmore, G. Cockton, and B. Shackel, editors, *Proc. of the 3rd IFIP TC 13 Conf. On Human Computer Interaction Interact '90 (Cambridge, 27-31 August 1990)*, pages 163–168, Amsterdam, 1990. Elsevier.

18. D. Thevenin and J. Coutaz. Plasticity of user interfaces: Framework and research agenda. In A. Sasse and C.W. Johnson, editors, *Proceedings of 7th IFIP TC 13 International Conference on Human-Computer Interaction Interact'99 (Edinburgh, August 30-September 3, 1999)*, pages 110–117, London, 1999. IOS Press.

19. M. van Welie, C.G. van der Veer, and A. Eliens. An ontology for task world models. In *Proc.of the 5th Int. Workshop on Design, Specification and Verification of Interactive Systems DSV-IS'98 (Abingdon, 3-5 June 1998)*, pages 57–70, Vienna, 1998. Springer Verlag.

Industrial User Interface Evaluation Based on Coloured Petri Nets Modelling and Analysis

Maria de F.Q.V. Turnell, Alexandre Scaico, Marckson R.F. de Sousa, and
Angelo Perkusich

Departamento de Engenharia Elétrica
Universidade Federal da Paraíba
Caixa Postal 10105 Campina Grande – Paraíba – Brasil
{turnellm,scaico,marckson,perkusic}@dee.ufpb.br

Abstract. This paper presents and discusses a generic navigation model
built with Coloured Petri net (CPN) to support the analysis of the navigation component in human interface design. The modelling and analysis
is developed in the context of supervisory control systems for industrial
plants. The paper discusses the results of using this navigation model in
an industrial application case study.

1   Introduction

In the search for human computer interaction quality the designer needs a solid
base to match the user's abilities and limitations with those of the interactive
system's technology. Faced with the growing number of implementation choices,
designers need to evaluate alternative solutions before the implementation phase.

The task of appropriately representing the user interface component of a
system goes through the full understanding of its functionality and behaviour,
and to support this task many formalisms and methods have been proposed.

Turnell and Sousa in [11] proposed a user interface design method that begins by identifying the user profile followed by a series of steps, the first of which
is the task analysis. Task analysis [6] has been an approach extensively used to
support designers in this understanding. It consists of a detailed study in order
to determine a task's nature, purpose and components (subtasks and states)
as well as the sequence of execution. The sequence of execution is particularly
important as it represents the user's action plan (or scenario) to solve a problem [12]. The method follows with the description of the interaction model that
specifies amongst other aspects the navigation structure of the interface. This
navigation structure, modelled in CPN, is presented and discussed in this paper. The resulting model is verified according to a set of specified properties
of navigation to ensure its usability, such as reversibility of user actions within
the specified context and access to specific points in the interaction sequence.
In the method, to each step of conception is associated an evaluation phase to
determine the specification adequacy to the user profile, to the task description
and to ergonomic criteria. The last step in the method consists in building a
prototype to be validated by the user during usability tests.

C. Johnson (Ed.): DSV-IS 2001, LNCS 2220, pp. 69–87, 2001.
© Springer-Verlag Berlin Heidelberg 2001

The use of formal methods in the design of human machine interfaces allows investigating the behaviour of a mathematical model of the interface early in the design phase. It has already been shown that Petri Nets (PN) [3] is an adequate modelling tool for human interfaces [1][5][8], for it provides graphical and formal representation that facilitate the analysis of these systems. They also offers support tools for building the model and verifying the net properties through simulation.

From the study of the interface sequencing, the authors built a model to support the analysis of the navigation between interface states during a task (or subtasks) execution [10]. This model, built in Coloured Petri Net (CPN) [2], intends to be a generic representation of the navigation structure of a user interface. Though it has already been used to model the navigation aspects of an internet browser's interface, in order to evaluate its generality and usefulness this work presents and discusses the results of its use in the context of industrial systems human-interface. This paper presents the results of applying the model to this context.

Industrial human interfaces, though similar to other applications interfaces, have characteristics that demand a closer study, in order to choose an adequate modelling tool. The volume of information presented to the plant operator is usually high, some, of which with hard deadlines and navigation restrictions imposing a high cognitive load. Also, the operator has to react to events and complete a task considering a deadline and safety conditions [13]. Therefore, the optimisation of the interaction navigation design could lead into more efficient task completion and an overall raise in the quality of system's performance and safety operation.

The paper is organised in 5 sections. In section 2 the original navigation model is briefly introduced. Section 3 describes an industrial user interface built to represent a set of characteristics typically found in industrial applications. It represents objects and aspects of interest for the context of study present in this paper. Section 4 presents the model applied to the industrial context and discusses its analysis, which was supported by the tool Design/CPN [14]. The work concludes with a discussion of the applicability of this model to the conception of the human interface component of industrial systems, and proposes future directions for this research work.

2   A Generic Interface Navigation Model in CPN

Petri Nets are a mathematical and graphical modelling tool that can be used in a variety of systems [3], in particular in systems that are asynchronous, parallel and concurrent. A Coloured Petri Net (CPN) [2] is a high level net which introduces the concept of data types (colours). This allows the designer of a system to build models that can be more compact. In the context of this paper this characteristic has allowed the simplification of the structure of the model. This was possible because interface systems have a high number of very similar elements and functions, which otherwise would result in repetitive structures. Moreover, there is a computational tool, named Design/CPN [14] that provides a graphical environment for editing, syntax verification, as well as behaviour analysis and verification of CPN models.

The CPN, shown in Fig. 1 [10], models the navigation in a windows-based interface where a colour set was chosen to represent the elements typically found in these interfaces such as windows, buttons and menus. In this model, the interface active windows and navigation options are modelled as state variables (places); the navigation between windows is modelled as transitions and the System State is represented by the net markings.

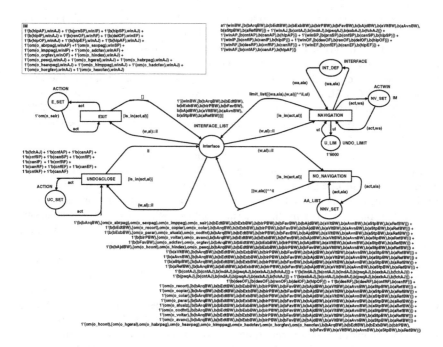

Fig. 1. CPN Navigation Model, for a Browser

This model has a single token that represents the Interface State, which colour set is **INTERFACE_LIST**. This colour defines a list that is used as a stack, in order to allow for the return navigation to a previous state (undo) in the interaction. The first element in the list represents the current state (the active window and the corresponding navigation options), whereas the other elements are stored in the reverse order of the interaction sequence states. In the specific case of industrial interfaces, this does not pose a problem during the analysis, since no matter how many windows the interface might have, only few windows will be simultaneously open. This restriction on the number of windows simultaneously open is found in most cases in order to reduce the user disorientation during interface navigation, for system safety reasons. Therefore, although the place behaves as a stack, during the model analysis there will not be a state space explosion.

Two functions were defined in order to manipulate the list described above: **is_in** and **new_interface**. The **is_in** function searches for an interface element in the action list. The **new_interface** function inserts an interface element in this list. Each time an interface element is acted upon, such as a button press, the interface goes to a new state, i.e. a new interface (window) becomes active. In the navigation model, each net arc has an associated expression to define the flow of information.

In the browser navigation model, shown in Fig. 1, the value of the input element is always the value of the active interface. That is, the interface changes according to the action executed by the user. For instance, if the transition **NEW_WINDOW** fires, a new interface (window, action list) defined by the function **new_interface** is added to the interface list. On the other hand, if the transition **UNDO&CLOSE** fires, the interface returns to the previous state, removing the element from the head of the interface list. Finally, if the transition **EXIT** fires, the interface reaches the Exit State in the interaction sequence, stopping the system's execution.

The transitions in this model represents four navigation situations: **NAVIGA-TION** - navigate between windows; **NO_NAVIGATION** - navigate within the same window; **UNDO&CLOSE** - close a window, and; **EXIT** - stop system's execution. Each transition is associated to the interface place and to one or more other places. The places represent the interface options when one of the transitions fires. For instance, for the transition **NAVIGATION** the places are: **U_LIM** which poses an upper limit to the number of UNDO requests that the system can execute; **INT_DEF** which holds the description of all the system's windows, and; **NV_SET** which holds pairs of elements, associating a window with the action that the user must perform in order to reach it. Thus, to enable the transition **NAVIGATION**, the user action (menu selection or button pressing) must correspond to the action listed in the pair represented in the place **NV_SET**. When this transition fires, a copy of the corresponding window is inserted in the list represented by the token in the place **Interface**, and a token is deposited in **INT_DEF**.

To enable transition **NO_NAVIGATION**, the element in the head of the list is removed from the interface list, and the corresponding options are compared with one of the navigation options in the place **NNV_SET**. If the option is in the list, the transition fires, indicating that the option was chosen. This selection might cause or not, a change in the list of available choices. Thus, this item (interface and options list) is returned to the interface place.

The transition **UNDO&CLOSE**, models the closing of a window and the return to a previous state in the interaction navigation. When it fires, the first item in the Interface place is removed, recovering the previous state. The corresponding place is **UC_SET**, which holds a set of the user navigation choices that must match one of the choices represented in the list associated to the element in the head of the interface list.

When transition **EXIT** fires, the system reaches the Exit state, finishing its execution, modelled by an empty list (**[]** in place **Interface**). The place **E_SET** has only one token that corresponds to the systems' exit option. This option must match one of those present in the list belonging to the element in the head of the interface list.

3   Industrial Human Interfaces

In supervisory software, the synoptic representation of an industrial plant allows the user to access plant activity information coming from different types of equipment and systems, such as diagrams, set points, alarm lists and other synoptic representations of equal complexity level [13].

The industrial human interface presented in this paper is based on a demo distributed with the software ©*InTouch* [1]. This was chosen because it offers the typical resources of this type of interface. It allows the operator to interact with a chemical process that consists in producing and storing a radioactive material. The interface consists of nine windows where the user can set variables, navigate between windows, and monitor through text and graphics the status of various aspects of the plant. The plant production consists in mixing a chemical concentrate inside of a reactor, which is followed by storing the final product into barrels. In the process, the operator performs a set of activities such as: monitoring the process by means of an animated synoptical view of the plant (see Fig. 2) and trend diagrams related to the plant's variable under control; controlling the percentage values of the components in the mix; filling and storing barrels (see Fig. 3); and handling alarms during plant operation.

WinReactor: Main system window. It presents an animated synoptic of the industrial plant. In this window it is displayed the current concentration of chemicals used in the process mix and the temperature and storage levels in a reservoir where the final mix is stored. In this window, the plant operator interacts with the system through a set of six buttons that are mainly used for navigation between windows.

WinReactorHelp: Help window that is superposed on the *WinReactor*. This particular window displays a help text about the synoptic.

WinBatch: Window where the user defines the concentration mix using a slide bar and a set of buttons for fine adjustments. This window overlaps the original active window on the screen.

WinBatchSet: Window where the user can (alternatively) define the mix concentration, using the keyboard. When displayed, it overlaps the *WinBatch* window.

WinHist: Window that shows a history graphic about the process. It offers buttons for navigation and bars for setting the graphic presentation characteristics.

---

[1] Software distributed by the *Wonderware Corporation*

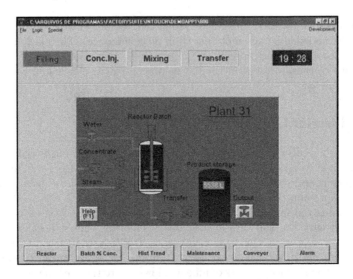

Fig. 2. Window Reactor from Intouch Demo

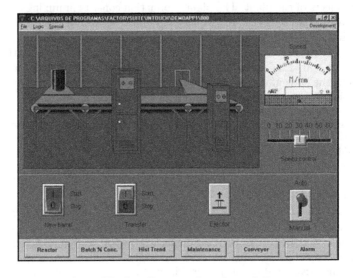

Fig. 3. Window Conveyor from Intouch Demo

WinHistHelp: Help window about the window *WinHist.*

WinMaintence: Window that shows the status of some aspects of the plant. When the user exits it, the system returns to the window where it was originally called.

WinConveyor: This window shows, through animation, the filling of barrels with the process mix being produced in the plant. It offers a button to toggle between manual and automatic filling, buttons to navigate between windows, and buttons to control the variables of the process such as the speed of the conveyor belts transporting the barrels.

WinAlarm: Displays all the alarm messages. It offers buttons to acknowledge the alarms individually or as a group, and buttons to navigate between windows.

4   Industrial Human Interface CPN Model

In the navigation model presented in section 2, all interface objects were assumed active at any time, i.e. available to the user. The model's new version, shown in Fig. 4, allows to represent the state (enabled/disabled) of the interface objects used for navigation purposes as a result of the navigation path taken by the user. Therefore it is possible to represent and analyse the status of all interface objects, whether they are related or not to the current active interface window. In order to model the industrial interface described in the previous section it was necessary to introduce two new types of navigation between windows: one that closes the current active window and opens another, and one that superposes the current active window with a new one.

4.1   Model Description

The resulting new version of the navigation model, applied to the industrial interface is presented in Figure 4.

It follows the declaration node for the CPN Industrial Interface Navigation Model:

```
color Window = with WinReactor | WinBatch | WinHist | WinMaintance |
                    WinBatch | WinHist | WinMaintance | WinConveyor |
                    WinAlarme | WinBatchSet | WinReactorHelp |
                    WinHistHelp;
color Button = with ButReactorHelp | ButBatchExit | ButBatchSet |
                    ButBatchOK | ButBatchUp | ButBatchDown | ButBatchBar |
                    ButMaintExit | ButAlarmConc | ButAlarmTemp |
                    ButAlarmLevel | ButReactor | ButBatch | ButHist |
                    ButMaint | ButConveyor | ButEndProgram | ButBatchSetOK |
                    ButReactorHelpExit | ButConveyorMA | ButConveyorEst1 |
                    ButConveyorEst2 | ButConveyorEjet | ButConveyorBar |
                    ButHistCTime | ButHistDefault | ButHistV100 |
                    ButHistV50 | ButHist3m | ButHist1m | ButHistBarVert |
                    ButHistBarHor | ButHistHelp | ButAlarm |
                    ButHistHelpExit | ButAlarmClose | ButAlarmAckAll;
color Status = with enabled | disabled; color Button_Status =
product Button*Status; color Options = product
Window*Button_Status; color List_Button_Status = list
Button_Status; color Interface = product
Window*List_Button_Status; color List_Interface = list Interface;
color Prob_Alarm = bool; color Which_Alarm = int with 1..3;

var y: Prob_Alarm;  var Win, Win1: Window;
var But, But1:List_Button_Status;  var act: Button;
var status, status1: Status;  var list: List_Interface;
var ProbAl: Prob_Alarm;  var t: Which_Alarm;
var interface: Interface;  var but_stat: Button_Status;
```

76   M. de F.Q.V. Turnell et al.

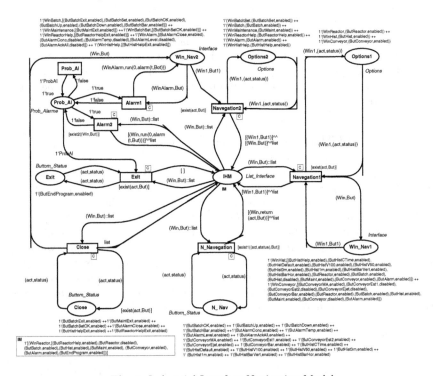

Fig. 4. Industrial Interface Navigation Model

The meaning of each colour set is as follows:

Window: Set with all the windows in the interface.
Button: Set with all the buttons in the interface.
Status: associated to a button, enabled or disabled.
Button_Status: Pair that represents the name of a button and its status.
Options: Triplet (window, button, status) which associates a window name to a button name and its status.
List_Button_Status: List with button status elements.
Interface: Product, with a window name as the first element, and a status button list as the second element.
Interface_List: List of elements of the type interface.
Prob_Alarm: (Alarm Probability) Boolean value.
Which_Alarm: Integer ranging from 1 to 3, to identify the type of alarm.

4.2 Model Functions

A new set of functions was defined to deal with the new navigation situations as well as the specific behaviour of the industrial interface modelled. These functions were defined to generate alarms and to alter the status of the alarm acknowledge buttons, allowing the operator to acknowledge the alarms individually and as a group and to change the current status in the barrel filling process (automatic/manual). These groups of functions are listed below:

exist: Verifies if the interaction element to be selected is in the current active window.

exist1: Verifies if the interaction element to be selected is in the current active window and if it is also active (for those elements which can be able or disabled).

test_AckAll: Verifies if the interaction element *ButAlarmAckAll* is enabled, if so, disables it.

change_status: Verifies if the selected interaction element is an alarm acknowledge, disables it and runs the function **test_AckAll**.

change_status1: Disables all the alarm acknowledge (including the *ButAlarmAckAll*).

change_status2: Toggles the status of all interaction elements *ButConveyorEst1*, *ButConveyorEst2* and *ButConveyorEjet* from able to disable (represents the toggle switch that chooses between automatic and manual filling of barrels).

return: Verifies which interaction element was selected, and executes the corresponding function. If the element is either *ButAlarmConc, ButAlarmTemp* or *ButAlarmLevel* the function executed is **change_status**. If the element is *ButAlarmAckAll* function **change_status2** is executed; and if the element is *ButConveyorMA* the function **change_status2** is executed.

alarm: Generates a random alarm.

run: Generates a random alarm probability.

exist2: Verifies if *WinAlarm* is the current active window.

As in the previous version of the model described in Section 2, the place **IHM** holds the information on which window is currently active. In this case, the initial active window is *WinReactor*, from this place in the net it can occur one of the five types of navigation transition that follows:

Navigation Type1. Consists of the navigation between windows, with the closing of the current active window and the opening of the requested window. In this case, the list in the **IHM** place has only one element, which must be replaced by the new one.

The transitions **Navegation1**, and the places **Win_Nav1** and **Options1**, model this navigation.

Win_Nav1: holds tokens that indicate which windows can cause this type of navigation.

Options1: holds tokens which associate an action on an interface navigation object (eg. button pressing) with the corresponding destination window.

Thes guard for this transition's is the **"exist"** function, which verifies if the navigation triggering action is available in the current active window, in other words, if the corresponding action is available in this window.

Navigation Type 2. Navigation between windows, with the requested window superposing the current active window, and becoming the new active window. This new active window is added to the interface list.

The transition **Navegation2** and the two places described below model this navigation.

Win_Nav2: This place has tokens that represent which windows can superpose the current active window, and thus become the new active window.

Options2: this place has tokens, which relate a navigation interface action to a window that must be opened superpose the current active window.

This transition's guard is the **"exist"** function, which verifies if the navigation triggering action is available in the current active window.

NoNavigation. Consists on navigating between options within the current active window. The transition **N_Navegation** and the place **N_NAV** model this situation. Tokens in place **N_NAV** determine internal navigation actions to a particular window. Note that all the tokens have buttons, which are enabled.

This guard of this transition is the **"exist1"** function, which verifies if the triggering action is available in the current active window, and if its status is enabled (i.e. available to the user). This transition leads into four possible routes of events in the interface list. Which one will be taken is decided by the **"return"** function in the transition's arc connecting it to the interface place:

If the action to be taken is the selection of the button *ButConveyorMA*, the buttons *ButConveyorEst1*, *ButConveyorEst2* e *ButConveyorEjet* will toggle their status (enabled/disabled or vice versa).

If the action to be taken is the selection of the button *ButAlarmConc* or, *ButAlarmTemp* or, *ButAlarmeLevel*; the selected button will have its status changed to disabled. This change occurs through the function **"change status"** which executes whenever one of the alarm buttons is pressed.

If the action to be taken is the selection of the button *ButAlarmAck-All* (available only when the three types of alarms have occurred), the buttons *ButAlarmAckAll*, *ButAlarmConc*, *ButAlarmTemp* and *ButAlarmLevel* will have their status changed to disabled. This change occurs through the function **"change_status1"** which executes whenever the button *ButAlarmAckAll* is pressed.

If the action to be taken is the selection of a button which does not change its own status or that of any other button in the same window, the information is returned to the top of the list unaltered, just indicating that a selection has been made.

Close. Consists on closing the current active window, which might have been superposed by another window. This navigation is modelled by the transition **Close** and by the place **Close**. This place holds tokens which relate a navigation action to a window indicating which window must be closed if a specific option is selected by the user in the current active window. This transition's guard is the **"exist"** function, which verifies if the navigation triggering action is available in the current active window.

Exit. The transition **Exit** and the place **Exit** model this type of navigation. When this transition fires the application execution is resumed. Place **Exit** has only one token that represents the navigation action of resuming the running of the application.

Three more transitions were introduced into this new version of the model in order to generate the random alarms: **Alarm1**, **Alarm2** and **Prob_Al**, needed to run the model, as it will be described as follows.

4.3 Random Alarm Generation

A function was defined in order to simulate the alarms that occur in an industrial plant. In this particular case there are three alarms related respectively to the level of concentration in the mix, to process temperature level and to the mix level. In the event of an alarm, the corresponding button in the interface must become enabled.

The alarms are modelled by the transitions **Prob_Al**, **Alarm1** and **Alarm 2**, and by the place **Prob_Al**, detailed as follows:

Prob_Al: The token in this place has a Boolean value used as a restriction on the alarm firing, since it must only happen when the token value is true.

Prob_Al: This transition generates the probability of occurrence of an alarm by replacing the false valued token in the place **Prob_Al**, with a Boolean random value (true or false).

Alarm1: This transition models the alarm generation when the window *WinAlarm* is not active. It has as input parameters the tokens from **Prob_Alarme** and *WinAlarm* and its navigation options. If all three types of alarm have occurred, this transition changes the status of the button **ButAlarmAckAll** to "enabled".

Alarm2: This transition models the alarm generation when the window *WinAlarme* is active. In this case, the input parameters are the head element of the **IHM** list and the *Prob_Alarme* place token.

In a synthetic view of the model presented above, a navigation request can only be executed in the active interface if it exists and if it is available (for those options that can be enabled/disabled). The model simulation cycle is interwoven by alarm occurrences until the occurrence of the event request to exit from the system.

5 Model Analysis

Among many aspects of interest to the area of interface design, this work focuses on the analysis of Interaction State Transitions through model verification. With this model the authors expect to be able to analyse an interface's interaction sequences whether intentionally introduced in its original specification or as a consequence of design flaws. Model analysis is particularly important for large systems, such as industrial applications where other types of analysis might be not feasible. The objective of the navigation component analysis is to be able to detect design problems such as deadlocks, non-existence of access path between interface states, overestimation or underestimation of paths between interaction states, non-optimized access path between states (path complexity or extent) and non-availability of reverse path between states.

The proposed analysis is based upon the Occurrence Graph (Occ) which is useful to analyse from an initial state (or marking) all the net markings, and all the available transitions for each net marking. Associated to the Occ graph, the tool *Design/CPN* provides a list with the entire Occ node and arc descriptors as well as a report with the Occ statistics. It is also possible to verify the interface model based upon the model's properties, as follows.

5.1 Navigation Model's Properties

This section presents a set of net properties that are associated to the navigation usability requirements. The properties informally presented in this section represent the navigation net behaviour and were used in the navigation model analysis.

Given that an interface navigation is represented by the CPN model described above, its characteristics can be express in terms of the net properties, as it is illustrated below.

Reversibility - Reversibility is the ability to return in the interaction, cancelling unwanted actions. It does not necessarily apply to all the net states. This property can be verified by means of the net reachability.

Existence of access paths to specific points in the interaction - For usability reasons [4], the access to help facilities must be available at any point during an interaction. The analysis of this navigation aspect is possible through the analysis of the net markings, verifying if from a state M_k is possible to reach the state M_j, where the first element in the token **INTERFACE_LIST** corresponds to the request for help.

Reinitialization - Ability to return to the beginning of the interaction. This behaviour is verified through the analysis of the net markings. If the initial marking is in the list of home markings, shown in the Occ report, this property is satisfied by the navigation net. Note that if all the net markings are home markings this could be interpreted as the existence of connecting paths between all the interface states.

Access to Exit - From the usability point of view systems should offer more than one exit point in the interface. To analyse the access to exit points in the interface is necessary to verify if all the dead markings in the Occ report correspond to the exit status. This status is characterised by the firing of the Exit transition. When this transition fires, the interface list is cleared, therefore the corresponding marking is a dead marking. This dead marking must always be reachable if there must be an exit from any point in the interaction. In this situation, the exit marking must be in the list of dead markings and in the list of home markings, but this is not true for all systems.

5.2   Automatic and Interactive Simulations

The model analysis consisted in a sequence of interactive and automatic simulations, followed by the generation of occurrence graphs and Messages Sequence Charts that enabled the analysis of the interface navigation scenarios.

Interactive simulations were done during model building in order to verify the logic correctness of its parts such as the navigation types between windows, alarm generation, change of state in the Conveyor window, and the availability of exit points. The automatic simulations were done in the complete model in order to test for deadlocks (other than the exit situation).

5.3   Occurrence Graph – Occ

The Occ was used to analyze the logic behaviour of the navigation model. The report of the Occ generation follows:

```
Statistics
----------------------------------------------------------------------
  Occurrence Graph
    Nodes:   560
    Arcs:    3388
    Secs:    8
    Status: Full
Boundedness Properties
----------------------------------------------------------------------
  Best Integers Bounds          Upper        Lower
  IHM_Industrial'Close 1        6            6
  IHM_Industrial'Exit 1         1            1
  IHM_Industrial'N_Nav 1        21           21
  IHM_Industrial'IHM 1          1            1
  IHM_Industrial'Win_Nav1 1     2            2
  IHM_Industrial'Win_Nav2 1     6            4
  IHM_Industrial'Options1 1     3            3
  IHM_Industrial'Options2 1     6            6
  IHM_Industrial'Prob_Al 1      1            0
Liveness Properties
----------------------------------------------------------------------
  Dead Markings:   16 [8,545,455,453,451,...]
  Dead Transitions Instances: None
```

The places upper and lower bounds were the expected ones. In the places **Close, Exit, N_Navigation, Options1** and **Options2**, the maximum and minimum number of tokens coincides, as it was expected since the tokens in those places are only used for verification purposes. That is to check if the requested navigation action exists in the main window and returned after this test.

Two tokens are the upper and lower bounds in the place **Win_Nav1** since there are only three windows from which this navigation can occur, implying the closing of the current active window and the swapping the tokens relative to two windows in this place.

In the place **Win_Nav2** the upper bound is of six tokens, which happen when none of the six windows from which this navigation type is possible is active, and the lower bound is four indicating the superposition of two windows on the current active window.

From the point of view of the liveness property, there are no dead transitions, therefore all the transitions can fire at least once. The system modelled has 16 dead markings, referring to the state of the buttons status, which can be either enabled or disabled when the exit transition fires. This will cause the return an empty list to the **IHM** place and cause a deadlock.

Each of the three alarm buttons can assume one of the status (enabled/disabled). For the three alarm buttons there are 8 possible status. The change of status of alarm button *ButAlarmAckAll* is not considered since it depends on the status of the other three buttons. The navigation buttons in the *WinConveyor* window change status simultaneously, according to the button *ButConveyorMA* into one of two possibilities, which with the alarm status add to the 16 possibilities of dead markings, mentioned above.

5.4   Generating Messages Sequence Charts

Message Sequence Charts (MSC) are a graphical and textual language for the description and specification of the interactions between system components. It contains the description of the asynchronous communication between instances and can be used as an overview specification of the communication behavior of real-time systems [9].

In this model analysis, an MSC was automatically generated using a library for the Design/CPN and was used for simulation and validation purposes. It was particularly helpful in the analysis of the system's behaviour under specific conditions such as: after an alarm, navigation from point to point, toggling between manual and automatic modes; and a general appraisal of the overall system behaviour until its exit.

5.5   MSC of the Industrial Interface from the Navigation Point of View

Since people unfamiliar with PN usually do the interface specification analysis, systems behaviour explained through MSC becomes a very useful approach. The representation of an event by means of a message is more intuitive than the analysis of the markings in a CPN model.

A Basic Message Sequence Chart contains a (partial) description of the communication behavior of a number of instances. An instance is an abstract entity of which one can observe (part of) the interaction with other instances or with the environment. An instance is denoted by a vertical axis. The time along each axis runs from top to bottom [9].

The Message Sequence Chart displayed in Figures 5 and 6, illustrates the system's behaviour when there are no restrictions on the navigation paths. It defines the communication behavior between instances *Win_Nav1*, *Win_Nav2* and *IHM*, making possible to analyze the functioning of the system, from the viewpoints: types of navigation between windows, alarm generation, navigation within the window and exiting the application.

In MSC1, the operator enters the supervisory program in the window **WinReactor**. Then he/she checks the trend graph for the process opening the window **WinHist**, where the zoom facility is selected. In the mean time an alarm occurs related to the concentration mix. The operator chooses to ignore the alarm and opens the window **WinConveyor** in order to adjust the speed of filling the barrels with the product. This is done by adjusting the speed in the slide bar (*ButConveyorBar*). Notice that the alarms that occur during the analysis are generated at random, and the decision on when to acknowledge them is a prerogative of the plant operator.

Next there is the need to verify the current status of system's parts such as conveyor belt and motor in the maintenance window **WinMaintance**. In this point a new concentration alarm is issued by the system. Next, the operator closes **WinMaintence** and alternates the view between the two windows **WinReactor** and **WinConveyor** in order to set the barrel filling process to manual control. In this stage the system issues a concentration level alarm. In this stage, since the filling process is now manual, the operator must return to it in order to continue the barrel filling. During the filling, he/she returns to **WinReactor** and opens the alarms window **WinAlarm** and acknowledges the concentration alarms. The operator closes **WinAlarm**, since it superposes the window **WinReactor**, and navigates to the window **WinHist** in order to check the trend graph.

In MSC2 - A new concentration level alarm is issued. The operator zooms the trend graph and a new alarm is displayed informing the process temperature. Then he/she asks for help on the trend graph, which causes the opening of the window **WinHistHelp**. Next he/she closes **WinHistHelp** and verifies the process mixture opening **WinReactor** and the filling process opening **WinConveyor** (which automatically closes **WinReactor**). The operator then opens **WinHist** and the system displays again a temperature alarm. Next the operator checks the status of the system's parts in **WinMaintence** and returns to monitor the reaction process in **WinReactor**. The operator navigates to **WinAlarm** when a new concentration alarm is issued by the system, and he/she acknowledges all the alarms. Finally the user closes **WinAlarm** and exits the system.

6   Connections

This paper is in the research area of Model-based design and evaluation of interactive applications, similarly to the work of Navarre et al, **Tool Suite for In-**

System Behaviour MSC (1)

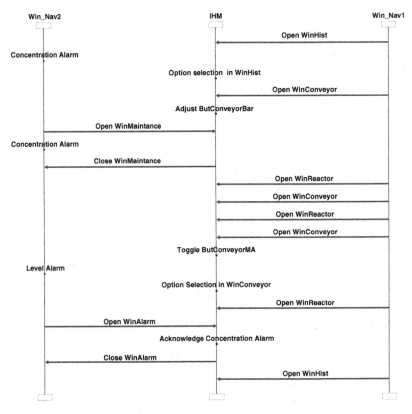

Fig. 5. System's behaviour MSC (1)

tegrating Task and System Models Through Scenarios, D. Navarre, P. Palanque, F. Paternó, C. Santoro and R. Bastide.. It also uses high level Petri Nets to model the dynamic aspects of interactive systems, but concentrates on the navigation component. But unlike it, since the model was built using Colored Petri Nets, it does not propose new tools for analyses. It uses a well know tool in the Petri Net community - Design/CPN. The authors were also concerned with the effort required to develop a new model for different applications and to support the design and evaluation of real systems. Thus, the generic navigation model at the basis of the evaluation process was built to facilitate model reuse and to ease the modelling process for interface developers who are not necessarily familiar with Petri Net theory. Also similar to Navarre et al, the model is fully executable allowing testing the application's navigation before it is implemented. The specification is also validated using analysis and proof tools developed within the Petri

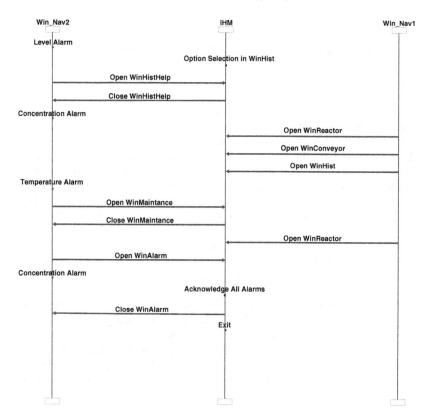

Fig. 6. System's behaviour MSC (2)

Net community, but in order to ease the semantic understanding, this model can be analysed by means of Message Sequence Charts.

Similarly to the model presented by Muller and Forbrig, in **Model-Based User Interface Design Using Markup Concepts, A. P. Muller and C Cap Forbrig**, this model is also device independent and based on User task.

The model presented treats in an abstract level the navigation mechanisms normally found in User Interfaces (UI). It was built based upon a study in which common navigation elements and strategies were isolated from multiple navigation applications in a similar fashion to the strategy used by Pribeanu et al in **Task Modelling for Context-Sensitive User Interfaces, C. Pribeanu, Q. Limbourg and J. Vanderdonckt**, where common elements across contexts were isolated in order to propose their model.

The generic UI navigation model proved to be adequate to represent User Interfaces for discrete interaction, as categorized by Doherty et al, in **Reasoning**

about Interactive Systems with Stochastic Models, G. Doherty, M. Massink, and G. Faconti, such as the industrial user interface presented in this paper.

7   Final Considerations and Future Directions

The CPN interaction state transition model presented in this work has a generic character. As it was shown with this work this model can be used to represent different interface situations provided that the colour set is adjusted to represent the new set of objects (buttons, windows) and actions.

This model's main limitation is the need for a high number of tokens in order to describe the interfaces making difficult the analysis of the system's interface behaviour. One possible approach to overcame this limitation would be to build the model in a hierarchical CPN where the navigation aspects would be represented in the higher level and the functional aspects in the lower levels. This approach would also reduce the set of functions built to deal with the token values.

As future directions for this work, the authors intend to extend the model in order to incorporate the functionality of other interface objects and in particular to include new interaction sequencing situations such as interruption states and wait states.

Finally, the authors major research interest consists of applying this interface model to more complex cases and to introduce time considerations in order to analyse user performances during task execution.

The authors would like to thank CNPq (Conselho Nacional de Desenvolvimento Científico e Tecnológico, Brazil) and CAPES (Coordenação de Aperfeiçoamento de Pessoal do Ensino superior) for supporting this research with scholarships for two of the authors.

References

1. Bastide, R.; Palanque, P., *A Petri Net Based Environment for the Design of Event-Driven Interfaces*. Proceedings of the 16th International Conference on Application and Theory of Petri Nets, p. 66-83, Turin, June, 1995.
2. Jensen. K., *Coloured Petri Nets - Basic Concepts, Analysis Methods and Practical Use, Volume 1, Basic Concepts*. Monographs in Theoretical Computer Science, Springer-Verlag, 1992.
3. Murata. T., *Petri Nets: Properties, Analysis and Applications*. Proceedings of the IEEE, Vol. 77, No 4, April 1989.
4. Nielsen J., *Usability Engineering*. Academic Press, Cambridge, MA, 1993.
5. Palanque, P.; Bastide, R., A Design Life-Cycle for the Formal Design of User Interfaces. (FAHCI'96) BCS-FACS Workshop on the Formal Aspects of the Human-Computer Interface, Sheffield, UK, September, 1996.
6. Palanque P.; Bastide R.; V. Senges, *Validating Interactive System Design Through the Verification of Formal Task and System Models.*. 6th IFIP Working Conference on Engineering for Human-Computer Interaction (EHCI'95) Grand Targhee Resort, Wyoming, U.S.A. 14-18 August 1995.

7. Peterson, J.L., *Petri Net Theory and the Modeling of Systems*. Prentice-Hall, Inc., Englewood Cliffs, 290p, 1981.
8. Rosis, F. de, *A Tool to Support Specification and Evaluation of Context-Customizes Interfaces*. SIGCHI Bulletin, 82-88, July 1996.
9. Anderson, M.; Bergstrand, J., *Formalizing Use Cases with Message Sequence Charts*. Department of Communication Systems at Lund Institute of Technology, May 1995.
10. Sousa, M.R.F. and Turnell, M.F.Q.V., *User Interface Evaluation Based on Coloured Petri Nets Modelling and Analysis*. In IEEE -SMC'98 Proceedings, October 1998, SanDiego - CA, EUA.
11. Sousa, M. R. F., *Avaliação Iterativa da Especificação de Interfaces com Ênfase na Navegação*. Doctoral Thesis, Electrical Engineering Department, at Federal University of Paraiba, Brazil, December 1999.
12. Treu S., *User Interface Design: A Structured Approach*. Plenum Press, New York, NY, 1994.
13. Turnell, Maria de Fátima Q. V.; Farias, Giovanni F. *The use of Supervisory Software in the Industrial Automation Process Control from the User Interface Perspective*. 1996 IEEE International Conference on Systems, Man and Cybernetics; Beijing China, October, 1996.
14. University of Aarhus, *Design/CPN Occurrence Graph Manual, Version 3.0*, Computer Science Department, 1996.

A Tool Suite for Integrating Task and System Models through Scenarios

David Navarre[2], Philippe Palanque[2], Fabio Paternò[1], Carmen Santoro[1], and Rémi Bastide[2]

[1] CNUCE-CNR,
Via V. Alfieri 1, 56010 Ghezzano, Pisa, Italy
[2] LIHS, Université Toulouse 1,
Place Anatole France, 31042 Toulouse Cedex, France
{navarre, palanque, bastide}@univ-tlse1.fr
{f.paterno, c.santoro}@cnuce.cnr.it

Abstract. This paper presents a set of tools supporting the development of interactive systems using two different notations. One of these notations, called ConcurTaskTrees (CTT), is used for task modelling. The other notation, called Interactive Cooperative Objects (ICO), is used for system modelling. Even though these two kinds of models represent two different views of the same world (users interacting with interactive systems), they are built by different people and used independently. The aim of this paper is to propose the use of scenarios as a bridge between these two views. On the task modelling side, scenarios are seen as possible traces of activities, while on the system side, they are viewed as traces of actions. This generic approach is presented in a case study in the domain of Air Traffic Control.

1 Introduction

The research area of model-based design and evaluation of interactive applications [12] aims at identifying models able to support design, development, and evaluation of interactive applications. Such models highlight important aspects that should be taken into account by designers. Various types of models, such as user, context, and task models, have proved to be useful in the design and development of interactive applications.

In particular, interactive systems are highly concurrent systems, which support several devices media and tools, and are characterised by dialogues and the presentations they provide for communicating information to users. However, to build effective presentations it is important to understand the activities that users want to perform with them. Such activities can be highly concurrent with even multi-user interactions and such concurrency is a source of flexibility but at the same time has to be carefully designed and controlled.

In addition, we have to take into account that the concurrency provided to users needs to be supported by the system underneath. Thus we need not only models for specifying user activities while interacting with the system, but also

C. Johnson (Ed.): DSV-IS 2001, LNCS 2220, pp. 88–113, 2001.

for specifying the underlying system. Such models should allow different levels of refinement depending on the needs of the users and should be powerful enough to express all the different relationships occurring among the various components without introducing too many low-level details.

Having models is not sufficient to support a formal analysis, methods and tools are strongly requested to help designers use the information contained in such models during their work. In particular, in the field of model-based approaches to human-computer interaction only recently tools supporting such approaches have started to be developed. Unfortunately, often such tools are rather rudimentary, usable only by the groups that developed them. Even less attention has been paid to the integration of models and tools developed for different purposes. In this paper we present the results of a work that aims to overcome this limitation. In particular, we show and discuss how we have reached the integration of a set of tools for task modelling with a set of tools for user interface system modelling through the use of abstract scenarios. The goal of such integration is to provide designers with an environment enabling them to see, for example, how a sequence of user tasks can be related to the specification of the behaviour of the underlying system's interconnecting components.

In the paper, after a short discussion of related works, we recall the basic concepts of the approaches and tools that we aim to integrate. Then, we discuss the architecture of the solution identified. As both the CTT and ICO notations are tool supported (the environments are respectively CTTE and PetShop), an integration tool (implemented at LIHS) based on this notion of scenarios is presented. An application example of the integrated set of tools is discussed before drawing some concluding remarks. The case study presented has been addressed in the European Project MEFISTO, which is a long-term research project dedicated to the design of safety critical interactive systems with the support of formal methods. In particular, the project has focused on the air traffic control domain from which this case study has been drawn.

2 Related Work

The use of models has often been criticised for the effort required to develop them and the difficulties in using the information that they contain to support design and evaluation. After having carefully evaluated the need for introducing a new notation, the first concern should be providing users with tools to make its use easier and more effective. The problem is that getting used to another notation involves a significant amount of effort and time spent by the potential users in order to understand features, semantics and meaning of the notation's conventions. In addition, even when users have understood the main features of the notation, there is still the risk that their effort might be wasted if they find that using it is difficult and not really feasible or appropriate for intensive use and real case studies.

Indeed, one of the strengths of a notation is the possibility of supporting it through automatic tools. Developing a formal model can be a long process, which requires a considerable effort. Automatic tools can ease such activity and can help designers to get information from the models, which is useful for supporting the design cycle.

Some research prototype was developed years ago to show the feasibility of the development of such tools, however the first prototypes were rather limited in terms of functionality and usable mainly by the people who develop them. Only in recent years some more engineered tools have been developed, in some cases they are also publicly available. For example, Euterpe [18] is a tool supporting GTA (Groupware Task Analysis) where task models are developed in the horizontal dimension with different panels to edit task, objects, actors. A simulator of task models of single user applications has been given with the support of an object-oriented modelling language [3].

Mobi-D [16] and Trident [4] are examples of tools aiming to use information contained in models to support design and development of user interfaces. In particular, in Mobi-D the designer can choose different strategies in using the information contained in task and domain model to derive the user interface design.

In our work we envision a solution based on the use of two tools (CTTE and PetShop) developed to support two different types of models. The former is a tool for task modelling supporting a unique set of functionality (simulation of models of cooperative applications, comparison of task models, support of use of scenarios to develop task models, ...). The latter supports system models described using Petri nets in an object-oriented environment. PetShop is able to support editing of a Petri Net controlling the dialogues of a user interface even at run-time thus allowing dynamic change of its behaviour. Their integration allows thorough support to designers since early conceptual design until evaluation of a full prototype.

3   Our Approach

Various models have been proposed in the human-computer interaction field. Task and system models are particularly important when designing and developing interactive software systems. In both industrial and academic communities there is a wide agreement on the relevance of task models as they allow expressing the intentions of the users and the activities they should perform to reach their goals. These models also allow designers to develop an integrated description of both functional and interactive aspects. Within the development lifecycle of an application the task-modelling phase is supposed to be performed after having gathered information on the application domain and an informal task analysis phase. The result of the latter one is an informal list of tasks that have been identified as relevant for the application domain.

After this step, in developing a task model designers should be able to clarify many aspects related to tasks and their relationships. In some cases task models are first developed and then used to drive the system design. In other cases designers have to address an existing system and need to develop a task model to better understand and evaluate its behaviour [11].

System models describe important aspects of the user interface. In this work we pay particular attention to the dialogue supported by the system: how user actions and system feedback can be sequenced. Thus, the purpose of these models is to support the analysis of the user interface system, rather than the related task model. They provide description of the objects making up the user interface and the underlying system and how they behave, whereas in the task model there is a description of the logical activities supported. There is an intersection between the aspects described by the two models (the actions that can be performed at the user interface level) but each of them also captures aspects that are not represented in the other one. The task model also describes cognitive user activities (such as deciding a strategy to find information) and the system model contains a description of the system architecture.

Scenarios [5] are a well-known technique in the human-computer interaction area. They provide a description of one specific use of a given system, in a given context. They are an example of usage. Their limited scope is their strength because they can easily highlight some specific aspect and are easily understood and remembered. Thus, they can also be considered as a useful tool to compare different models and analyse their relationships.

In the design process, one important goal is to check if the task model fulfills the expected requirements and if the system model matches the planned behaviour. However, what cannot be missed is checking if both two models are consistent, which means if both specifications really refer to the same user interface. This requires checking if for each user action assumed in the system model there is an actual counterpart in the task model, and each system output provided to the user has been foreseen in the task model specification.

Another relevant point that has to be highlighted is that these two models can be specified by different people and in distinct moments of the design cycle of the user interface development process. Indeed, especially in real case studies sometimes the task models will be developed at first, sometimes they might be specified after the system model has already been obtained. So, we need an approach that does not have specific constraints and requirements on what is assumed to be available at a certain phase of the system design, as it can be equally used efficiently in both cases.

In our approach, we used abstract scenarios as the common "lingua franca" to ensure that there is actual correspondence between what has been specified within the task model and what has been specified in the system model. The idea is to focus the attention on specific examples of usage either on the system side or on the tasks side and to check if on these simple examples of the system use such correspondence exists.

Considering the task model-side, in our approach we used the ConcurTask-Trees notation for specifying tasks. The formal semantics of the operators used in this notation is in [13]. This notation allows users to explicitly express how the allocation of the different tasks has been assumed in the system design.

Such allocation could be on the user alone (user tasks), on the application alone (application tasks), on the interaction between the user and the application (interaction tasks), or if the activity is too general to be specifically allocated on each of them (abstract task). Explicit indication of task allocation is one aspect which makes the notation very suitable for designers of interactive systems, because they have to explicitly indicate which part of the interactive system (user, application, interaction between them) has to undertake each task.

This aspect proves to be effective especially when both comparison and integration of different models has to be carried out, such as in our case. The notation provides the ability to specify in the task model when system support is requested on the user interface. This allows comparing and cross-checking if the task model reflects and is adequately supported by the corresponding system model. More specifically, the points that have to be carefully checked in the task model specification are the interaction and application tasks. Application tasks indicate that at a certain point during a session a specific behaviour of the system is expected. This behaviour can be expressed in terms of a specific feedback of an action the user has performed while interacting with the system; in terms of a result the system has produced after some elaboration; in terms of availability of a specific input needed to users in order to perform their tasks. All those possibilities have to be carefully supported especially if the considered domain is vast and complex as the air traffic control field considered in our case study. Such domain is composed of a number of entities that maintain a complex relationship structure, due to their internal structure and to the dynamic behaviour they follow, which has to be appropriately presented to the users.

4   A Case Study

This case study has been considered in the European Project MEFISTO which is a long term research project dedicated to the design of safety critical interactive systems, with particular attention to the air traffic control application domain.

After a short overview of the case study in sub-section 4.1, this section presents the various models built in order to represent both predictive user activities and the system under consideration. Sub-section 4.2 presents the use of CTT and its environment for tasks modelling and simulation as well as the identification of scenarios from the task models. Sub-section 4.3 presents the use of the ICO formalism and its support environment PetShop for modelling and executing interactive systems.

4.1   Informal Description of the Case Study

This example is taken from a case study related to En-route Air Traffic Control with the support of data-link technologies in the ATC field. Using such applications air traffic controllers can communicate with pilots in a sector (a portion of the airspace) through digital commands. In particular, we focus on the activities related to when an aircraft changes air sector.

A representation of the radar image is shown in Figure 1. On the radar image each plane is represented by a graphical element providing air traffic controllers with useful information for handling air traffic in a sector. In the simplified version of the radar image we are considering, each graphical representation of a plane is made up of three components: a label (providing precise information about the plane such as ID, speed, cleared flight level, ...), a dot (representing the current position of the plane in the sector) and a speed vector (a graphical line from the dot which represent the envisioned position of the plane in 3 minutes).

An Air Traffic Control simulator is in charge of reproducing the arrival of new planes in the sector while in reality they would be instantiated on the user interface by calls from the functional core of the application processing information provided by physical radars.

Initially the radar image is empty. Each time a new plane is randomly generated it is graphically represented on the radar image. It is possible for the user to select planes by *clicking* on its graphical representation. *Clicking* on the flight representation will change its state to the *Assume* state meaning that the air traffic controller is now in charge of the plane. Assuming the plane changes its graphical representation as it can be seen on the right-hand side of Figure 1. Once a plane is assumed, the controller can send clearances to this plane. In this case study we only consider the change of frequency functionality corresponding to the controller's activity of transferring a plane to an adjacent sector. When the plane has been taken on, the button FREQ is enabled (see plane 1123 on the right-hand side of Figure 1). Clicking on this button opens a menu allowing the controller selecting the new value for the frequency.

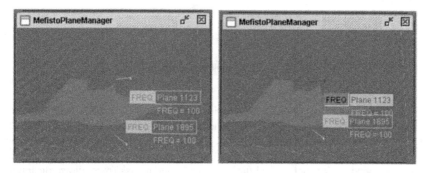

Fig. 1. A screen shot of the radar screen with planes (right-hand side, one the planes 1123 is assumed)

4.2   The ConcurTaskTrees Notation and Environment Used in the Case Study

We first introduce the notation for task modelling that has been used and the related environment.

The ConcurTasktrees Notation

There are various approaches that aim to specify tasks. They differ in aspects such as the type of formalism they use, the type of knowledge they capture, and how they support the design and development of interactive systems. In this paper we consider task models that have been represented using the Concur-TaskTrees notation [12]. In ConcurTaskTrees activities are described at different abstraction levels in a hierarchical manner, represented graphically in a tree-like format (see Figure 2 for an example). In contrast to previous approaches, such as Hierarchical Task Analysis, ConcurTaskTrees provides a rich set of operators, with precise meaning, able to describe many possible temporal relationships (concurrency, interruption, disabling, iteration, and so on). The notation allows designers to obtain concise representations describing many possible evolutions over a user session. The formal semantics of the operators has been given in [13]. The notation also supports the possibility of using icons or geometrical shapes to indicate how the performance of the tasks is allocated.

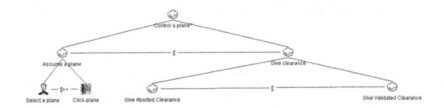

Fig. 2. The abstract task model of the case study

For each task it is possible to provide additional information including the objects manipulated (for both the user interface and the application) and attributes such as frequency. In addition, as in the design of complex cooperative environments more and more attention is being paid to the horizontal mechanism of coordination between different roles, ConcurTaskTrees allows designers to specify explicitly how the cooperation among different users is performed.

We give an overview of the main features of the notation by commenting on two excerpts of specification from the considered case study.

The activity of controlling a plane (*Control a plane*) is an iterative task (∗ is the iterative operator) which consists of either assuming a plane (*Assume a plane* task) or giving clearance to the plane (*Give clearance task*). Those two activities are mutually exclusive, as you can see from the choice operator [].

The activity of assuming a plane is composed of deciding which plane has to be assumed (*Select a plane* task, the associated icon emphasizes the cognitive nature of this *user* task). Once this activity has been performed it is possible to select the button related to the plan (see the Enabling operator with information passing [] >>, which highlights that only after the first activity has been carried out and delivered information to the second task, the latter can be performed). In addition, the *Click plane* task requires an explicit action of the controller on an element of the user interface so it belongs to the category of *interaction* tasks and the appropriate icon has been used. The *Give clearance* task is composed of two different activities: *Give Aborted Clearance* and *Give Validated Clearance*, depending on whether the clearance has been aborted or not. Each of these two activities is a high-level one, whose performance cannot be entirely allocated either to the application alone, or to the user alone, or to an interaction between the user and the system: this is expressed by using a cloud-shape icon associated to the so-called *abstract tasks*. The specification of each of these two tasks is described in Figure 3.

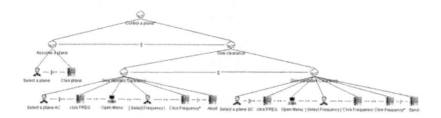

Fig. 3. The concrete and detailed task model of the case study

The *Give Aborted Clearance* task is composed of the controller's cognitive activity of selecting a plane (*Select a plane AC*), then they select the button related to the frequency (*Click FREQ*). This triggers the opening of the associated menu on the controller's user interface (*Open Menu*, note the icon associated to the category of the *application* tasks), then the controller can think about a specific frequency (in the task model the possibility of performing or not this task is expressed by the option operator represented by squared brackets [*T*], see the *Select Frequency* task). Then, controllers choose the appropriate value of frequency within the user interface (*Click Frequency* task, which can be performed more than one time, as you can see from the iterative operator *) until they decide to interrupt the entire activity (see the Disabling operator [> which refers to the possibility for the second task to disable the first one), by selecting the related object in the user interface (*Abort task*).

In case of a clearance that is sent to the pilot (*Give Validated Clearance*), the sequence of actions is mainly the same, apart from the last one (*Send task*), with which the controller sends the clearance to the pilot.

The ConcurTasktrees Environment (CTTE)

A set of tools have been developed to specify task models for co-operative applications in ConcurTaskTrees and to analyse their content. The CTTE tool [15] has various features supporting editing of task models. It can automatically check the syntax of the specification, give statistical information, compare task models, simulate their behaviour and give examples of scenarios of use. The CTTE editing environment is intended as a computer-based support tool for CTT, and is freely downloadable from http://giove.cnuce.cnr.it/ctte.html.

The tool has been used in a number of projects and at several universities for teaching purposes. It was used to support design of an adaptable web museum application. The application provided different ways to navigate and present information depending on the current user model (tourist, expert, student). We developed a task model for each type of user. The task models also shared some portions for tasks that were common to different types of users. In the MEFISTO project, CTTE has been used to model various air traffic control applications and support their design and evaluation. Large specifications, including hundreds of tasks, were developed. In this project the tool was proposed to several teams belonging to organizations that design and develop systems for air traffic control; in some cases the teams also included people with different backgrounds. At the University of York an evaluation exercise was developed using a number of techniques (including cognitive dimensions for notations and cooperative evaluation). In the GUITARE project, various teams from software companies have used the tool for different application domains. Some of these teams included people without any background in computer science, who nevertheless were able to use the tool satisfactorily. Methods have also been developed for supporting user interface design and generation starting with task models specified by CTTE.

With this tool becomes very intuitive and effective to exploit the graphical and hierarchical nature (tree-like format) features of the notation by all the operations (cut, paste, insert) that are possible on tree-like structures. In addition, even the specific layout selected for the tool conveys further useful information about the notation. For instance, the relative positions of the user interface objects presenting the operators within the tool convey information about their priorities (sorted top to bottom from highest to lowest operator priority). In addition, it is possible to recall the meaning of any operator by means of useful tool tips available within the environment (such feature is found very useful especially by users who are rather new to the notation and unable to recall the meaning of the operators). Finally, the ability to structure the specification with some tasks that can be referenced both in the single-user and cooperative parts is well supported by the environment because it allows easy switching between these different views. These simple examples, relative to the case of the CTT notation, serve to highlight the extent to which the use of a suitable tool can support users while building the task specifications.

In Figure 4 the simulator provided in the CTT Environment is shown. The simulator has been implemented following the formal semantics of the CTT

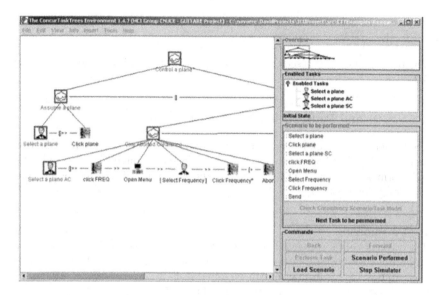

Fig. 4. CTTE for extracting scenarios

notation. When this tool is activated, in the left-hand part of the window it is possible to highlight (by means of a different colour) all the tasks that are enabled at any moment of the simulation. This means all the tasks that can be performed at a specific time, depending on the tasks that have been previously carried out. The execution of a task can be performed either within the graphical panel on the left (a task can be executed by double-clicking on the related task icon), or by selecting the task name within the list of "Enabled tasks" panel on the right. In addition, it is possible to load a previously created scenario. Its composing tasks will appear in the "Scenario to be performed" list from where it is possible to simulate its performance again.

As an example of scenario we have chosen to extract from the task model of Figure 3 the following trace of low-level tasks (this scenario has been generated using CTTE and is displayed on the right-hand side of Figure 4):

- First the controller selects one of the planes not assumed yet (this is a user task)
- Then the controller clicks on this plane to assume it (interaction task)
- Then the controller decides to change the current frequency of one of the flight assumed (user task)
- Then the controller clicks on the label FREQ to open the data-link menu (interaction task)
- Then the controller selects (in his /her head) a new frequency for this plane (user task)
- Then the controller clicks on one of the available frequencies for this plane (interaction task)

- Then the controller clicks on the SEND button to send the new frequency to the aircraft (interaction task)

The performance of this scenario on the system model will be detailed in section 5.2.

4.3   ICOs and PetShop Used in the Case Study

System modelling is done using the ICO formalism and its development environment is called PetShop. Both of them are presented through the case study. The ICO formalism is the continuation of early work on dialogue modelling using high-level Petri nets [1].

ICO formalism

The various components of the formalism are introduced informally hereafter and all of them are fully exemplified on the case study. A complete and formal presentation of this formalism can be found in
http://lihs.univ-tlse1.fr/palanque/Ps/ICOFormalDef.pdf.

The Interactive Cooperative Objects (ICOs) formalism is a formal notation dedicated to the specification of interactive systems. ICOs use concepts borrowed from the object-oriented approach (dynamic instantiation, classification, encapsulation, inheritance, client/server relationship) to describe the structural or static aspects of systems, and uses high-level Petri nets to describe their dynamic or behavioural aspects. ICOs were originally devised for the modelling and implementation of event-driven interfaces. An ICO model of a system is made up of several communicating objects, Petri nets describe both behaviour of objects and communication protocol between objects. In the ICO formalism, an object is an entity featuring four components: services, behaviour, state and presentation.

Services (or Interface): The interface specifies at a syntactic level the services that a client object can request from a server object that implements this interface. The interface details the services supported and their signature: a list of parameters with their type and parameter-passing mode, the type of the return value, the exceptions that may possibly be raised during the processing of the service. For describing this interface we use the CORBA-IDL language [7]. An ICO offers a set of services that define the interface (in the programming language meaning) offered by the object to its environment. In the case of user-driven application, this environment may be either the user or other objects of the application. The ICO formalism distinguishes between two kinds of services: services offered to the user (user services) and services offered to other objects.

Behaviour: The behaviour of an ICO defines how the object reacts to external stimuli according to its inner state. This behaviour is described by a high-level Petri net called the Object Control Structure (ObCS) of the object.

State: The state of an ICO is the distribution and the value of the tokens (called the marking) in the places of the ObCS. This defines how the current state influences the availability of services, and conversely how the performance of a service influences the state of the object.

Presentation: The Presentation of an object states its external appearance. It is made up of three components: the widgets, the activation function and the rendering function. This Presentation is a structured set of widgets organized in a set of windows. The user - system interaction will only take place through those widgets. Each user action on a widget may trigger one of the ICO's user services. The relation between user services and widgets is fully stated by the activation function that associates the service to be triggered to each couple (widget, user action). The rendering function is in charge of presenting information according to the state changes that occur. It is thus related to the representation of states in the behavioural description i.e. places in the high-level Petri net.

ICOs are used to provide a formal description of the dynamic behaviour of an interactive application. An ICO specification fully describes the potential interactions that users may have with the application. The specification encompasses both the "input" aspects of the interaction (i.e. how user actions impact on the inner state of the application, and which actions are enabled at any given time) and its "output" aspects (i.e. when and how the application displays information that is relevant to the user). An ICO specification is fully executable, which gives the possibility of prototyping and testing quickly an application before it is fully implemented. The specification can also be validated using analysis and proof tools developed within the Petri nets community.

ICO environment (PetShop)

In this section we introduce the PetShop environment and the design process it supports. The interested reader can find more information in [17].

Figure 5 presents the general architecture of PetShop. The rectangles represent the functional modules of PetShop. The documents-like shapes represent the models produced and used by the modules.

Presentation of ICOs and PetShop on the case study

In this section we only present a subset of the set of classes and objects of the case study specification. However, a complete description of the specification can be found in [6].

In this paper the case study is modelled as a set of three cooperating classes: MefistoPlaneManager, MefistoPlane and MefistoMenu. These three classes are full fledged and we will describe successively their components.

The class MefistoPlaneManager

The class MefistoPlaneManager is the class in charge of handling the set of planes in a sector. Each time a new plane arrives in the sector the MefistoPlane-Manager instantiates it from the class MefistoPlane (see paragraph *The class*

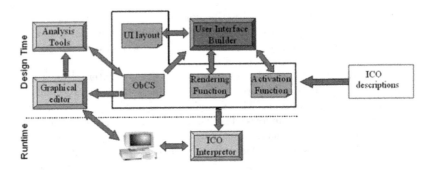

Fig. 5. Tools available for designers in PetShop Environment

MefistoPlane). During the execution this class will only have one instance. The set of services offered by this class is described in Figure 6.

```
interface MefistoPlaneManager {
        void closePlane(in MefistoPlane p);
        void terminatePlane(in MefistoPlane p);
        void addPlane(in MefistoPlane p);
};
```

Fig. 6. IDL description of the class MefistoPlaneManager

This IDL description shows that the class offers three services dealing with the managing of the planes in a sector: adding a plane, terminating a plane (when it leaves a sector) and closing the menu of a plane.

Figure 7 presents the behaviour of this i.e. the state of the class and, according to the current state, what the services available to the other objects of the application are. The transition *UserOpenPlane* has an input arc from place *AssumedPlanes* meaning that a controller can only open a menu on a plane that has previously been assumed. The inhibitor arc between that transition and the place OpenedPlanes states that only one plane at a time can have the data-link menu opened.

Figure 8 and Figure 9 describe the presentation part of the ICO Mefisto-PlaneManager. From the rendering function it can be seen that this class only triggers rendering through the class MefistoPlane as each time a new token enters in the place Planes the graphical function Show is triggered on the corresponding plane.

The class MefistoPlane

The class MefistoPlane is also an ICO class. Graphical information is added with respect to the class MefistoPlaneManager in order to describe how the plane

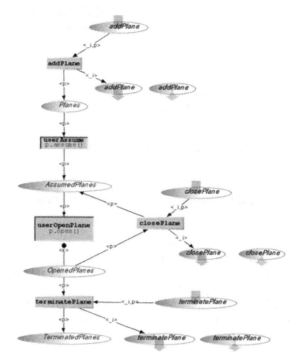

Fig. 7. ObCS description of the class MefistoPlaneManager

is rendered on the screen. This information is given on Figure 12 while Figure 10 gives the IDL description, Figure 11 describes the behaviour of MefistoPlane and Figure 13 presents the rendering function. It is interesting to notice that this class does not feature an activation function. This is due to the fact that all the user interaction on a plane takes place through the MefistoPlaneManager class.

The class MefistoMenu

This class is in charge of the interaction taking place through the data-link menu that is opened by clicking on the button FREQ on the plane label.

Widget		Event	Service
Place	Type		
Planes	Plane	LabelClick	userAssume
AssumedPlanes	Plane	ButtonClick	userOpenMenu

Fig. 8. The activation function of the class MefistoPlaneManager

ObCS Element	Feature	Rendering method
Place Planes	token $< p >$ enterred	p.show()

Fig. 9. Rendering function of the MefistoPlaneManager

```
interface MefistoPlane {
        void open();
        void close();
        void assume();
        void validate(in short x);
};
```

Fig. 10. IDL description of the class MefistoPlane

Figure 14 provides the set of services offered to the other objects of the application; Figure 15 describes its behaviour.

Figure 16, Figure 17 and Figure 18 give the presentation part of the class MefistoPlane.

This description still lacks the code of the functions given in Figure 16 and in Figure 12 for describing precisely the graphical behaviour of the classes. This is not given here for space reasons.

5   The Integration of the Models: CTT-ICO Integration

5.1   Integration Framework

The integration framework we have followed takes full advantage of the specific tools that we have developed initially in a separate manner. One advantage of this separation is that it allows for independent modification of the tools, provided that the interchange format remains the same.

We have previously investigated the relationship between task and system models. For instance in [10] we proposed a transformation mechanism for translating UAN tasks descriptions into Petri nets and then checking whether this Petri net description was compatible with system modelling also done using Petri nets. In [9] we presented the use of CTT for abstract task modelling and high level Petri nets for low-level task modelling. In that paper the low-level task model was used in order to evaluate the "complexity" of the tasks to be performed, by means of performance evaluation techniques available in Petri net theory.

The two notations model slightly different aspects: CTT is a notation for task modelling whereas ICO is a notation for specifying concurrent systems, thus an automatic conversion from one notation to the other one would have been difficult. We have preferred a different solution that is easier to implement and better refers to the practise of user interface designers. Indeed, often designers

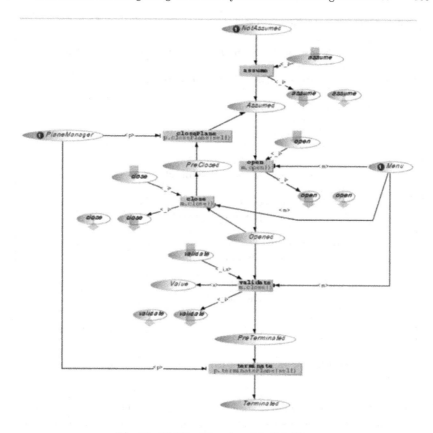

Fig. 11. ObCS of the class MerfistoPlane

use scenarios for many purposes and to move among the various phases of the design cycle. So, they can be considered a key element in comparing design solution from different viewpoints.

CTT Environment

The different parts of the framework for CTT-PetShop integration are shown in Figure 19 and referred by means of numbers. For instance, the outputs provided by CTT environment and their processing are highlighted on Figure 19 as part 1 and part 2. As described above, CTT environment provides a set of tools for engineering task models. For the purpose of integration we only use the interactive tool for editing the tasks and the simulation tool for task models that allows scenario construction from the task models. Thus the two main outputs are a set of task models and a set of scenarios. These two sets are exploited in the following way:

```
public class WidgetPlane {
        //Attributes
                //A button to open the menu for the change of frequency
                Button freqButton;
                //A label to display the name of the plane
                Label label;
        //Rendering methods
                void show() {
                        //show plane
                }
                void showAssumed() {
                        //show plane as assumed
                }
                void showOpened() {
                        //show plane as opened
                }
                void showTerminated() {
                        //show plane as terminated
                }
                void setFreq(short x) {
                        //show the new frequency
                }
}
```

Fig. 12. The presentation part of the class MefistoPlane

- from the ConcurTaskTrees specification a set of interaction tasks is extracted. This set represents a set of manipulations that can be performed by the user on the system (part 1 of Figure 19),
- the set of scenario is used as is by the integration tool (part 2 of Figure 19).

ICO Environment

The outputs of the ICO environment and their processing are highlighted by part 3 and part 4 of Figure 19). Amongst the features of the ICO environment (PetShop), the one that is used for the integration is the tool for editing the system model. It allows executing the system model.

ObCS Element	Feature	Rendering method
Place Assumed	token entered	showAssumed
Place Opened	token entered	showOpened
Place Terminated	token entered	showTerminated
Place Value	token $< x >$ entered	setFreq(x)

Fig. 13. The rendering function of the class MefistoPlane

```
interface MefistoMenu {
        void open();
        void close();
        void send();
        void setValue(in short x);
};
```

Fig. 14. IDL description of the class MefistoMenu

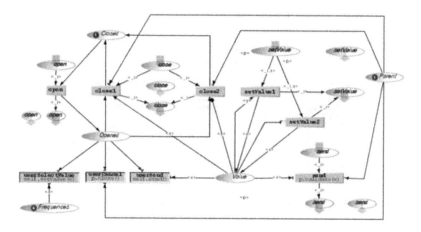

Fig. 15. ObCS of the class MefistoMenu

From this specification we extract a set of user services (part 3 of Figure 19) and from the ICO environment we use the prototype of the system modelled (part 4 of Figure 19).

A user service is a set of particular transitions that represents the functionalities offered to the user by the system. These transitions are performed when and only when they are fireable and the corresponding user actions are performed (which is represented by the activation function in the ICO formalism).

The Correspondence Editor

The activities that are managed by the correspondence editor correspond to part 5 and part 6 of Figure 19.

The first component of the correspondence editor relates interaction tasks in the task model to user services in the system model (part 5 of Figure 19). When the task model is refined enough, the leaves of the task tree represent low-level interactions on the artifacts. It is then possible to relate those low-level interactive tasks to user actions in the system model that are represented, in the ICO formalism, by user services.

```
public class WidgetMenu {
    //Attributes
        //Button to validate or cancel the current choice for frequency
        Button sendButton, cancelButton;
        //A comboBox to show the set of possible frequency
        ComboBox freqComboBox;
    //Rendering methods
        void show() {
            //show menu as opened
        }
        void hide() {
            //hide menu
        }
}
```

Fig. 16. The presentation part of the class MefistoMenu

Widget		Event	Service
Place	Type		
	sendButton	actionPerformed	userSend
	abortButton	actionPerformed	userCancel
	freqComboBox	select	userSelectValue

Fig. 17. The activation function of the class MefistoMenu

In order to check that this correspondence is valid we have developed a model checker (part 6 of Figure 19). The properties checked by the model checker correspond to the verification and validation phase in the development process. Validation phase relates to the question "do we have modelled the right system?" while the verification phase address the question "do we have modelled the system right?". In the context of ICO-CTT integration for the verification phase the model checker addresses the following two questions:

a. "are there at least as many user services in the ICO specification as interaction tasks in the CTT model ?",
b. "are all the possible scenarios from the task model available in the system modelled ?".

In the context of ICO-CTT integration for the validation phase the tool addresses the following two questions:

ObCS Element	Feature	Rendering method
Place Opened	token entered	show
Place Closed	token entered	hide

Fig. 18. Rendering function of the class MefistoMenu

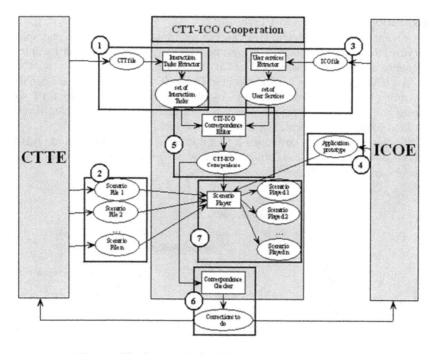

Fig. 19. The framework for CTTE - PetShop integration

a. "are there more user services in the ICO specification than interaction tasks in the CTT model ?", and,

b. "are there scenarios available in the system model that are not available in the task model?".

If the answer is yes for one of these two sub rules, the system modelled offers more functionalities than expected by the task model described with CTT. This leads to two possible mistakes in the design process. Either the system implements more functions that needed or the set of task models built is incomplete. In the former case the useless functionalities must be removed. In the latter case either task models using this functionality are added or the use of this functionality will never appear in any of the scenarios to be built.

The role of the correspondence checker is to notify any inconsistency between the CTT and the ICO specifications. Future work will be dedicated to provide recommendations on how to correct these mistakes.

In this part a CTT-ICO correspondence file that stores the mapping between elements in the task and system models is produced.

Execution: The Scenario Player

As a scenario is a sequence of tasks and as we are able to put a task and a user service into correspondence, it is now possible to convert the scenarios into a sequence of firing of transitions in the ICO specification.

An ICO specification can be executed in the ICO environment and behaves according to the high-level Petri net describing its behaviour. As the CTT scenarios can be converted into a sequence of firing of transitions, it can directly be used to drive the execution of the ICO specification.

To this end we have developed a tool dedicated to the execution of an ICO formal description of a case study driven by a scenario extracted from a task model (see Part 7 of Figure 19).

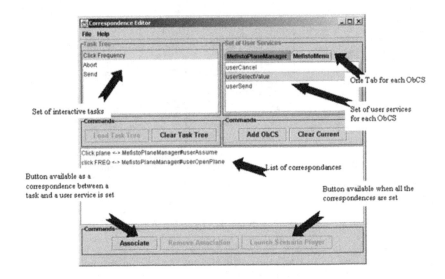

Fig. 20. Association of interactive tasks and user services

5.2   Application on the Case Study

This section presents the application of the integration framework presented in section 5.1 to the Air Traffic Control case study presented in 4.1.

Figure 20 presents the correspondence editor introduced in previous section (called *The Correspondence Editor*). The left-hand side of the window contains the task model that has been introduced in section 4.2 and loaded into the correspondence editor. In the case study under consideration only one task model can be loaded. However, if cooperative task models are considered the correspondence editor makes it possible to include several task models. In such a case, the "Task Tree" panel includes tabs widget for each task model. In this panel the set of interactive tasks are displayed. On the right-hand side of Figure 20 the panel "Set of User Services" displays the set of user services in the ICO specification that has been loaded. Here again it is possible to load several ICOs. The set of user services of each ICO appears in a separate tab widget.

The lower part of the window in Figure 20 lists the set of associations that have been created when all the user services loaded in the ICOs have been associated with all the interactive tasks loaded in the "Task Tree" panel. Then, the "Launch Scenario Player" button is available.

Clicking on this button opens the window presented in Figure 21 corresponding to the scenario player. This tool allows for loading a scenario (produced using CTTE tool presented in Figure 4) and executing it in PetShop. The scenario can thus be used to replace user interactions that would normally drive the execution of the ICO specification.

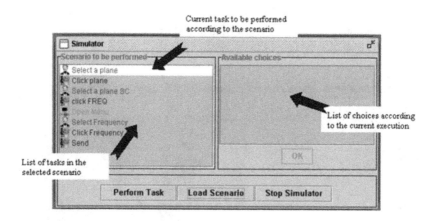

Fig. 21. The scenario player

The left-hand side of Figure 21 presents the set of actions in the selected scenario. The first line in the scenario represents the current task in the scenario. In Figure 21 the current task is "Select a plane" and is a user tasks i.e. the task is performed entirely by the user without interacting with the system. Clicking on the "Perform Task" button triggers the task and next task in the scenario becomes the current task. Figure 22 shows the scenario player in use. The right-hand side of the figure shows the execution of the ICOs specification with the two main components: the Air Traffic Control application with the radar screen and the ATC simulator allowing for test purpose to add planes in the sector.

Some tasks of interactive or application category require runtime information to be performed. For instance this is the case of interactive task "Click plane" that corresponds to the user's action of clicking on a plane. Of course the click can only occur on one of the "current" planes in the sector and thus, the identification

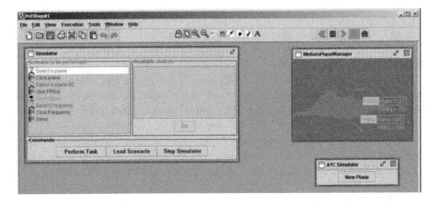

Fig. 22. Execution of the scenario of the system

number cannot be known at design time and thus cannot be represented in the task model.

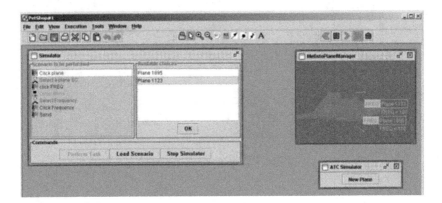

Fig. 23. Interaction between scenario and current execution: planes IDs are selected at runtime

Figure 23 provides an example of this aspect. Triggering the action "Click plane" in the task model requires a parameter i.e. a plane identifier. As this interactive task has been related to the user service "userAssume" (in the correspondence editor) the triggering of this task starts off the corresponding user service. However, the triggering of this service requires one of the values in the input place of the transition userAssume in the ObCS of the class MefistoPlane-Manager (see Figure 7) i.e. one of the objects planes in the place Planes. In order to provide those values to the scenario player the set of all the objects in the place Planes is displayed on the right-hand side of the scenario player (see Figure 23).

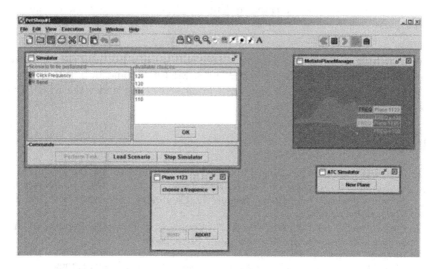

Fig. 24. Interaction between scenario and current execution: values for frequency are selected at runtime

Figure 24 shows the same interaction occurring while selecting a value for the frequency. The set of frequencies in the place Frequencies (see Figure 15) is displayed for user's selection in the scenario player.

The tool shows a dialogue window when the scenario has been successfully played on the description of the application using the ICO formalism. A scenario fails when at some point no action can be performed and the list of actions still to be performed is not empty.

6 Conclusions

This paper has presented work that has been done in order to bridge the gap between task modelling and system modelling. The bridge is created by means of scenarios, which are considered here as sequences of tasks mapped onto sequences of actions in the system model. The use of scenarios is common practise in the design of interactive applications. We can thus obtain a design cycle that is thoroughly supported by dedicated software tools.

The environment proposed for both task modelling and scenarios generation supports the editing of cooperative tasks, while that for editing and executing the formal description of system models supports distributed execution of models according to the CORBA standard. On the system modelling side, further work is currently under way in order to ease the editing of the presentation part of the ICO models. Indeed, currently both activation and rendering functions are edited in a textual way, while graphical editing through direct manipulation would make this task easier.

Future work will be dedicated to defining formal mappings between the two notations.

Acknowledgements. The work presented in this paper has been partly funded by ESPRIT Reactive LTR project #24963, MEFISTO and by FT R&D (formerly CNET), the Research Centre of France Telecom, under the SERPICO project, grant number 98 1B 059.

References

1. Bastide, Rémi, and Palanque, Philippe. "Petri Net Objects for the Design, Validation and Prototyping of User-Driver Interfaces." In *3rd IFIP Conference on Human-Computer Interaction, Interact'90*, Cambridge, UK, Aug. 1990, 625-31. North-Holland, 1990.
2. Baumeister L., John B. and Byrne M. "A Comparison of Tools for Building GOMS Models." In *Proceedings CHI'2000*, ACM Press, 2000.
3. Biere, M., Bomsdorf, B., Szwillus G. "Specification and Simulation of Task Models with VTMB." In *Proceedings CHI'99*, Extended Abstracts, pp.1-2, 1999.
4. Bodart F., A-M. Hennebert, Leheureux J-M., I. Provot, and J. Vanderdonckt. "A Model-Based Approach to Presentation: A Continuum From Task Analysis to Prototype." In *1st. EUROGRAPHICS Workshop on Design Specification and Verification of Interactive System (DSV-IS'94)*, Bocca di Magra, Italy, 8-10 June 1994.
5. Carroll, John (ed.). "Scenario-based Design." John Wiley and Sons, 1995.
6. Navarre, D., Palanque, P., Bastide, R., Sy, O. "Specification of Middles Touch Screen using Interactive Cooperative Objects." In *Working Paper 2.5*, MEFISTO Project: `http://giove.cnuce.cnr.it/mefisto/wp2-5.html`, (2000)
7. Object Management Group. "The Common Object Request Broker: Architecture and Specification." CORBA IIOP 2.2 /98-02-01, Framingham, MA (1998).
8. Palanque, P., Paternò, F., Bastide, R. and Mezzanotte, M. "Towards an Integrated Proposal for Interactive Systems design based on TLIM and MICO." In *Proceedings of DSV-IS'96*, Springer Verlag 1996.
9. Palanque, Philippe, Rémi Bastide, and Fabio Paternò. "Formal Specification As a Tool for the Objective Assessment of Safety Critical Interactive Systems." In *Interact'97, 6th IFIP TC13 Conference on Human-Computer Interaction*, Sydney, Australia, 14 July 1997-18 July 1997, 323-30. Chapman et Hall, 1997.
10. Palanque, Philippe, Rémi Bastide, and Valérie Sengès. "Validating Interactive System Design Through the Verification of Formal Task and System Models." In *6th IFIP Conference on Engineering for Human-Computer Interaction, EHCI'95*, Garn Targhee Resort, Wyoming, USA, August 14-18. Chapman et Hall, 1995.
11. Palanque, Philippe, and Rémi Bastide. "Synergistic Modelling of Tasks, Users and Systems Using Formal Specification Techniques." In *Interacting With Computers* 9, no. 2, 129-53, 1997.
12. Paternò, F. "Model-Based Design and Evaluation of Interactive Application." Springer Verlag, ISBN 1-85233-155-0, 1999.

13. Paternò, F. "The specification of the ConcurTaskTrees notation." GUITARE Working Paper, March 2000.
14. Paternò, F., Santoro, C., Sabbatino, V. "Using Information in Task Models to Support Design of Interactive Safety-Critical Applications." In *Proceedings AVI'2000*, pp.120-127, ACM Press, May 2000, Palermo, 2000.
15. Paternò, F., Mori, G., Galimberti, R. "CTTE: An Environment for Analysis and Development of Task Models of Cooperative Applications." In *Proceedings ACM CHI'01*, Vol.2, ACM Press, Seattle, 2001.
16. Puerta, A.R., Eisenstein, J. "Towards a General Computational Framework for Model-Based Interface Development Systems." In *IUI99: International Conference on Intelligent User Interfaces*, pp.171-178, ACM Press, January 1999.
17. Sy, Ousmane, Bastide, Rémi, Palanque, Philippe, Le, Duc-Hoa, Navarre, David. "PetShop: a CASE Tool for the Petri Net Based Specification and Prototyping of CORBA Systems." In *20th International Conference on Applications and Theory of Petri Nets, ICATPN'99*, Williamsburg, VA, USA. 1999.
18. van Welie M., van der Veer G.C., Eliëns A. "An Ontology for Task World Models." In *Proceedings DSV-IS'98*, pp.57-70, Springer Verlag, 1998.
19. Wilson, S., Johnson, P., Kelly, C., Cunningham, J., and Markopoulos, P. "Beyond Hacking: a Model Based Approach to User Interface Design." In *HCI'93*, Loughborough, U.K., 217-31. Cambridge University Press, 1993.

Temporal Patterns for Complex Interaction Design

Min Du and David England

School of Computing and Mathematical Sciences, Liverpool John Moores University,
Liverpool, L3 3AF, UK d.england@livjm.ac.uk

Abstract. Patterns have emerged as a useful organising mechanism for
component re-use in Software Engineering. There is, however, less agreement about how patterns might be used in the Human-Computer Interaction design process. In this paper we look at one way that patterns
might be used to augment an existing user interface design notation.
XUAN is a useful notation for expressing temporal problems in interaction. However, XUAN has showed its limitations in the design process,
requiring the repeated description of common situations. This notation
bureaucracy makes it hard to redesign during the UI development process. To overcome this limitation, we proposed the exploitation of the
pattern technique. The combination of pattern language and XUAN is
PUAN. The PUAN inherits most features of XUAN and also, like patterns, can be reused where tasks repeatedly occur in scenarios.

1 Introduction

Our overall aim is to deliver a set of validated design patterns of the eXecutable
User Action Notation, which can be used by application and systems designers
in a range of multi-media, virtual reality and mobile computing developments.
The pattern-based User Action Notation is referred to as PUAN in this paper.
Our work concentrates on the temporal specification of interaction. The issue
of simple response time is generally dealt with in HCI texts, but more general
issues of temporal relations and durations are usually ignored. The effects of this
omission can be seen in numerous interactive systems that display unpredictable
temporal behaviours. Such systems cause confusion and frustration to end-users.
In order to fill this gap in design knowledge our work has three stages; firstly
we have defined our temporal pattern notation, PUAN, which enables designers
to reason about temporal issues, secondly we will write a pattern reader and
engine to build interactive prototypes described in PUAN and finally we will
validate a small range of patterns against actual usage of the prototypes. This
paper describes the first stage of our work

Historically, software engineers and programmers designed most of the user
interface as part of the software in an interactive system. The result was that
interfaces often varied in quality and usability. Much work in the field of human
-computer interaction has been directed toward new approaches to user interface
development in the hopes of improving quality and usability. With the advent

C. Johnson (Ed.): DSV-IS 2001, LNCS 2220, pp. 114–127, 2001.

of the Web and mobile computing we have a new generation of designers and implementers who are faced with the challenges of user interface design. The challenge for HCI researchers is how to reach this new audience so that the lessons learned over the last 15-20 years can be re-used with the new presentation platforms.

One of these new concepts is the notion that the design of software to construct a user interface is different from design of the interface itself. Using software-engineering methods cannot necessarily produce user interfaces with high usability. Designers need behavioural specification tools to develop user-centred interface design. By the integration of behavioural techniques into the constructional method, they can create useful and usable user interfaces. One approach is based on notations such as the User Action Notation (UAN) [3]. UAN is a task and user-oriented notation for behavioural representation of temporal properties and asynchronous tasks, has been used to design direct manipulation interface designs.

In the UAN's tabular task diagrams, one of the main problems is that the temporal relationships within and across tasks are not stated explicitly. The ordering of tasks, feedback and system operations are represented loosely. Hence, some important temporal relationships are often represented implicitly. Furthermore, temporal relationship within UAN concentrated primarily on user actions, thus neglecting the temporal aspects of task categories not considered user actions.

The eXecutable User Action Notation (XUAN) [3, 8] is a variant of the User Action Notation (UAN). It is mixed graphical and textual notation and introduced temporal relations and temporal constraints to capture descriptions of user interface with time-varying media. XUAN inherited most of the advantages and resolved some of the limitations of UAN, especially in temporal relations and ordering of the tasks. It adds more features on temporal relations by defining new constraints to assist in the evaluation of various hypotheses regarding the time dependence of usability [7].

XUAN represents tasks as tabular diagram table. The diagram table contains three categories (columns), which represent a set of the actions making up the task. The columns have been systematised in order to make clearer their roles and their relationship to one and another. The left/ right/ -top/down ordering of the table elements may be viewed as a partial representation of temporal ordering of actions and the columnar organisation as modelling the task agents. For example in table1.1, the three columns represent the communications between those categories while the rows represent the temporal ordering of actions. We can use XUAN to help us deal with designs that involve notions of concurrency and time.

2   Patterns

The user interface (UI) design development process is a cycle of the design of the UI via some notation or scenario modeling, the development of a prototype, and the evaluation of the UI. Ideally we should be able to refine our notation description from the results of evaluation. However, our experiences with teaching XUAN and UAN to final year students, have shown their limitations in some applications, such as repeatedly applying descriptions of common task situations, for example, when common buttons or menu actions are re-described at the task level of design. This notation bureaucracy makes redesign of the user interface more difficult. By contrast pattern notations describe a problem, which occurs and reoccurs again in our environment, and then describe the core of the solution to that problem in such a way that one could use this solution many times over. With usability patterns we can also capture requirements information about tasks.

The pattern languages introduced by Christopher Alexander [1] are representations that have been used in architecture and urban design for about twenty years. Architectural Design patterns help the designer choose design alternatives that make an environment more livable and avoid alternatives that compromise the enjoyment a space. Software designers have adopted design patterns where software patterns record experience in designing object-oriented software. Design patterns [4] make it easier to reuse successful designs and software architectures.

Pattern languages have the potential to organise and effectively communicate user interface design solutions. For example, a small, domain specific pattern language was created and used for en-route air traffic control project [11]. In Human Computer Interaction (HCI), the purpose of using patterns is not only to help programmers and designers but also the users. The programmers can use patterns to design different kind of user interfaces for different users. Users, however, will pick up a copy of those HCI patterns ultimately and use them to redefine and customise their own private computing interfaces.

Patterns have also used in Virtual environments and present a set of design patterns to assistant the virtual environment designers to solve recurrent design problems, e.g. in interacting with remote objects. It provides solutions to the design in many aspects, such as virtual space, mobility and other issues. Patterns are also used to describe business domains, processes and tasks to aid early system definition and conceptual design.

In general, Pattern languages have mainly been used to deal with recurrent situations and complicated tasks in computer programming. It makes programming work simpler and easier and enables the reuse of intelligent and good ideas. The challenge for HCI researcher is going beyond guidelines and find concrete ways of capturing re-usable ideas about interaction in order to better server our design community.

3   Examples

In this section we present some examples of using patterns to solve a set of common requirement problems. Our general patterns are derived from Tidwell's informal pattern and we have expanded her patterns and made them more precise.

We first present a non-temporal and then a temporal pattern.XUAN example: An Equal Opportunity Chocolate Vending machine

In our first example we want to show how XUAN can be used to specify an interaction scenario. We wish to show the reader how temporal relations and temporal durations can be used to model interactions with a novel vending machine. Our inspiration for this machine comes from two requirements; firstly the issue of equal opportunity interaction raised by Thimbleby [12] and secondly the notion of two-handed interaction proposed by Bill Buxton [13]. Our machine will meet the requirements of these two authors by allowing the user use both hands to operator the machine and also allowing the user to choose interleave the actions of choosing the chocolate and entering the cash. Firstly we specify the operations with the partial ordering of the XUAN table:

Table 1.1. A partially ordered Chocolate Vending Machine in XUAN

User Action	Feedback	System State
Enter Cash(M)		Cash = Cash+M
	Display (Cash)	
Choose Choc(C)		Choc= C
		If Cash greater than Price(C) then (Delivery(C), Change(Cash - Price (C)))
Cancel		Change(Cash), Reset
	Display(0)	

Now the above description requires that the money be entered before the chocolate is chosen, counter to the principal of equal opportunity. We can further specify the ordering of tasks using temporal constraints to both allow equal opportunity and two-handed operation:

1) Allow two-handed operation and concurrency of cash entry and product choice:

 − Choice = (Enter Cash(M) | | Choose Choc(C))

2) Allow interleaving of delivery of the product and change

 − Delivery = (Deliver(C) | Change(X))
 − 3) Choice must be completed before delivery Choice, Delivery

4) Choice can be interrupted by Cancellation followed by the return of change

 − Choice <= Cancel, Change(X)

5) If the user takes too long (e.g. 5 minutes) reset the machine and return the change

 − If Elapsed(Choice) greater than 5:00 then
   Change(X)
   Reset()

By examining the above we might begin to see where re-usable patterns may emerge. For example, we might begin to develop a pattern for equal opportunities that always includes constraint (1) in its specification. We might also reuse constraint (5) if we wished to always specify a time-out. However, these "micro" patterns or interaction sequences fall short of being full patterns. They do, however, indicate the process by which new patterns may arise, by examining useful temporal sequences in novel applications. The next stage in the process would be to validate that the patterns actually improve the usability of interfaces designed from them.

Note that the word "complex" in our title is relative. We are aiming at interaction designers, who may or may not be computing professionals. We wish to give a wide range of designers the tools to deal with temporal issues. The challenge of our work is to codify re-usable interaction sequences and scenarios for use by less experienced designers. Note also that we are not dealing with temporal systems issues such as deadlock or liveliness. Such issues will affect the usability of a system but our perspective is to view such issues at the interface between user and system. In addition our work is aimed at "soft" real-time issues. We may set constraints but we cannot guarantee that they can be met, we can only flag when constraints have be broken. Furthermore there may be instances where we cannot detect that a constraint has be broken, e.g. a time event is lost by the underlying system. This means that we can only specify capturable events with our notation.

3.1   Pattern Example 1: Drawing Shapes

Our next (XUAN) example (table 1.2) is called Toolbox [Shape]. In this simple example, we try to show the advantages of PUAN over XUAN in dealing with common situations.

Many application packages, such as PowerPoint, Illustrator, Word (draw tool) etc. have a tool-kit or toolbox to aid selection of operations. The toolbox is often used for:

1. Creating objects that are different in kind from ordinary actions performed upon existing objects.
2. Allowing users to know how many tools are available.
3. Allowing users to know where to put it when the users to bring in new tools.
4. Allowing users easy to access all tools

A user can draw any shape by choosing the shape from the toolbox. The Toolbox (shape) operation is common interaction sequence across many applications.

When users use a drawing program to draw a shape (such as line, circle etc.), they need to choose the symbol of the shape from toolbox, and then move the mouse to draw the shape on canvas. table 1.2 shows the common operation of drawing shapes.

From the table (table 1.3), we can see that drawing a Line or drawing a Circle is a similar action. However, in the XUAN diagram table (table 1.3), every step

Table 1.2. Selecting a shape via Toolbox [shape]

User Action	Feedback	Ssytem State
Click toolbox [Shape]	Shape-button selected	Get Shape
Mouse-down (x, y)	Cursor (x, y)	Start-point (x, y)
Mouse-move (x", y")	Cursor (x", y")	
Mouse-release (x', y')	Cursor (x', y') par drawing Shape(x1,y1)	End-point (x', y') par Shape (x1, y1) = End-point (x, y) - Start-point (x', y')

Table 1.3. Drawing line(s) and circle(s) described in XUAN

Head	Head	Head
Click Line	Line button selected	
Mouse-down (x, y)	Cursor (x, y)	Start-point(x, y)
(Mouse-move (x ", y")	Cursor (x", y")	Potential-point(x", y"))*
Mouse-release(x', y')	Cursor (x', y') par Draw Line (x1, y1)	Line (x', y')= (End-point (x', y')) - Start-point (x, y))
Click Circle	Circle button selected	
Mouse-down (x, y)	Cursor (x, y)	Start-point (x, y)
(Mouse-move (x ", y")	Cursor (x", y")	Potential-point(x", y"))*
Mouse-release(x', y')	Cursor (x', y') par Draw Circle (x1, y1)	Circle (x', y') = (End-point (x', y')) - Start-point (x, y))

for each drawing has to be described separately. Therefore the common action was repeated twice in this example and would have to repeat many times for all similar actions.

Table 1.4. An Interaction pattern for drawing line(s) and circle(s) by PUAN

Head	Head	Head
Click Toolbox [Line]	Line-button selected	
(Move mouse (x, y)	Draw Line (x, y)	Line (x, y)) *
Click Toolbox[Circle]	Circle-button selected	
(Move mouse (x, y —	Draw Circle (x, y)	Circle (x, y))*

If the same task is represented by PUAN (see table 1.4), both drawing Line and drawing Circle can be represented by a simple Toolbox [shape] pattern. This basic drawing operation can also be extended to other drawing tasks. This example demonstrates that PUAN could save the repeated descriptions of XUAN and maintain interaction sequence consistency across similar operations.

3.2   Pattern Example 2: Task Switching and Progress Monitoring

The following example deals with timely feedback to user input [6]. In this pattern response to user feedback must demonstrate either:

1. Immediate feedback with a short sensory cue on successful completion
2. An indication of progress and an estimate of completion for delayed responses
3. An indication of task status and the steps needed for termination in the case of abnormally delayed response.

These criteria can be parameterized to define acceptable time delays, either for different sensory modes of interaction or for different task contexts. The reader has probably met interaction scenarios where the above requirements were not demonstrated, for example, in MS Outlook - when pressing Send/receive; if no new messages are present the status message disappears before it can be read

In this example we examine the case of waiting for the completion of lengthy tasks. We show how our pattern can be applied to these tasks. We then go onto show how we might meet the requirement for monitoring multiple lengthy tasks.

The first part of this XUAN example (table 1.5) is Show- progress [task]. In this example we present the general scenario of a user waiting for a lengthy task and monitoring the progress of that task, for example, when the user transfers or downloads a file through the Internet or is awaiting the delivery of email. The feedback is important information to the user. The user needs to know whether the process has been completed or not, and how long they have to wait for the process to be finished, and if the task has been completed successfully.

In this example we have set some parameters for the minimum (S) and maximum (M) waiting times for task feedback. We have specified a minimum waiting time so that some feedback always occurs.

In Show-progress [task]: the task is an application, it could be started clicking a button or starting an application. It can also be used as sub-task within another task. The key pattern-like aspects of the above description are the feedback requirements of the task which specify that the user is made aware of

- Normal progress of the task
- Completion of the task
- Abnormal delays to the task

Completion of the task is also shown even when the task time is very short. Some applications (e.g. MS Outlook), flash up completion messages within the same timescale of the task, which maybe too short for the user to observe.

M = maximum time, S = minimum time

In our second part of the example, we consider an XUAN fragment for multitasking between tasks. In the example the tasks are exemplified by using Word to write a document, which includes an image, downloaded from the Internet. The document is to be sent by email on completion (figure 1.).

The key feature of this example is that the requirements from the Show-progress [task] task are inherited by the image saving task and the email delivery

Table 1.5. General Pattern: Show-progress [task]

Head	Head	Head
Click on (icon)	Highlight icon	Access application

	if (process is being made) (
	if (time less than S)
	show process is finished
	else if ((time greater than M)
	par (unknown time))
	(show process is stopped)
	(show file size, speed, time)
	)
	else
	(process is being hung)
		Process is made
		Process finished
		
		Process is stopped
		
		Process is hung

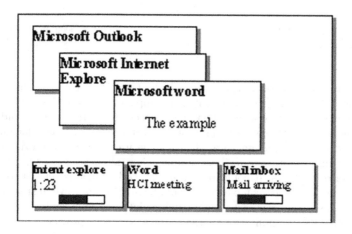

Fig. 1. Screen Display of Switching between tasks ext

task. The re-design of the interface presentation has been driven by the requirements specified in our general task monitoring pattern. This has implications for the implementation of the tasks as we show below (table 1.6).

The requirement set by the inclusion of the task monitoring, Show-progress [task] pattern are inherited by the task-switching example. In a conventional Windows interface, the user would accomplish task monitoring by switching between tasks to observe they state. This introduces an overhead in task switching. However, we already have screen real estate permanently presented to the user in the form of the task bar. One possible design solution to our Show-progress [task] requirement is shown in table 1.6 where each task bar item shows the progress of its respective task. There are three progressing state bars on the bottom of the screen (table 1.6) along with the taskbar. These state bars represent the present

Table 1.6. Switch between tasks

Head	Head	Head
Click Explore	Explore is active par Word is inactive par Mail is inactive	Explore active
Right click on image	Menu appeared	
click save as	Save dialogue box	entry
click save	Show-progress [save] par (Word is active)	Image saved entry
(click Word Typing click save as click save	Show text Choose directory save file) *	Word active entry File saved
click Mail choose a file to attach click attach file click send	Mail is active par Word is inactive par Explore is inactive Show-progress [send]	Mail active file has been attached file has been sent

state of their applications. No matter which application the user is using, he or she is aware of what is happening in other applications from the taskbar.

This example demonstrates the way PUAN can be used to identify and reason about interaction problems arising from concurrence tasks. It also demonstrates how a general pattern can be applied and be used to generate a design solution. The important point in this example is how Show-progress [task] has been reused in other tasks. It could be use in any task, which is related to process monitoring. Therefore, complex task could be divided into several small or basic tasks. Also several basic tasks could combine into one complex task. Each basic task represents an application of the pattern. Patterns provide a good format for capturing background information and describing generically good solutions. Patterns are also a good way of capturing the knowledge of good designs, thus allowing transmission and reuse of this knowledge.

3.3   Example 3: Online Ordering and Time-Outs Ext

According to a recent report [9] 39\% of attempts at on-line purchasing fail. Many of these failures are ascribed to difficulties in site navigation and searching. Further problems are time-related, for example, long delays in delivering the next web page and time-outs during the ordering process. In the former problem the user has some control in that they can stop the downloading of the delayed page. However, it is the latter problem that is of more interest here as it breaks our progress monitoring and control requirements. This kind of time-out behaviour is often seen on ticket ordering sites. The user is given a finite time (usually not specified to the user) between login on to the site and making a purchase. If the user attempts to make a purchase after their allotted time has elapsed their order is refused and they must sign in again. This is quite frustrating to the user, as they may have spent several minutes entering ordering information. This information may have to be re-entered, as they session details have been lost when their time expired. The expiration process does not take account of whether the user's time passed in useful activity (entering data) or wasted activity (waiting for the next page from the site). The rationale for the expiration process seems to be driven by the need to conserve system resources rather than user needs.

If we accept that the expiration process is necessary (which is doubtful), this scenario demands a requirement that is the mirror image of our second progress monitoring statement, i.e.

- If the user is faced with a time limit, progress towards task completion should be provided, during the time limit

In fact, this requirement is often met in computer games where the user is playing against the clock. Let us now express this requirement in PUAN in table 1.7.

Table 1.7. Figure 1. PUAN Time-limited purchasing

Head	Head	Head
Sign on to site	Show Successful login on	Begin expiration count
(Perform data entry	Show-progress [Expiration count] par Validate data entry) *	
Complete data entry and purchase		If count not expired
	Show purchase accepted	
		Else
	Show purchase rejected	
		Store data entered
	Request re-purchase	

Here the user is always aware of the time limit they may face and can abandon attempts at purchasing if they cannot complete their purchase in the allotted time.

4   Discussion

We believe we have met our first requirement for patterns, namely, cutting down on notation bureaucracy. This has an important benefit of making notations more appealing and usable by designers. So far we have only discussed one pattern relating to temporal aspects of interaction and we will investigate others such as

- Synchronization of user actions and system actions in dynamic applications (e.g. simulations) and multi-threaded applications
- Awareness of user status between users in multi-user environments
- Synchronization of user actions in multi-user environments

It is important that we investigate scenarios like these and express solutions to them in a notation like PUAN so that other designers can me made aware of common temporal interactions problems that their users will face. If we fail in this task we risk condemning the new generation of designers to repeating design mistakes, such as not providing timely feedback or now giving warnings of delayed system responses. In the attempt to formulate patterns we may find that we cannot find patterns that are full generalized and re-usable. However, we may find that the process of looking for such patterns may sharpen our focus on the design choices that need to be exercised when dealing with temporal issues. Another risk of patterns is of them being too readily accepted as easy design solutions. We then risk them being used as a short-cut for design and an appropriate design process.

Papers at the recent workshop on Patterns in HCI [10] highlighted different philosophies in pattern use. Some authors argued that HCI patterns should retain the philosophy of Alexander's architectural patterns in that they should be about design and user issues. They argued for the practice of HCI as a separate discipline that drives down-stream development processes. We would argue that such a separation of activities is doomed to failure. Studies of usability methods such as, Delta [11] have shown that usability techniques, that are not fully integrated into the requirements specification and verification processes, will not be adopted. If patterns are to be adopted by HCI practitioners, researchers need to demonstrate how they can be integrated in the development process. We hope we have demonstrated here how one particular pattern, for progress and task monitoring, can be used to drive design solutions.

5   Connections

In this section we look connections with other authors' work at the DSVIS 20001 workshop. We have already seen a link between XUAN specifications and symmetry [12] in our first example. Equal opportunity is an example of symmetry between user and system tasks. Symmetry is also an important concept in Alexander's [2] original conception of patterns in Urban Architecture. However the architectural work points to a potential problem with symmetry. The overuse, via patterns, of similar spatial features can lead to a sense of dis-orientation as people cannot tell one location from another. Does this point to a role for asymmetry rather than symmetry in user interface design. Asymmetry can be used to draw the user's attention to alerts and other important features and also help in navigation of structures. Symmetry may have a temporal equivalent in the notion of pace as explored by Dix [14]. Here Dix argues that for successful interaction the pace of system responses should match the pace of the user.

This analysis can be expanded further to computer mediated co-operative work, where, for successful cooperation the users should be communicating and performing their tasks at the same pace. The challenge for patterns writers is to try to codify the notion of micro and macro pace so that we help other designers develop systems that support pace matching effectively. That is, we need patterns that express the good properties of temporal symmetry. trapprox

Muller et al [15] discuss the use of mark-up languages such as XML as a way of communicating user interface descriptions to a variety of devices. The lesson for our work is that PUAN could be re-written in an XML style. The Java PUAN engine could then be provided as an applet or Web servlet to provide a temporal constraint engine on different devices. Different parameters could be set up for different temporal conditions to take care of local temporal differences.

Personal Digital Assistants are one potential device for exploring different temporal conditions [16]. Firstly, they are of lower performance than desktop machines and thus have different response times. But, more importantly, as we move to PDA as mobile interfaces to other devices (e.g. a personal interface to our Chocolate machine) we have to be concerned about the temporal issues of interacting with remote devices. Not only do we have to worry about the speed of the wireless link but also about the potential non-availability of the network and hence the interface.

In Sutcliffe's work on website attractiveness [17] various heuristics were proposed to measure attractiveness but not mention temporal issues. This raises the question of the need for further study - if two users view a web site but in different temporal conditions will they produce different ratings of attractiveness? With a highly interactive page (containing say applets or flash objects) the user has to wait for the interaction objects to appear before the page can be used. Perhaps we need a further metric for website evaluation: before we consider affordance we need to consider, when and if, objects make themselves available for interaction.

Finally we consider the work of Garrido and Gea [18]. They use UML as a task modelling notation for group interaction. XUAN has been used to discuss group interaction previously [8]. In this paper PUAN and XUAN are used to model concurrent interactions between user and system. To model co-operative interactions we replace the system by the tasks of other users. This could be expanded by having cooperating PUAN engines exchanging temporal information about their client's environments. This information could be used to adapt the interactions between cooperating users.

6   Conclusions

In this paper we have explored the Gamma-style [4] component approach to patterns to aid in the production of tasks descriptions. In future we will first establish a system, which includes a tool for authoring patterns and Java engine to read pattern descriptions. In this system, we can produce executable PUAN that can be read by a Java-based simulator. We can also exploit the built-in thread capabilities of Java to investigate how we might validate the usability of interface solutions via rapid prototyping and evaluation of further complex, temporal interaction scenarios. Then we will produce a set of design patterns, which can be used in virtual reality, multi-media and mobile computing.

There are some remaining issues in this project, such as how well the pattern "reader" works and how well PUAN will fit into the "real" UI development process and most importantly, how useful and re-usable our patterns prove to be? The final stage of our project will aim to answer the latter question by validating our patterns against a range of design scenarios.

Acknowledgements. Min Du is supported by a PhD studentship funded by the School of Computing and Mathematical Sciences, Liverpool John Moores University.

References

1. Alexander Christopher. (1997). "Keynote Speech OOPSLA'97." OOPSLA '97Video, ACM, New York.
2. Alexander Christopher, I. S., Silverstein S. (1977). "A Pattern Language: Towns, Buildings, Construction." Oxford University Press.
3. England, D, P. Gray. (1998). "Temporal aspects of interaction in shared virtual worlds." Interacting with Computers, 11(pp), P87-105
4. Gamma E, H. R., Johnson R, Vlissides J. (1995). "Design Patterns: Elements of Reusable Object-Oriented Software", Addison-Wesley
5. H. Rex Hartson, P. D. Gray. (1992). "Temporal aspects of tasks in the User Action Notation." Human Computer Interaction, 7(92), P1-45.
6. Jennifer Tidwell. (1996). "Common Ground." http://www.mit.edu/~jtidwell/interaction_patterns.html, last accessed August, 2001
7. Paddy O'Donnell, S. W. Draper, (1996)"Temporal aspect of usability, How Machine Delays Change User Strategies." SIGCHI, 28(2), P39-46
8. Gray P D, England D, McGowan S, (1994). "XUAN: Enhancing the UAN to capture temporal relationships among Actions." Proceedings of BCS HCI '94, Cambridge University Press, 1(3), P26-49.
9. E-Commerce Times (1999), "Mistakes Could Cost E-tailers \$6 Billion This Holiday Season", http://www.ecommercetimes.com/news/articles/991008-2.shtml, last accessed August, 2001
10. Patterns Workshop (2000), "BCS/IEE Workshop on Patterns in HCI".
11. Carlshammre P, Rantzer M, (2001), "A narrative approach to User Requirements for Web Design", ACM Interactions, VIII.1, January 2001
12. Thimbleby H, (2001) "Symmetry as a connection between affordance and state space", in C.W. Johnson (ed) Proceedings of DSVIS 2001, Design, Specification and Verification of Interaction Systems, Lecture Notes in Computer Science, Springer Verlag.
13. Buxton, W, Mayers, B, (1986) "A Study in Two-Handed Input ", Proceedings of CHI '86, , 321-326.

14. Dix A J, (1992) "Pace and interaction", in proceedings of HCI'92: People and Computers VII, Eds. A. Monk, D. Diaper and M. Harrison. Cambridge University Press. 193-207.

15. Mueller A, Forbrig P, Cap C, (2001), "Model-based user interface design using markup concepts", in C.W. Johnson (ed) Proceedings of DSVIS 2001, Design, Specification and Verification of Interaction Systems, Lecture Notes in Computer Science, Springer Verlag.

16. Gray P D, Gardiner M, Sage M, Johnson C W, (2001), "Design models for clinical anaesthesia on a pen-based PDA" C.W. Johnson (ed) Preproceedings of DSVIS 2001, C.W. Johnson (ed.), Technical Report, University of Glasgow, Scotland.

17. Sutcliffe A, (2001), "Heuristic Evaluation of Website Attractiveness and Usability", in C.W. Johnson (ed) Proceedings of DSVIS 2001, Design, Specification and Verification of Interaction Systems, Lecture Notes in Computer Science, Springer Verlag.

18. Garrido J L, Gea M, (2001), "Modelling Dynamic group behaviours", in C.W. Johnson (ed) Proceedings of DSVIS 2001, Design, Specification and Verification of Interaction Systems, Lecture Notes in Computer Science, Springer Verlag.

Modelling Dynamic Group Behaviours

José Luis Garrido and Miguel Gea

Department of Lenguajes y Sistemas Informáticos, University of Granada,
E.T.S.I. Informática, Avda. Andalucía 38, 18071 Granada, Spain
{jgarrido,mgea}@ugr.es

Abstract. New technological challenges provoke continuous improvements in society, and thus, change the very conception of the world around us. Nowadays, communication and collaboration activities play an important role in the modern work organisation. The CSCW paradigm is a promising technology offering group support, but its success depends on the way in which real group organisation is captured. We propose a model to represent, describe and integrate the complex behaviour of groups in a suitable manner. After a review of the state of art, a conceptual framework to address the problem domain is presented, and a formalism is introduced by extending Unified Modelling Language (UML) notation to model foundations and peculiarities of groups.

1 Introduction

Information Technologies are influencing social protocols and communication. The so-called information society in the 21st century is based on the *global village* concept, Internet, electronic mail, mobile phones, etc. These media contribute to a new way of understanding our world, based on distributed interactive computing systems [32]. This technological challenge is accompanied by a new way to understand the workload, increasing group collaboration to achieve common goals. Traditionally, work is organised into groups where individuals interact with others in order to achieve better productivity and performance. This challenge in technology, allowing the user to be part of a widely networked community, moves Computer-Human Interaction research toward Human-Human Interaction by using the computer as a medium. Computer networks allow the designer to consider that the user is not isolated in his own world focusing on effective communication with the computer, but rather involved in a new world which he shares with other users and in which he can also communicate with them. In this context, several users can cooperate to perform their tasks by using this paradigm, also called *Computer Supported Cooperative Work* (CSCW) [18,24].

The development of computer programs for group support is more difficult than single-user application, because social protocols and group activities should be taken into account for a successful design [15]. Thus, in the study of workgroups, techniques oriented to enhance group interaction activities should be applied [13]. The inherent complexity of any Interactive System demands a great effort in the formulation of specifications, and formal methods may be used to

C. Johnson (Ed.): DSV-IS 2001, LNCS 2220, pp. 128–143, 2001.

achieve this goal [6,16]. Furthermore, this abstract specification stage should also cover group features, providing the study of the group organisation for the design phase [11].

Several approaches have been used for the interactive system specification, and these can be categorised as *architectural models* [2] or *task-based models* [25, 35]. In architectural specifications, the system is modelled as a set of components as well as the relationships between them. Examples of such models are Interactor Models [8,10], the Arch Model [1], PAC [4], or MVC [20]. For CSCW systems, extensions have been proposed such as PAC* [3], or new models such as the Dewan Architecture [5]. These system specifications allow us to break the system into small components in which its functionality is clearly defined and translated to an implementation phase using Object Oriented technology. A drawback of these models is that the description is focused on the system design, so a loss of abstraction and independence will arise.

The second approach is based on user perception, and the specification focuses on representing user tasks [22]. The system specification is a collection of user goals where each one is defined by the sequence of tasks that allow us to achieve a desired objective. Several notations have been proposed, and can be used for different purposes. For example, the CCT [19] allows us to describe the user learning process, while TAG [27] is used to validate a system design seeking consistency. Other notations such as GOMS and NGOMSL [17] measure system performance and they are suitable to express the user's knowledge. Task analysis models have also been proposed for CSCW systems, such as GTA (Groupware Task Analysis) [34] and CTT (ConcurTaskTrees) [28]. GTA proposes a system study based on the so-called *ontology for task world models* [36], that is, a framework in which participants (agents and user roles), artifacts (objects) and situations (goals, events) take place. Moreover, a set of relationships among them are clearly identified (uses, performed-by, play, etc). CTT provides a hierarchical graphical notation to describe concurrent tasks. An extension to CTT was proposed in [29] to specify cooperation by adding a hierarchical specification with temporal constraints for each cooperative task. These extensions aim to establish common tasks for several users and the relationships between them.

These task-based approaches study the system from the user's point of view, describing the user cognitive skills to be acquired for a correct use. However, these techniques cannot consider dynamical changes in the problem domain. For example, the user role may change throughout real situations (e.g. a change of responsibilities in an office department), and the ways in which the objectives are achieved (e.g. a new commercial strategy, different work organisation). In fact, group organisation and evolution in time should be taken into account in order to describe social organisations. In [23] a theory of groups is described. A group is defined as a "*complex, intact social system that engages in multiple interdependence functions, on multiple concurrent projects ...*" and these projects determine different role-net definitions and choices between interaction protocols to achieve the goals.

This paper presents a technique to model complex group organisations where temporal evolutions take place, focusing on the user role description [12]. The group behaviour is described in terms of the roles and their relationships (organisational constraints), group activities (collaboration) and group dynamics (coordination). The following section presents the conceptual framework for a group structure. Section 3 briefly describes the UML elements and their interpretation in the problem domain that we have used as the basis for the system specification. Section 4 introduces a case study and the core of this paper, that is, how our extension to UML can be used to specify behaviour evolution, identify collaboration between participants to achieve goals, and coordinate group behaviour to perform activities. Finally, some connections to the rest of this book are shown in Sect. 5, and in Sect. 6 the major contributions of this paper and future work are reviewed.

2   Framework

The study of group organisation demands a consistent framework for the correct analysis of any parameter that may affect its nature. Several definitions have been used for framework, with different meanings depending on the level where it is applied. In this context, a framework should give a higher common abstraction level between a family of related systems to be described in terms of general concepts. In this sense, a framework is a pattern encompassing the principal common concepts of a kind of system and the relationships between them [9].

In describing the framework, we define the basic terminology [38] as follows. An *action* is a basic unit of work executable atomically. An *activity* is a set of other related activities and/or actions. A *task* is a set of activities that aim to achieve certain goals. A *role* is a designator for one set of possible capabilities to carry out work, and hence covers tasks, skills, constraints and authority/responsibility. An *actor* is a user, program, or entity that can play roles in order to execute, to be responsible for or to be related in some way to tasks. Finally, a *cooperative task* is a task that has to be carried out by more than one actor.

From the user's point of view, the framework allows us to specify the system fulfilling the following objectives:

- *The learning process.* The user needs to learn about the system and its rules. This knowledge can be achieved from cognitive approaches based on task analysis. This point of view focuses on the learning process, seeking an answer to the question: *"How can I do it?"*
- *The capability approach.* This approach is focused on dynamic system behaviour. Once the user knows the system in which he is involved, he may accept new objectives that the system offers. This approach seeks an answer to the question: *"Will I do it?"*
- *The group behaviour.* Users play a role in the system. Each user follows a set of known rules in each specified task depending on the current role. These

roles determine the user's possibilities and limitations in the system. This approach seeks to answer the question: *"Can/Should I do it?"*

A subtle difference exists between the two latter questions. In the first case, the user wants to know the possibilities that the system offers (present and future), while the second one is an ontological question that determines the permission and prohibition for the role which the user is playing in the group. These two final questions are directly related to the group behaviour in which the user is involved.

In addition to this, specific features [14] for group support are provided in this conceptual framework:

- *Communication.* Emphasises the exchange of information between remote actors by using the available media (text, graphics, voice, etc.).
- *Collaboration* [33]. An inherent activity within groups. Effective collaboration demands that people share information. The information content is shared in the group context.
- *Coordination* [21]. The effectiveness of communication/collaboration is based on this feature, which is related to integration and the harmonious adjustment of individual work effort toward the accomplishment of a greater goal. It should be influenced only by social protocols. The coordination process determines the appropriate task model and role-net definition for a group.

This set of concepts, objectives and features makes up our group conception and justifies the choice of this conceptual framework as a basis for group behaviour modelling.

3   Notation

We now introduce the ideas behind our notation, based on UML [31]. Next section provides some examples of its use. UML can be defined as a general-purpose visual modelling language to specify, visualise, construct and document the artifacts of a software system. The strengths of UML we are interested in are summarised as follows:

- The language is a standard that includes semantic concepts, notation and guidelines.
- It has dynamic, environmental and organisational parts.
- It is supported by visual modelling tools that usually include code generators.
- It is not intended to be a complete development method.
- It allows a graphical specification for aspects that can be better stated in this way.
- Specification at different levels of abstraction is possible.
- One model may be translated into others automatically to achieve a more suitable representation (e.g. activity and state diagrams are isomorphic) or alternatively, it is possible to translate into any formal methods for analysis and verification purposes.

UML provides a technological focus to system development. However, we are more interested in modelling behaviour, so the UML notation is used as follows:

1. using the more abstract kind of diagrams (activity and state), that do not cover any structural aspects, to model concepts in the framework, and
2. combining these diagrams with text notation in order to simplify the specification and increase its expressiveness.

Table 1 summarises the main UML elements we are interested in and the interpretation of each in the problem domain. Basically, UML state diagrams are used to model how an actor can dynamically change his behaviour and influence group behaviour. Anything that may affect an actor is contemplated as an event. Each actor is treated as an individual entity that communicates with the rest of the world by detecting events and reacting to them in different ways. The reaction to an event may produce a new event that affects other actors. Thus, group behaviour may be affected indirectly. A change in the actor's behaviour can be produced by his own decision as well as by external events (conditions such as group decisions, etc).

Table 1. UML elements and their interpretation

UML Diagram	UML Element	Used for/to
State	State	Role
	Stub state	Set of interruptible substates in a role
	Internal transition	State or behaviour change in an actor playing a role (e.g. starting a new task execution)
	Transition between states	Role change
	Transition guard	Capability or condition enabling or disabling the behaviour change
	History pseudo-state	Remember last execution state of an actor in a particular role
Activity	State	Activity or action
	Branch-merge	Alternative behaviours on basis of guards
	Fork-join	Concurrent execution of activities
	Completion transition	Normal execution termination of an activity
	Comments	Add or modify behaviour rules, conditions, etc.

UML activity diagrams describe how a group is coordinated to accomplish a task. An activity diagram is considered a higher level notation than a state diagram. Activity states represent the states of executing a computation. Normally, the execution progresses without external events. In UML, activity diagrams may contain activity (interruptible) and action (atomic) states, branches and forking of control into concurrent activities and any other element of a state diagram (e.g. deferred events).

Below, activity diagrams are nested within state diagrams. The combination of these two kinds of diagrams poses no problem since the former is a special form of the latter. The submachine corresponding to a task is specified by an activity diagram, and the dynamic changes between tasks and roles by means of a state diagram.

4   Modelling Group Dynamics for Cooperative Systems

This section focuses on the main topics for work group modelling. For this purpose, we introduce a case study in which several roles and group activities are taken into account. Firstly, a brief introduction to the example is given. After that, the roles involved in the system are modelled. Finally, some of the most relevant cooperative tasks are described.

4.1   Case Study

Any work group is governed by social rules and protocols that should be taken into account in the analysis and design phase. As a study case, we have analyzed some staff members in a faculty. This scenario features several participants, to each of which a role is assigned (Lecturer, Director, Director Assistant and Secretary) and to each of which a task model is associated. In this group, several cooperative tasks are contemplated (to organize a Faculty Assembly, etc). In addition, one participant may play a different role in the future or he may play more than one role but alternately, i.e., only one at a given moment. For instance, a Lecturer nominated to be Director may play both roles but at different moments, note that the Director does not cease to be a Lecturer. Moreover, various protocols and policies are preserved (democratic statements, obligations to attend the Faculty Assembly, etc). For the sake of simplicity, this paper focuses on a limited set of roles and tasks.

4.2   Actor-Role Modelling

We start the behaviour modelling for the group from the roles involved as shown in Fig. 1(a). Each state in this diagram, specified as a submachine (`include` clause), represents one role, e.g., the `Lecturer` role matches the state that specifies a submachine with the same name. At any given moment, the actor's behaviour is defined by the role he is playing.

Behaviour Evolution. The set of possible behaviours for a group (of actors) is modelled by the state machine that stems from role connections by means of transitions. The dynamic change between two roles is represented by a transition and its corresponding *capability*, which enables an actor to change his role. This appears as a guard condition associated with the transition. For instance, an actor playing the role `Lecturer` may play the role `Director` if he satisfies the capability with the same name as this. The occurrence of external events may enable or disable capabilities. Hence, the set of possible behaviours that an actor can play is constrained by capabilities.

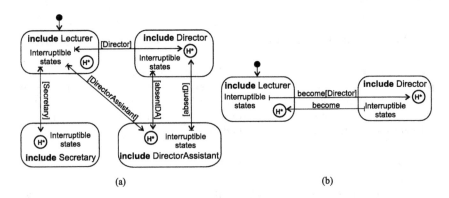

Fig. 1. Behaviour evolution

An actor playing a role may be interrupted in specific substates. This allows the actor to behave in a different way in order to perform other tasks, probably by changing to a different role. Each role is specified in the next section by a submachine containing activity states for tasks. A transition goes from a set of interruptible activity states (showed as a UML stub state) in the source role, to the history pseudo-state in the target role. Each possible change of role may have a different set of interruptible states. This is specified in detail below, in the role specification, and only the whole set is considered here for abstraction. The history pseudo-state is a deep history (shown as a small circle containing H∗), which remembers a state that may have been nested at some depth within a composite state. Thus, a transition to a deep history state restores the previous active state at any depth. The purpose of this pseudo-state is to be able to resume the last interrupted task of a role at the same place (the state at which the actor left it) after a behaviour change during its fulfillment.

To simplify the specification, we have introduced a double-headed arrow to represent two-way changes between two roles. We have also removed the stereotyped event `become` that causes transitions. Figure 1(b) shows the representation semantically equivalent to the transition between the `Lecturer` and `Director` roles in Fig. 1(a). In this example, an actor who is playing the role `Director` may always change (there is no capability) to the `Lecturer` role because becoming a Director always implies continuing being a Lecturer. Indeed, an inclusion relationship between them exists. On the other hand, the opposite is not true.

When the capability to change between roles has a different name from the target role to be reached, then the new role may still be kept when both the capability is satisfied and there are some tasks to be accomplished. For instance, the DirectorAssistant may play the role `Director` if the latter is absent (capability `absentD`) and some work related to this role must be performed. This characteristic allows us to influence the group behaviour. Hence, capabilities allow us to model interaction requirements such as:

– Users themselves may accept new challenges that the system offers (e.g. a Lecturer can become a Director).
– Users can modify their possibilities and limitations in the system according to other group members' behaviours, even without changing the role that they are playing.

Role Specification. Two role specifications are shown in Fig. 2. In each one, we must identify every task, together with:

– external events to start its execution,
– guard condition that enable its execution, and
– tasks that may interrupt its execution. These tasks can be in the same role or others. By default, a task cannot be interrupted.

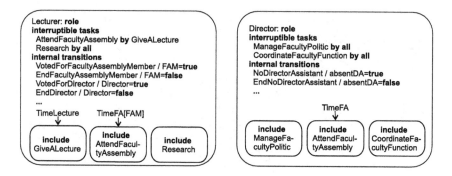

Fig. 2. Role specifications

The `Lecturer` role specification shows three tasks, each one described as a submachine: `GiveALecture`, `AttendFacultyAssembly` and `Research`. Each one specifies the event that leads the task to its execution, except the last one, which is to indicate that the execution is a consequence of an internal decision by the actor. Constraints for task execution are optional here, as in UML. Moreover, there is a section (`interruptible tasks`) intended to specify that tasks may be interrupted and which are the interrupting tasks for each one. For instance, the task `Research` may be interrupted by the other tasks (clause `by` followed by reserved word `all`), even by tasks in other connected roles.

Internal transitions may be described in the same way as does UML. In our model, they are intended to control the evolution of behaviour by means of capabilities for both role changes and guard conditions of task executions. For instance, `Director` is a capability that is enabled or disabled by external events. `FAM` (for Faculty Assembly Member) is another capability that affects the guard condition for the task `AttendFacultyAssembly`. It is also modified by external events.

Comparison of the two role specifications in Fig. 2 reveals that both contain the same task `AttendFacultyAssembly`. This match clearly indicates that it is a cooperative task. Moreover, it allows us to specify different events for each role to start its execution, as well as different guard conditions. For instance, a Lecturer has to be a member of the faculty assembly (capability `FAM`) to collaborate in this task fulfillment, so the guard condition is necessary for this role. On the other hand, the Director is enabled to collaborate because this role includes the task as a responsibility.

The equivalent specification in UML is shown in Fig. 3. The diagram complexity increases according to the specification. This arises from the larger number of arcs that must be handled. Every role follows the same specification pattern. All the differences can be specified in a simpler way by using the text notation. Thus, the specification in Fig. 2 abstracts implementation details and hence is more convenient from the user's point of view.

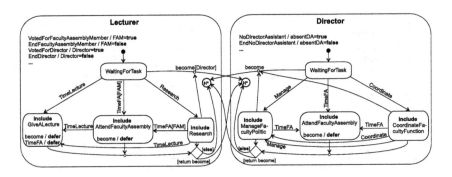

Fig. 3. UML state machine

4.3   Task Modelling

We now focus on tasks to complete the behaviour modelling. To model tasks, an extension to UML activity diagrams is proposed. A UML activity diagram is suitable to model a system where no event-driven transitions exist. External events are already captured at a higher level in the previous actor-role modelling. One of the main features of task modelling is coordination to obtain suitable collaboration. Coordination is present during the whole modelling process, but especially here. Coordination between activities implies coordination between actors, too.

At first, task starting/completion depends on the task itself. However, actors playing a role may decide to start/leave/finish a task by themselves or it may be produced as a consequence of certain external events.

There are two kinds of tasks: *individual* and *cooperative*. The latter need more than one actor to be accomplished. An individual task can be considered a special case of a cooperative task. Thus, the specification of the former is usually simpler than that of the latter. Hence, we prefer to address cooperative tasks directly in order to show a wider vision of the problem domain.

Cooperative Tasks. An example of cooperative task specification is given in Fig. 4(a). First, the task is divided into general activity states in order to model every step in its execution. The task `AttendFacultyAssembly` consists of a simple sequence of composite activity states. However, it may include any other UML element apart from those that appear in Table 1 (e.g. conditional threads, deferred events, etc). For some submachines (e.g. `Inform()`) we have introduced the new element `[i:1..NumTopics]` to indicate that `Inform()` is the sequential execution of an array of `NumTopics` submachines; each element `Inform()[i]` has a different value for `i`, which is implicitly declared.

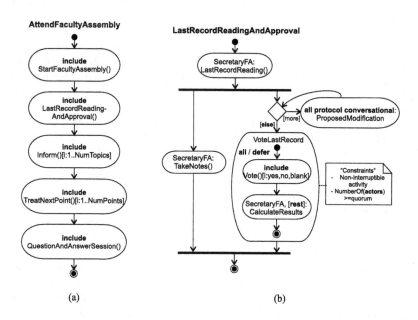

Fig. 4. Cooperative task

Another interesting property in groups is the relationship between roles and responsibilities for tasks. Thus, the identification and assignation of relevant activities on the basis of roles or groups of roles is useful to describe group dynamics. These relationships are described as follows for the task `AttendFacultyAssembly`:

```
Responsibility/Role
  Chairman = Director
  SecretaryFA = Secretary
  VotedMember = MemberAdministrativeStaff
                + Student + Lecturer
```

As shown in Fig. 4(b), a submachine may contain other submachines (e.g. `VoteLastRecord`) and activity states (e.g. `LastRecordReading()`). Of course, these submachines may also include any other UML element. For instance, a forking and joining of control specifies that the activity `TakeNotes()` and activities in submachine `VoteLastRecord` are executed concurrently. Moreover, our notation allows us to specify which participant is in charge of accomplishing an activity as well as the type of participation: compulsory or optional. The activity `CalculateResults` must be carried out by the `SecretaryFA` and optionally, the other actors (reserved word **rest**) may also do the calculation in parallel. This notation and its semantics are an extension of the UML. In addition, the way of specifying the (participant) responsible for each activity is a clearer alternative to the UML swimlanes notation because it avoids larger and more complicated diagrams.

Although UML comments have no specific semantics, they may give very useful semantic information here, such as a constraint. The standard stereotype **constraint** of UML can be applied to comments, which allows us to add or modify new or current rules, respectively. In Fig. 4(b) two constraints are associated with the `VoteLastRecord` submachine. One specifies that no activity within this submachine can be interrupted once it starts its execution. Note that the task to which the submachine belongs is interruptible at any place by the `Lecturer` role. On the other hand, this is not the case for the `Director` role. The other constraint specifies a condition that must be satisfied for the group to perform the activity.

Interaction Protocol. Up until now, we have not explicitly taken into account the interaction between actors. The type of interaction that occurs when a task, or specific activity in it, is being carried out depends on its nature.

Initially, we have implicitly assumed a multicast communication for the whole `AttendFacultyAssembly` task; that is, a send message from an actor who is collaborating in the task is received by the other participants in this task. In addition, we assume the actors can see each other as in real life. For instance, `TakeNotes` implies that the `SecretaryFA` can hear and see everything that is happening, i.e., the consequences of performing the other parallel activities.

In any case, it is possible to specify a particular communication protocol for an activity. A protocol specification consists of:

1. a participant description on the basis of responsibilities (e.g. in Fig. 5(a) `all-Chairman/Chairman`) identifying source and target for the interaction,
2. type of rules to guide the interaction (`Request/Reply`), and
3. contents of interaction, i.e., objects involved in the activity (`QuestionAbout(Topic[i])`).

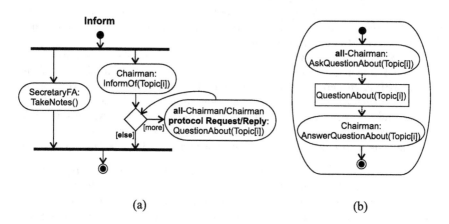

(a)   (b)

Fig. 5. Interaction protocol

Figure 5(b) describes in detail the equivalent submachine for the activity that has the protocol specification in Fig. 5(a). In any case, the `QuestionAbout(Topic[i])` message is still received by all participants in the task. However, it specifies who may perform the action that generates the message, who may perform the action that processes it, and the temporal ordering of these activities (i.e. the interaction rules to accomplish this activity). We have identified some standard protocols, but others may be incorporated in the future:

− Request/Reply as commented above.
− Conversational. Any participant may formulate a question, sentence or request, and reply to a given one. There is no specific order for interventions.
− Queued messages. Similar to Request/Reply, but allowing asynchronous interaction between participants. Each request must be replied to but not immediately.

These protocol specifications aim to be as abstract as possible, since technological aspects should be left for the system design. In addition, it allows us to disconnect interaction properties from specific media. Thus, its binding may be resolved dynamically during the use of the system.

5   Connections

The design of interactive systems is a complex task which involves a previous knowledge about human behaviour. This book includes several contributions related with the human nature and the way in which the work is performed, and it can be classified as follows:

- *Human behaviour*. In [7] stochastic models are used to describe the user's behaviour. In fact, the user's reaction may be unpredictable to certain stimuli from the environment (changes in the scenario, system errors). The user's response is conditioned by previous knowledge and the capability to react when the scenario has been modified. This approach can also be extended to describe the group behaviour.
- *Task modelling*. In [30] and [26] are proposed notations to describe the ordered sequence of activities that the user has to perform in order to achieve a goal. Each paper focuses on important aspect of the proper work organisation such as the context and the scenario in which the user is involved. A common feature of these papers is the importance of the workgroup (cooperative task) due to the current work organisation. People work in groups, and this feature has to be taken into account for the task modelling phase.

In our paper we propose a notation to describe the complex relationships between humans on groups (the dynamic group behaviour) and their tasks. Task modelling is done extending UML (instead of using CTT) to describe social protocols. We have chosen UML because it is a standard in fact for software engineering, although this notation can also be translated to CTT easily.

6   Conclusions and Future Work

Task analysis helps the designer to understand and validate the underlying system, and focuses on those aspects of interest for the user in order to describe how tasks are performed. However, a frequent drawback is the operational approach by which tasks are described. This kind of information helps us to explain how to perform certain tasks, but no information is given about the user's intentions (permission or obligation to perform certain tasks). This kind of information is related to the different roles that can be played in the system rather than to the task itself.

We have developed a formalism to model interactions between users in order to accomplish a project. Although state diagrams are used in the design of a system to model object behaviour, we show how an extended notation based on UML can be applied to the analysis phase by modelling concepts such as roles, capabilities, etc. The same is true for activity diagrams, when they are normally used to implement operations or use cases. Only these two types of UML diagrams are used to model the system. Moreover, the combination of them poses no problem because both are state machines though focusing on different aspects. We believe this diagrammatic modelling to be very clear and hence satisfactory for requirement negotiation with users, especially because it avoids technical aspects.

Role modelling by means of state diagrams allows us to specify dynamic behaviour. It is only necessary to detect events that may provoke changes and under what conditions this may occur. Unlike other models, our model clearly isolates the parts reserved for cooperation (i.e. cooperative tasks) from those that are bound to capabilities or intentions of participants (role specification). This notation allows us to disconnect the two parts to obtain a system that is a little more flexible and reusable. Our main goal is to produce a simpler specification and facilitate study of the system and its subsequent design. This work presents an approach to address some important aspects in the analysis of complex systems rather than a complete methodology to develop them.

UML includes roles, stereotype messages and collaboration diagrams to model dynamic changes between roles. Nevertheless, the use of these elements implies dealing with other aspects such as scenarios (several diagrams are needed to specify these) and specific operations related to structural issues (classes and structural relationships between them, interfaces, etc). Moreover, UML collaboration diagrams do not embody concurrent constructions. UML also has different possibilities to describe interaction, namely, collaborations and sequence diagrams. These elements are very helpful to specify more complicated interaction cases in detail. However, the use of these elements should be avoided at a higher abstraction level because they are focused on the design phase.

Petri Nets also offer good visual modelling facilities together with a degree of formalism to support them. On the other hand, Petri Nets require low-level details to capture an entire system. Future work is oriented towards developing tools to automatically translate these state machines into Petri Nets, so that properties such as inconsistencies, safeness, deadlocks, liveness, and reachability can be easily studied. Tools for design and implementation are also being considered. In addition, we are applying the model to other complex systems such as Air Traffic Control Systems, Virtual Learning Systems and Emergency Coordination Centres [34]. In the last, the team's cognitive tasks, to assess an event and to dispatch adequate resources, are achieved by mutual awareness, joint situation assessment and the coordinate use of technology.

References

1. Arch: A metamodel for runtime architecture of an interactive system. The UIMS Tool Developers' Workshop. SIGCHI Bulletin 24(1), ACM (1992) 32-37
2. Bass, L., Clements, P., Kazman, R.: Software Architecture in Practice. SEI Series in Software Engineering. Addison-Wesley (1998)
3. Calvary, G., Coutaz, J., Nigay, L.: From Single-User Architectural Design to PAC*: a Generic Software Architecture Model for CSCW. Proceedings CHI'97. ACM Press (1997) 242-249
4. Coutaz, J.: PAC-ing the architecture of your user interface. In Proceedings of the Fourth Eurographics Workshop on Design, Specification and Verification of Interactive Systems (DSVIS'97). Sringer-Verlag (1997) 15-32

5. Dewan, P.: Multiuser Architectures. IFIP Conference on Engineering for Human-Computer Interaction (1995)
6. Dix, A.: "Formal Methods for Interactive Systems". Academic Press (1991)
7. Doherty, G., Massink, M., Faconti, G.: Reasoning about Interactive Systems with Stochastic Models. In C.W. Johnson (ed.) Design, Specification and Verification of Interactive System (DSVIS'2001). Lecture Notes in Computer Science, Springer-Verlag (2001)
8. Duke, D., Harrison, M.: Abstract Interaction Objects. Computer Graphics Forum, 12 (3), (1993) 25-36
9. Ellis, C.: A Framework and Taxonomy for Workflow Architecture. In: Dieng, R., Giboin, A., Karsenty, L., De Michelis, G. (eds.): Designing Cooperative Systems - The Use of Theories and Models. IOS Press-Ohmsha (2000) 99-112
10. Faconti, G., Paterno, F.: An approach to the formal specification of the component of the interaction. Proceeding of Eurographics 1990. North-Holland (1990)
11. Garrido, J.L., Gea, M., Gutiérrez, F.L., Padilla, N.: Designing Cooperative Systems for Human Collaboration. In: Dieng, R., Giboin, A., Karsenty, L., De Michelis, G. (eds.): Designing Cooperative Systems - The Use of Theories and Models. IOS Press-Ohmsha (2000) 399-412
12. Garrido, J.L., Gea, M.: Analysis and Design of Cooperative Systems. Technical Report LSI-2001-1. Department of Computer Science. University of Granada (2001)
13. Gea, M., Garrido, J.L., Gutiérrez, F.L., Padilla, N.: World Wide Users: Exploring New Approaches to Active a Better Design Strategy. Proceedings of Basic Research Symposium at CHI'2000, The Hague, The Netherlands (April 2000)
14. Gea, M., Padilla, N., Garrido, J.L., Gutiérrez, F.L.: Diseño de entornos cooperativos. In: Arinyo, R.J., Navazo, I., Quirós, R. (eds.) X Congreso Español de Informática Gráfica (CEIG'2000). Castellon, Spain (June 2000) 143-156
15. Grudin, J.: Groupware and Cooperative Work: Problems and Prospect. The Art of Human Computer Interface. Addison-Wesley (1990)
16. Harrison, M., Thimbleby, H. (eds.): Formal Methods in Human-Computer Interaction. Cambridge University Press (1990)
17. John, B.E., Kieras, D.E.: The GOMS Family of user Interface Analysis Techniques: Comparison and Contrast. ACM Transactions on Human-Computer Interaction, vol 3, n° 4 (1996)
18. Jordan, B.: Ethnographic Workplace Studies and CSCW. In: Shapiro, D., Tauber, M.J., Traunmueller, R. (eds.): The Design of Computer Supported Cooperative Work and Groupware System. North-Holland, Amsterdam (1996) 17-42
19. Kieras, D.E., Polson, P.G.: An approach to the formal analysis of user complexity. International Journal Man-Machine Studies, 22 (1985)
20. Krasner, G.E., Pope, S.T. A cookbook for using the Model-View-Controller user interface paradigm in Smalltalk-80. Journal of Object-Oriented Programming, 1(3) (August-September 1988) 26-49
21. Malone, T.W., Crowston, K.: What is Coordination Theory and How Can It Help Design Cooperative Work Systems. Proceedings of the Conference on Computer Supported Cooperative Work (CSCW'90). ACM Press, New York (1990) 357-370
22. Markopoulos, P., Johnson, P., Rowson, J.: Formal Aspects of Task based Design. In Design, Specification and Verification of Interactive System (DSVIS'97). Springer Computer Science (1997)
23. McGrath, J.: Time, Interaction and Performance: a theory of groups. In Readings in Groupware and Computer-Supported Cooperative Work. R. Baecker (ed). Morgan Kauffman (1993)

24. Mills, K.L.: Introduction to the Electronic Symposium on Computer-Supported Cooperative Work. ACM Computing Surveys, Vol. 31, n° 2, (June 1999) 105-116
25. Nardi, B. (ed): Context and Consciousness: Activity Theory and Human Computer Interaction. MIT Press, Cambridge MA (1995)
26. Navarre, D., Palanque, P., Paternò, F., Santoro, C., Bastide, R.: A Tool Suite for Integrating Task and System Models through Scenarios. In C.W. Johnson (ed.) Design, Specification and Verification of Interactive System (DSVIS'2001). Lecture Notes in Computer Science, Springer-Verlag (2001)
27. Paine, S.J., Green, T.: Task-Action Grammars: A model of the mental representation of task languages. Human-Computer Interaction, 2 (1986)
28. Paternò, F., Mancini, C., Meniconi, S.: ConcurTaskTrees: A Diagrammatic Notation for Specifying Task Models. Proceeding of Interact '97. (July 1997) 362-369
29. Paternò, F., Santoro, C., Tahmassebi C.: Formal Models for Cooperative Tasks: Concepts and Application for En-Route Air-Traffic Control. In Design, Specification and Verification of Interactive Systems (DSVIS'98). Springer Computer Science (1998) 71-86
30. Pribeanu, C., Limbourg, Q., Vanderdonckt, J.: Task Modelling for Context-Sensitive User Interfaces. In C.W. Johnson (ed.) Design, Specification and Verification of Interactive System (DSVIS'2001). Lecture Notes in Computer Science, Springer-Verlag (2001)
31. Rumbaugh, J., Jacobson, I., Booch, G.: The Unified Modeling Language - Reference Manual. Addison-Wesley (1999)
32. Salvendy, G.: The Human Factors of the Information Society. In Proceeding of the 6th ERCIM Workshop of User Interfaces for All (2000)
33. Terveen, L.G.: An Overview of Human-Computer Collaboration. In Knowledge-Based Systems Journal, Special Issue on Human-Computer Collaboration (1995) 67-81
34. van der Veer, G., Lenting, B., Bergevoet B.: GTA: Groupware Task Analysis - Modelling Complexity. Acta Psycologica, 91 (1996)
35. van der Veer, G.C., van Vliet, J.C., Lenting, B.F.: Designing complex systems - a structured activity. In: Olson, G.M., Schuon, S. (eds.): Symposium on Designing Interactive Systems (DIS'95). ACM Press, New York (1995) 207-217
36. van Welie, M., van der Veer, G.C., Eliens, A.: An Ontology for Task World Models. In Design, Specification and Verification of Interactive System (DSV-IS'98). Springer Computer Science (1998) 57-70
37. Whalen, J.: Expert systems versus system for experts. Computer-aided dispatch as a support system in real-world environments. In: Thomas, P.J. (eds.): The social and interactional dimensions of human-computer interfaces. Cambridge University Press (1995) 161-183
38. Workflow Management Coalition (WfMC): Coalition Overview, Reference Model, and Glossary. Document Numbers WfMC TC-1003 - TC-1016 (1994-1998) http://www.aiai.ed.ac.uk/WfMC

Reasoning about Interactive Systems with Stochastic Models

G. Doherty[1], M. Massink[2], and G. Faconti[2]

[1] Rutherford Appleton Laboratory, Oxfordshire, UK,
[2] Istituto CNUCE, Pisa, Italy
G.J.Doherty@rl.ac.uk, {M.Massink,G.Faconti}@cnuce.cnr.it

Abstract. Several techniques for specification exist to capture certain aspects of user behaviour, with the goal of reasoning about the usability of the system and other human-factors related issues. One such approach is to encode a set of assumptions about user behaviour in a user model. A difficulty with this approach is that human behaviour is inherently non-deterministic; humans make errors, perform unexpected actions, and, taken individually, both the occurrence of errors and response times can be unpredictable. Such factors, however can be expected to follow probability distributions, and so an interesting possibility is to apply stochastic or probabilistic techniques that allow the modelling of uncertainty in user models. Recently, a number of process algebra based approaches to specifying stochastic systems have been proposed and in this paper we examine the possibility of applying these stochastic modelling techniques to reasoning about performance aspects of interactive systems.

1 Introduction

Interactive systems in the modern world are becoming both increasingly pervasive, and increasingly rich in the variety of tasks supported, the amount of information potentially available, and the different ways in which the user can interact with them. Interacting with such systems can involve multiple media and interaction devices, supporting a continuous flow of information rather than discrete interactions. By discrete interactions we mean those interactions where the user communicates his intentions in the form of separate events such as commands sent when hitting the "return" button and mouse clicks. They are events of relatively short duration and the user usually has control over the time needed to observe the effect of the event and decide the next event.

Continuous interaction differs from discrete interaction in the sense that the interaction takes place over a relatively long period of time in which there is an ongoing exchange of information between the user and the system at a relatively high rate, such as in vision based gestural interaction or haptic interfaces, that cannot be modelled appropriately as a series of discrete events. This shift towards more continuous interaction between user and system means that important properties of such systems are better expressed in terms of some quality of service parameter rather than static "yes or no" properties. Time can play

C. Johnson (Ed.): DSV-IS 2001, LNCS 2220, pp. 144–163, 2001.

a particularly important role - properties such as latency and jitter (variance of latency) are often critical to the usability of a system. With this motivation, a possible approach to modelling is to apply timed specification and analysis techniques [5].

Time-based properties are certainly relevant to the usability of the system from the human perspective. However, these properties and associated approaches to modelling consider only the system, and the properties are system properties. We would like to investigate timing issues while considering explicitly the role of the user, and the performance of the system as a whole with respect to the user's performance and capabilities. We can enhance the usefulness of such techniques by including partial user models, which encode assumptions about the user's behaviour with respect to time. Such an approach is described in [12], which applies a specification language for hybrid systems to the analysis of a human-operated critical system. It describes the construction of models to represent both system and user. Properties of the combined models are explored with a model checker, for example supporting analysis of the inferences involved in user diagnosis of system failure. However, in the hybrid systems approach, constraints on variables (including timing variables) are given as upper and lower bounds, with no way of determining the likelihood of a given value occurring.

1.1   Behaviour as a Stochastic Process

An important observation with regard to timed modelling is that user behaviour is typically stochastic. While it is certainly not deterministic, it is not completely random, and hence we would expect a variable based on user performance, such as reaction time, to follow a certain probability distribution. Note that such a distribution could be for the general population, or for more restricted groups of users. Although the user behaviour is stochastic rather than deterministic, we do not preclude deterministic time to model relevant parts of system behaviour or of the environment.

We propose that given a set of statistical assumptions about both system and user performance, we can use stochastic modelling techniques to understand the character of the interaction between user and system, in a richer manner than timed modelling techniques can support. In this way, answers to design questions can be both easier to relate to empirical performance data from human factors and usability studies, and also the results of the analysis can be more meaningful for interpretation by human factors experts. Additionally, much modern and emerging user interface technology is stochastic in nature, which provides further motivation for the application of stochastic techniques to modelling interaction.

For the usability analysis of *discrete* interactive devices, probabilistic approaches have been used for analyses based on the possible choices the user may make. For example, one can compare two interface designs with a measure of the average number of state transitions (i.e. button presses and the like) required of a user to achieve some goal [7]. It has been shown that formal approaches of this kind provide a useful complementary assessment of real interfaces that is scalable and applicable throughout the software design cycle.

In this paper we apply the stochastic time approach to address continuous rather than discrete interfaces. For those interfaces the performance in time is critical to their usability.

1.2 Overview

In Section 2, we look at different sources of stochastic uncertainty in interactive systems and discuss how stochastic modelling approaches can be applied to reasoning about interactive systems. In Section 3 we examine how we might apply stochastic modelling techniques based on stochastic process algebra. In Section 4 we look at an example application. We conclude with a discussion of the strengths and limitations of the approach and identify areas for future work.

2 Reasoning about Interactive Systems

The approach we take is to model both the system and aspects of user behaviour using stochastic modelling techniques. We can see these specifications as a means of making explicit the *assumptions* we make about the capabilities of both user and system, and exploring the behaviour of the combination of system and user on the basis of these assumptions. Modelling the system, and quality of service parameters within the system, is an issue which has already been explored in some preliminary case studies on the application of stochastic modelling such as [4]. A quality of service parameter may be directly related to the usability of the system (for example system response time). We may also have certain quantitative requirements (stochastic or otherwise) which the system must meet. Particular to this context is how we might model aspects of the user's behaviour, and the forms of property of the combined model of user and system which we can investigate.

2.1 Stochastic Variables in Interaction

Let us consider the kind of stochastic variables which are involved in human performance. Two common measures used in human performance are *performance with respect to time* and *performance with respect to errors*. In practically all cases there is some form of tradeoff between the two. It is important to remember the distinction between the overall measure of performance applied to the users operation of the system and stochastic variables identified in modelling the behaviour of both user and system.

Examples of stochastic variables at this micro- or behavioural level include response times to some stimulus or request from the system, frequencies with which certain operations are invoked and so on. Certain actions are more likely to be invoked than others, and hence selection from some set can also be expected to follow a distribution. Likewise, how often "correct" or "incorrect" operations are chosen can also be expected to follow a distribution. Another possibility concerns "efficiency"; how is the length of an interaction trajectory distributed beyond the canonical or optimal trajectory [16].

2.2 Use of Performance Data

A necessary facet of stochastic modelling is the use of performance data, and particularly human performance data. The distributions of variables modelling user performance can be based on experimentally derived data. While a large body of data exists, which it should be possible to use immediately, another possibility is to use the process to identify and motivate appropriate experiments to carry out in the context of the development of a certain type of application - for example where novel interaction devices are in use, for which precise performance data from users is not yet available.

Requirements on the performance of a system may also be derived from human factors knowledge. In the case of media streams these might include the performance necessary to preserve a sense of continuity. The performance could be with respect to the noise present in an audio stream, or the synchronisation of video and audio output. We can then relate the predicted results from our stochastic model to the human factors generated performance requirements. Finally we have the opportunity to test the validity of a model by experiment with a system once constructed.

Thus we have a number of roles that performance data (whether it concerns user or system) can play in the analysis of a system (illustrated in figure 1).

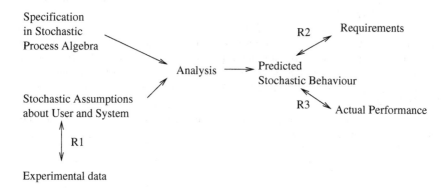

Fig. 1. Analysis process

- R1: Incorporating known data into specification, and also motivating experimentation where appropriate data is not available.
- R2: From assumptions about distribution of stochastic variables, ascertain whether system would meet performance requirements, which might for example be expressed as goodness of fit to a distribution.
- R3: Validation of a model with respect to actual performance of user and system.

From the point of view of the overall development process, introducing performance data at an early stage is an attractive proposition since it encourages consideration of problems which might otherwise only emerge during testing, since neither prototypes nor high-specification development platforms are constructed with such issues in mind. Hence, we see such analysis as allowing an interactive development and validation loop to occur much earlier in the process.

2.3   Distributions of Human Performance Variables

Assigning distributions to aspects of human performance is no simple task. While there is a wealth of experimental data concerning motor skills, response times, and so on, experimental conditions rarely map directly on to real-world conditions. Swain and Guttmann [33] recommend that the lognormal distribution be used for probabilistic risk assessment concerning human performance. This applies both for performance variables based on time (particularly response times) or quality (such as error rate). Although some performance measures conform to other distributions such as the normal, Weibull, Gamma and exponential distributions [24], in general the lognormal tends to provide a good fit for human performance since competent or skilled workers will tend to have performance around the low (better) end of the performance distribution. An example of a (not so smooth) lognormal distribution is presented in Fig. 3. A lognormal distribution is essentially a normal distribution skewed to the left, i.e. to the 'faster' end of the distribution.

It is useful to consider some of the factors which may alter the shape of the distribution. When tasks become more complicated, the lognormal distribution tends to become skewed and approaches the normal for very complex tasks. High stress situations will shift the entire performance distribution to the right, with a skew towards the left. Another possibility is that where there are two or more possible behaviours (eg. two possible diagnoses of a fault) then we may get two clusters of values for a measure such as performance time, and hence we may obtain a bimodal distribution.

2.4   Motor Skills

With a wide variety of interaction technologies likely to be based around physical (real-world) artefacts, we expect future computing systems to make greater and more varied use of the users' perceptual-motor skills.

There is a substantial literature dealing with these skills; perhaps the best known result in HCI is Fitts' Law, which relates mean movement time to movement amplitude and target size. The relationship has been validated for a wide range of tasks and contexts. Within the Fitts' Law literature, of particular interest are studies on variations due to the scale of a movement [26]. Where output is mediated by a computer, lag makes final corrective submovements more difficult and can dramatically increase movement times. Ware and Balakrishnan [35] give a formula for movement time including lag as a parameter. Other variations in sensory-motor performance concern manual control situations; for example the index of performance is lower for a velocity control than it is with a position control [23].

While Fitts' Law provides us with mean movement times, a problem for the stochastic modelling of motor performance is that Fitts' Law studies typically do not talk about the distribution or variability of movement times. While the distribution in space of "hits" around a target will be normal, the data we have available suggests the lognormal distribution gives a better fit for movement times.

2.5   Human Error

One area in which probabilistic issues have received a lot of attention is that of human error, especially for critical tasks, and hence we review here some basic concepts and measurement figures from this area. We would stress that the use of stochastic modeling techniques is not restricted to this domain, but a significant body of research and empirical data is available, which can be incorporated into approaches using eg. stochastic model checking and discrete event simulation.

Human error is defined [31] as: *"A failure on the part of the human to perform a prescribed act (or performance of a prohibited act) within specified limits of accuracy, sequence or time, which could result in damage to equipment and property, or disruption of scheduled operations"*. This applies to both continuous and discrete tasks. In terms of sequencing problems traditional approaches to HCI have considered the behaviour of the system under sequencing errors, eg. omission, commission and transposition [22] and the impact of such errors in some depth [10]. Probabilities associated with such errors have also received attention, but dealing with complex user-system interactions involving different sources and types of error is extremely difficult.

There are a number of different quantities which can be measured when analysing human error, each of which may have a given distribution. Two fundamental concepts - human error probability and reliability - can be defined for both discrete and continuous-time tasks. Human reliability can be expressed in terms of demand reliability for the first, and time reliability for the second.

2.6   Analysis

In the above we have considered briefly some different aspects of human computer interaction which are suitable candidates for representation as stochastic processes. Since the models are constructed in order to facilitate analysis, the level of abstraction and appropriate detail depends on the performance issues of relevance to the analyst. Because of the difficulty in obtaining performance data which precisely matches a given application and context, we would recommend a focus on *qualitative* differences and features in both modelling and simulation. In modelling these would include different modes of use, different modalities and so on. In simulation these would include brittleness and sensitivity with respect to model parameters, the appearance of bimodal distributions and so on.

3   Stochastic Modelling

Our discussion of stochastic modelling up to this point has not been based on a particular modelling language. Now that we come to consider the mechanics of construction and analysis of stochastic models, it is appropriate to look at the available technology. Recently, there has been much progress in the verification and analysis of system models that reflect qualitative and performance aspects in the same behavioural model. Much of this work has been developed in the context of process algebras, automata theory and Petri-Nets [9,20]. The aim is to have a single system model on which different kinds of analysis can be performed by simply adding further details about system behaviour such as real-time aspects and stochastic time features. In traditional approaches qualitative models and performance models have been developed separately giving results that are often difficult to relate to each other. For example, correctness results obtained for the qualitative models could not be assumed to hold for the performance models because they were too different in nature.

Most of the work we have examined on the specification of probabilistic systems has centred on stochastic time process algebras and stochastic automata. The models that are dealt with are essentially of two kinds: Markovian models, i.e. models where the next system state depends only on the current system state, and non-Markovian models. Markovian models have a sound and well-understood mathematical theory, but are restricted in the sense that they must satisfy the memoryless property. In the stochastic time extension of Markov models this leads to the restriction that only (negative) exponential distributions can be used to model stochastic time variables. Tools based on this approach are for example TIPP [19], ETMCC [18], PEPA [14] and PEPP [17]. The advantage of the Markovian approach is that numeric solutions can often be obtained.

In non-Markovian models the next state may depend on the history of how the state is reached, which is the case in the majority of systems. In the timed case this means that distributions other than the exponential can be used to model stochastic time. In general this also means that no numerical solutions can be obtained and that analysis relies on less precise and more laborious (discrete event) simulation techniques. In the context of user modelling Bayesian Networks (BN) [30] have been used quite extensively to model hypotheses or beliefs about human behaviour and to calculate dependencies between these. A drawback of these models is that they give a static view of a situation rather than modelling dynamic aspects of behaviour. Timed extensions of BN [32] have been proposed to deal also with dynamic aspects, but in that setting time is modelled as discrete slots and not as a stochastic variable.

Among specification oriented approaches, stochastic process algebras have a number of advantages over stochastic Petri-nets, particularly in terms of compositionality [20]. In this paper we use a variant of the stochastic time process algebra SPADES (Stochastic Process Algebra for Discrete Event Simulation) [9] that allows the use of arbitrary distributions and in particular normal distributions and lognormal distributions that have shown to fit many human performance variables [33]. A prototype tool for performance analysis of SPADES specifications provides discrete event simulation. In the remainder of this section we give an overview of SPADES and an example. Much of what follows, however, is equally applicable to other stochastic time modelling techniques that allow general distributions.

3.1   Stochastic Process Algebra Representation

The SPADES ($\spadesuit$) representation has many similarities to standard process algebraic specifications such as those in Communicating Sequential Processes (CSP) [21], but with the addition of clocks. Expressions may include the initialisation of clocks (according to a probability distribution associated with the clock), following which they begin to decrease uniformly towards zero, at which point they expire. Expressions may be guarded by more than one clock, in which case the expression is not enabled until all the clocks in the guard have expired. The guards may contain clocks that have been set previously in the same process or by other processes, i.e. clocks are global variables in SPADES. The language of SPADES is restricted to the minimum needed to model stochastic processes in order to study the concepts of such an algebra and its prototype simulation tool. There is ongoing work to extend the language to a richer version and a tool with a proper graphical interface[1]. While we do not intend to go into detail on the stochastic modeling techniques themselves, we give here a short overview of the $\spadesuit$ process algebra language and automata language, which we use to illustrate the use of such techniques in interactive systems.

The syntax of the language is as follows, for processes p, clocks C and process variables X.

$$process ::= \textbf{stop} \mid a;p \mid C \mapsto p \mid p+p \mid \{C\}p \mid p\|_L p \mid p[f] \mid X$$

We can summarise the meaning of these expressions as follows:

the **stop** process performs no action.
$a;p$ - the process performs action a then behaves like p.
$C \mapsto p$ - after the clocks in C reach zero, the process behaves like p.
$p+q$ the first of p or q to be enabled is selected.
$\{C\}p$ - initialise clocks in C, then behaves like p
$p\|_L q$ - p and q are performed in parallel, synchronised on actions listed in L
$p[f]$ - process p with actions renamed according to renaming function f.

As with early work on modelling interaction through process algebra [1], actions can correspond to user operations, system operations, or synchronised operations involving both user and system. The process algebraic representation is compositional, which facilitates the interpretation of the specifications. Process algebraic representations can also be obtained from a graphical representation of stochastic automata which are composed in parallel. Such a graphical representation can be very useful in facilitating discussions on the models in an

---

[1] For more information, see http://fmt.cs.utwente.nl/HaaST/

interdisciplinary setting, in particular when the automata involved are not too complex.

To illustrate the SPADES algebra and the graphical representation, consider a small example involving polling behaviour, where the user checks periodically for an output from the system. We specify this in the process algebra as the parallel composition of two expressions, representing system and user, synchronised on the action where the user 'notices' that the system has produced an output.

$$stochastic\_sys == system \|_{notice} user$$
$$system == \{st\} st \mapsto (notice; system)$$
$$user == \{ut\} ut \mapsto ((check; user) + (notice; user))$$

The system is ready for the user to notice that it has finished at any time after clock st has expired. The user specification states that the user can only participate in the *notice* action when ut has expired; if the system is not also ready to participate in the action, then ut is reset and the user continues waiting and checking.

Stochastic automata representation. The process algebraic specification can be represented graphically as a set of communicating automata as shown in Fig. 2. The semantics of those automata are such that on entry into a given location, the clocks listed for that location are initialised according to their distributions. Associated with outward transitions are both labels which can be synchronised with other automata, and the set of clocks which must have expired before the transition can be taken. Given a choice between different transitions, the first transition to become enabled is taken.

Where we specify a system involving more than one automaton, they are assumed to be composed in parallel, and synchronised as defined by the composition rule in the configuration box at the right in Fig. 2. Also the clocks and their distribution functions are defined in this box. Initial states of the automata are indicated by a double concentric circle. It is important to note however that stochastic process algebra allows hierarchical parallel composition, which is awkward to represent and reason about using graphical automata languages.

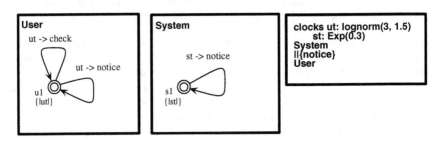

Fig. 2. Stochastic automata for polling

In this example, the left hand automaton represents the behaviour of the user, and the right hand automaton represents the behaviour of the system. As in the SPADES model above, the two automata are synchronised on the *notice* action, which is guarded by the *ut* clock in the user automaton, and the *st* clock in the system automaton. The user automaton may also execute the *check* action, in which case the *notice* action may not take place until the *ut* clock has expired once more.

3.2 Analysis

Stochastic automata and stochastic process algebra specifications are amenable to model checking techniques for reachability analysis if the memoryless condition is satisfied [2,17,20,19]. When *general* distributions are used in the stochastic specification model checking becomes much harder. Preliminary work on model checking of stochastic process algebras with generalised distributions may be found in [6]. When clocks are used in a global way discrete event simulation techniques may be used to obtain the characteristics of the stochastic behaviour of the model. This is the approach we follow in this paper. The use of stochastic modeling is concerned with random or non-deterministic variables with given distributions. All non-determinism in the specification, which is not represented by such variables, must be removed. In the SPADES approach, this is achieved by means of *adversaries*, which are external processes which decide the outcome of non-deterministic choices. In terms of system modeling the use of adversaries can be seen as representing the implementation architecture (including scheduling policy) of the system. Thus a complete SPADES specification consists of the combination of the stochastic model plus the adversary.

In the case of interactive systems, we can see a possible use of adversaries to model environmental factors, which affect the performance of the system, but which are not part of the system itself. The adversaries may be used to regulate the priority of actions with respect to other actions. For example, in the polling specification in Fig. 2 it is possible that both the action *notice* and the action *check* are enabled. In that case priority could be given to the action *notice*, modelling that if the system is ready and the user is consciously looking at the system to see whether it is ready, then the user notices that it is ready.

Fig. 3 shows the results of simulation for the polling example where non-determinism is solved by an adversary that chooses between enabled actions with equal probability. The chart shows the distribution of the time it takes the user to notice that the system is ready. The results are based on 10,000 simulation runs. We can observe that in most cases the user notices that the system is ready within 8 time units (seconds). But we also observe that this is not a hard upperbound. It may happen quite often that more time is needed. The chart shows a clear lognormal distribution.

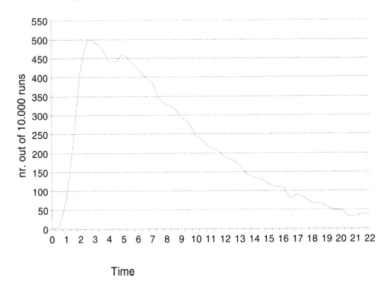

Fig. 3. Results of polling simulation

4   Application – Finger Tracking

The aim of the following example is to illustrate how stochastic models may be used to represent both user and system behaviour. The example we consider is based around MagicBoard, an augmented reality application of an interactive whiteboard with a gestural interface based on a computer vision finger tracker [3] and image projection.

What distinguishes this application from an electronic whiteboard is that the user draws directly on a board with real pens; what is drawn on the board may be scanned by the system by means of a camera. The user can use gestures to perform operations on what is drawn on the board, such as selection, copy, paste etc. The results of the operations are projected back on the board. Thus, from the interaction point of view, there is gestural input from user to system, and feedback both of the user's input (real ink on the board) and from the system ("digital ink" projected on the board) as illustrated in the data flow diagram in Fig. 4. The user's gestures are captured by the system using vision techniques that recognise and track the finger of the user after a calibration phase at the beginning of the session. A cursor is displayed (by projection) on the board when the system is tracking and gives the user feedback about whether it is able to accurately follow the position of the finger.

Jitter. A system which does not always keep up with the user (displaying "jitter") constrains the behaviour of the user. In the following we use the stochastic process algebra approach to model this aspect of the Magic Board interface and examine the relation between system performance and the

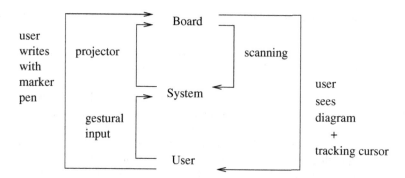

Fig. 4. Input/output flow in MagicBoard

constraints placed on the user's behaviour. The situation that we will examine is one in which the system never completely loses track of the finger, and does not fall behind so much that the user needs to stop moving their finger. So we consider the situation in which the user sometimes needs to slow down their movement to allow the system to keep up.

Modelling timing issues. In order to develop an abstract but realistic model we need to make a number of assumptions about the real-time behaviour and its variability of both system and user behaviour. Part of the necessary information can be obtained from the literature. In particular the delay generated by the tracker can most likely be assumed to be accurately modelled by an exponential distribution because each lag occurs independently from any previous lag (memoryless property).

The timing aspects related to the behaviour of the user are of a different nature. First of all we need to know how much time it takes for a user to move their finger from one point at the whiteboard to another point in an unconstrained way. Further we need to know how much the movement slows down when the user observes a lag in feedback. For small distances the first aspect has been addressed in many articles concerning Fitts' Law [27], however, to our best knowledge the variability has never been treated explicitly. This is somewhat surprising because human behaviour is intrinsically variable but not totally unpredictable, i.e. the variability often follows particular probability distributions. Taking variability explicitly into consideration may help us obtain a more informative assessment of the performance of human and system behaviour.

While it is not the focus of this work, in order to have reasonable data for our illustration, we require data on the human performance for moving a finger over large distances and in different directions. We have available experimental data collected at a real whiteboard at the University Joseph Fourier in Grenoble. To keep the amount of work needed to obtain the data within reasonable bounds, each trajectory was divided into three parts of equal length and the time to traverse each part during a single movement has been measured using digital video recordings of each session.

The results showed that the variability in time to move a finger from one place to another on the whiteboard follows an approximately lognormal distribution. Since the distances that are covered on the whiteboard are relatively long (33, 60 and 120 cm resp.) the initial part of the movement, covering the first two thirds of the distance, is performed very quickly; from the motor skills literature (see for example [31]) we take this as the initial, "open loop" or ballistic part of the movement. The last third of the movement is performed more slowly and we take this as corresponding to the visually guided part of the movement to precisely at the target on the whiteboard. In our model, following the (uninterruptible) "open loop" part of the movement, the user checks whether the cursor is managing to follow their finger. A delay may be introduced at this point before the final part of the movement.

Finally we must formulate our assumptions about the threshold of time for the user to take account of the lag (taken as cognitive delay) and the delay introduced by the user taken as a combination of cognitive and motor delay. For these delays we use the bounds data from the model human information processor [8]. Again we are not given the distribution, so we make the minimal assumption that it is somewhere between 25 and 170 ms, although we would expect it to follow a distribution with a more central tendency. A similar argument holds for the delay introduced by the user which we estimate to be between 55 ms and 270 ms, uniformly distributed.

Stochastic Model. We construct a stochastic process algebra model, presented as stochastic automata in Fig. 5, that describes the relevant parts of system and user behaviour. The starting point is when the system is ready to track the finger and the user is about to start moving. This is indicated by label *Start1* at the initial transitions of both processes modelling user and system. After the start the system is in tracking mode modelled by location *Track1* and tries to follow the user movement at least for the time it takes the user to reach the first two thirds of the movement. This time is modelled by the stochastic variable *H1* and has a lognormal distribution that has been derived from the experimental data. Given the values in the data, a good approximation of the distribution is a lognormal with parameters $\mu = 2.3$ and $\sigma = 1.4$, where μ is the mean of the distribution and σ the standard deviation of the distribution.

After the tracking phase, the system may show some delay updating the cursor position. This is modelled by stochastic time variable *Pt* that is set in location *Track2*. The second part of the tracking starts when the user starts the last part of the movement with or without delay. The time needed to finish this last part is modelled by the timed stochast *H2*. As soon as *H2* expires, the target is reached. This event is modelled by the synchronisation label *TargetReached*. Given the values in the experimental data, a good approximation for this part of the movement is a lognormal distribution with parameters $\mu = 4.4$ and $\sigma = 1.6$.

At the user side, after the first part of the movement has been performed we assume that the user observes whether the cursor is sufficiently close to the finger. If this is the case, the movement continues without observable delay due to inertia of the movement. If the cursor is behind, then the user slows down their movement. This is modelled by the stochastic variable *W*. Finally the user performs the last part of the movement to reach the target. Notice how in the model both the system and the user share the variables *H1* and *H2*. The user is the only process to set these variables as they reflect the user's movements. The system uses the variable to obtain the minimum time it would need to follow the user's finger on the whiteboard. This way the natural dependency of the system on the user's behaviour is modelled. The variable *Pt* models the dependency of the user on the system behaviour in a similar way.

The SPADES specification in Fig. 6 describes both the model and the kind of analysis that is performed. In this case we used the model to obtain a histogram of the distribution of the time it would take to reach the target for 10,000 different runs of the simulation of the model. We further specified that when more than one action is enabled, one is selected with equal probability by the adversary.

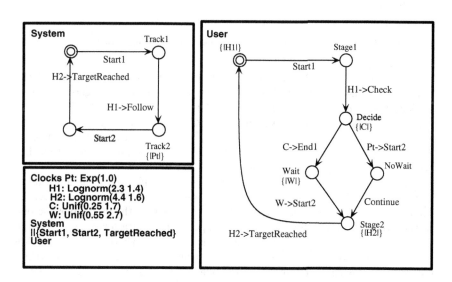

Fig. 5. Finger tracking model - jitter

4.1   Simulation

Presented in Fig. 7 are the simulation results for this model showing the distribution of time until the TargetReached action for a variety of values for system performance. As before, the horizontal axes represent the time and along the vertical axes the number of times that the target was reached is given, out of

```
actions Start1 Start2 Follow Check End1 TargetReached
        Continue
clocks  Pt:exp(0.1) H1:lognorm(2.3 1.4) H2:lognorm(4.4 1.6)
        C:unif(0.25 1.7) W: unif(0.55 2.7)
terms
system  = SSys ||Start1, Start2, TargetReached User
SSys    = Start1; Track1
Track1  = H1 -> Follow; Track2
Track2  = {|Pt|} Start2; Move2
Move2   = TargetReached; SSys
User    = {|H1|} Start1; Stage1
Stage1  = H1 -> Check; Decide
Decide  = {|C|}((C -> End1; Wait) + (Pt -> Start2; NoWait))
Wait    = {|W|} W -> Start2; Stage2
NoWait  = Continue; Stage2
Stage2  = {|H2|} H2 -> TargetReached; User
analysis
print action TargetReached as histogram(0.5, 45)
adversary EqProb
runs 10000
```

Fig. 6. SPADES model of finger tracking corresponding to that in Fig. 5

10,000 simulation runs. As we can see, there are two modes, corresponding to the waiting and non-waiting conditions. When system performance is good, the non-waiting mode dominates (curve on the left); as performance degrades it shifts to a bimodal distribution (curves in the middle), and as it degrades further the waiting mode dominates (curve on the right). In this case, the shift to a bimodal distribution occurs between $\lambda = 1.5$ and $\lambda = 0.5$ corresponding to a system that has an average delay of between ca. 60 and 200 ms.

This example illustrates the basic technique of identifying stochastic variables and available performance data, encoding these in a model, which can then be simulated, allowing us to investigate the effect of varying the model parameters. In the example above, we had available experimental data for some aspects of the model, but not all. Data on distributions is particularly difficult to find. We plan to collect more motor skills data, both using whiteboards, and also with a haptic input device which allows us to collect data at such a small granularity that we may plot effectively continuous movement trajectories.

5   Discussion

The tracking example above shows how stochastic models could help to visualise the possible impact of assumptions made about user and system behaviour on the overall interaction. The models allow us to study this impact using powerful software tools such as model checkers and simulators, helping us to investigate the consequences of design decisions in the early stages of interface development.

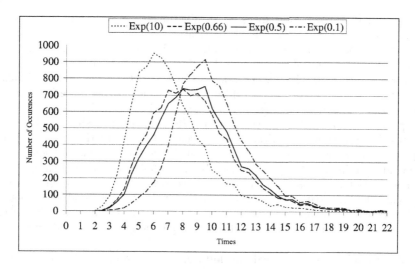

Fig. 7. Results for different tracking performance

However, the modelling of assumptions about user behaviour requires a very careful approach. There are a number of problems and limitations that have to be taken into account. The best choice of modelling approach may not always be evident, and tool support is still an active area of research. Currently, most available tools are prototypes rather than ready-to-use software packages. We briefly review some of these issues here.

Problems and limitations.   Although the analysis of human reliability according to procedures like those in Swain & Guttmann [33] is well established in areas such as process control, it is worth sounding a note of caution, particularly where critical applications are concerned. Wickens [36] cites a number of sources of difficulty in conducting this kind of analysis, including the following points:

1. *nonindependence of human errors.* An error which has been made at one point may either increase or decrease our likelihood of making an error in the period following. For example the increased stress may make us more likely to make another mistake, or conversely we might act with increased care and caution, making an error less likely.
2. *error monitoring.* People very often quickly correct capture errors or slips of action before they affect system performance.
3. *parallel components.* With multiple operators interacting at a social level (eg. in a cockpit or control room) operators do not work independently.
4. *integrating human and machine reliability.* Humans tend to adjust their behaviour according to the reliability of the system.

Most of these problems apply at a higher level of analysis than addressed in the current paper - where complex reasoning and decision making affect the overall level of performance. Our focus is on user behaviour and interactions with the system at a much lower level, particularly where there are soft real-time constraints on performance. Additionally, the first point requires both that we be interested in multiple errors, and that the user is immediately aware that an error has been made. The second point assumes that the errors are recoverable, and is again at a level of analysis which is not of immediate relevance for the real-time behaviours we are discussing in this paper. Also it is not just "mistakes" or slips by the user which may lead to poor performance or undesirable behaviour. Regarding the final point, it is certainly true that over time the user would adjust to the reliability of system. However, models for unadapted behaviour could provide a basis for a later comparison between this behaviour and the amount of adaptation that was required from the user to work with the system. Further, it would be interesting to see whether more complex models could be developed that reflect the adaptation process to a certain extend. In particular when questions can be answered under which conditions adaptation may be developed.

Analytical vs. behavioural modelling. Where simple error probabilities can be calculated for each source of error, their product can be taken to combine the probabilities. However, when the task to be performed is complex, involving different sources of error (with associated distributions), analysis by hand using statistical rules quickly becomes impractical. Conversely, processes described by distributions may be modelled directly, but by reducing a complex but well understood behaviour to a known distribution with given parameters, effort and complexity can be saved in constructing the model, and also the work facing the tools in automated analysis.

Tool support. Approaches which overcome the compositionality problem by limiting consideration to exponential distributions have better tool support at the moment, but seem limited in the longer term. Also, the knowledge of statistical theory required in approximating distributions seems to be a serious barrier to widespread use. The SPADES process algebra also needs some minimal language features added to allow realistic examples to be specified more easily. In particular, inclusion of a probabilistic choice operator would enhance the expressiveness of the language and allow the modelling of both stochastic time and probabilities related to human error.

6   Connections

The need for analysis of *user performance* is raised by a number of papers (eg. [34]). Of the papers in the session which examine temporal properties of interaction, the temporal patterns approach of [13] might be extended to consider stochastic time. The ICO formalism (for references see [28], this volume), is also of relevance as it is used as a basis for performance evaluation in [29]. With a stochastic formalism including probabilistic choice, such analysis can be conducted within the same framework, with the benefit of the ability to deal with stochastic time.

7   Conclusions

Stochastic modelling, simulation and analysis using stochastic automata is still a relatively new field. As such, the expressiveness of the specification languages based on the technology, the theories concerning analysis of such specifications, and the incorporation of these into automated support are still at an early stage of development. Due to the limitations of the language constructs currently available in SPADES we have been considering only stochastic time related aspects of interaction. An extension of the language with a probabilistic choice operator would allow the specification of probabilities related to human and system error.

Such techniques have an exciting potential for modelling performance in interactive systems, taking into account the abilities and limitations of both user and system. Stochastic models allow us to generate a richer set of answers to design questions, which enables more meaningful comparison of the results of an analysis to human factors data and other empirical evidence. We would like to explore further the different ways in which the approach can be used, and also look at sources of performance data and how they can be integrated.

A final area that needs careful consideration is the form of the specification language that can be used to describe the models. The design of interfaces is a multidisciplinary activity, where models need to be understood and discussed by designers with different expertise and backgrounds. A well-defined graphical modelling language could be a valuable tool for this purpose, especially when such a language is close to other languages used for the specification of software. In this context we have investigated a stochastic extension of UML statecharts [15] which can be mapped to a stochastic process algebra representation [11].

Acknowledgements. Many thanks are due to Leon Watts of UMIST for discussions concerning this work and access to his experimental data. This work was supported by the TACIT network under the European Union TMR programme, contract ERB FMRX CT97 0133.

References

1. H. Alexander. Structuring dialogues using CSP. In M. D. Harrison and H. W. Thimbleby, editors, *Formal methods in Human Computer Interaction*, pages 273–295. Cambridge University Press, 1990.
2. R. Alur, C. Courcoubetis, and D.L. Dill. Model-checking for probabilistic real-time systems. In *Automata, Languages and Programming: Proceedings of the 18th ICALP*, volume 510 of *Lecture Notes in Computer Science*, pages 115–136. Springer-Verlag, 1991.

3. François Bérard. *Vision par ordinateur pour l'interaction fortement couplée*. PhD thesis, L'Université Joseph Fourier Grenoble I, 1999.
4. H. Bowman, J. W. Bryans, and J. Derrick. Analysis of a multimedia stream using stochastic process algebra. In C. Priami, editor, *Proceedings of 6th International Workshop on Process Algebras and Performance Modelling*, Nice, France, pages 51–69, September 1998.
5. H. Bowman, G. P. Faconti, and M. Massink. Specification and verification of media constraints using UPPAAL. In P. Markopoulos and P. Johnson, editors, *Proceedings of the 5th Eurographics Workshop on Design, Specification, and Verification of Interactive Systems*, pages 261–277. Springer Wien, 1998.
6. J. Bryans, H. Bowman, and J. Derrick. A model checking algorithm for stochastic systems. Technical Report 4-00, University of Kent at Canterbury, January 2000.
7. P. Cairns, M. Jones, and H. Thimbleby. Reusable usability analysis with markov models. *ACM Transactions on Human-Computer Interaction*, (in press), 2001.
8. S. Card, T. Moran, and A. Newell. *The psychology of human computer interaction*. Lawrence Erlbaum Associates, 1983.
9. P. R. D'Argenio, J-P. Katoen, and E. Brinksma. A stochastic automaton model and its algebraic approach. In *Proceedings of 5th International Workshop on Process Algebra and Performance Modelling*, pages 1–17, 1997. CTIT Technical Report 97-09.
10. A.M. Dearden and M.D. Harrison. Using executable interactor specifications to explore the impact of operator interaction error. In P. Daniel, editor, *SAFECOMP 97: Proceedings of the 16th International Conference Computer Safety, Reliability and Security*, pages 138–147. Springer, 1997.
11. G. Doherty and M. Massink. Stochastic modelling of interactive systems with UML. TUPIS Workshop, UML 2000.
12. G. Doherty, M. Massink, and G. Faconti. Using hybrid automata to support human factors analysis in a critical system. *Formal Methods in System Design*, 19(2), September 2001.
13. M. Du and D. England. Temporal patterns for complex interaction design. In Johnson [25].
14. S. Gilmore and J. Hillston. The PEPA workbench: A tool to support a process algebra-based approach to performance modelling. In *Proceedings of the Seventh International Conference on Modelling Techniques and Tools for Computer Performance Evaluation*, volume 794 of *Lecture Notes in Computer Science*, pages 353–368. Springer-Verlag, 1994.
15. S. Gnesi, D. Latella, and M. Massink. A stochastic extension of a behavioural subset of UML statechart diagrams. In L. Palagi and R. Bilof, editors, *Fifth IEEE International High-Assurance Systems Engineering Symposium*, pages 55–64. IEEE Computer Society Press, 2000.
16. M.D. Harrison, A.E. Blandford, and P.J. Barnard. The requirements engineering of user freedom. In F. Paternó, editor, *Proceedings of Eurographics Workshop on Design Specification and Verification of Interactive Systems, Italy*, pages 181–194. Springer-Verlag, 1995.
17. F. Hartleb. Stochastic graph models for performance evaluation of parallel programs and the evaluation tool PEPP. In *Proceedings of the QMIPS Workshop on Formalisms, Principles and State-of-the-art, Erlangen/Pommersfelden, Germany*, number 14 in Arbeitsbericht Band 26, pages 207–224, March 1993.
18. H. Hermanns, J.P. Katoen, J. Meyer-Kayser, and M. Siegle. Tools and algorithms for the construction and analysis of systems. In *Proceedings of TACAS 2000*, volume 1785 of *LNCS*, pages 347–362. Springer-Verlag, 2000.

19. H. Hermanns, V. Mertsiotakis, and M. Siegle. TIPPtool: Compositional specification and analysis of markovian performance models. In *Proceedings of Compter Aided Verification (CAV) 99*, volume 1633 of *Lecture Notes in Computer Science*, pages 487–490. Springer-Verlag, 1999.

20. J. Hillston. *A Compositional Approach to Performance Modelling*. Distinguished Dissertations in Computer Science. Cambridge University Press, 1996.

21. C.A.R. Hoare. *Communicating Sequential Processes*. Prentice-Hall International, 1985.

22. E. Hollnagel. The phenotype of erroneous actions. *International Journal of Man-Machine Studies*, 39(1):1–32, July 1993.

23. R. Jagacinski, R.D. Repperger, M. Moran, S. Ward, and B. Glass. Fitts' law and the microstructure of rapid discrete movements. *Journal of Experimental Psychology: Human Perception and Performance*, 6(2):309–320, 1980.

24. R. Jain. *The art of computer systems performance analysis : techniques for experimental design, measurement, simulation, and modeling*. Wiley, New York, 1991.

25. C. Johnson, editor. *Proceedings of Design Specification and Verification of Interactive Systems, Glasgow*. Springer-Verlag, 2001.

26. G. Langolf, D. Chaffin, and J. Foulke. An investigation of Fitts' law. *Journal of Motor Behaviour*, 8:113–128, 1976.

27. I. Scott MacKenzie. Fitts' law as a research and design tool in human-computer interaction. *Human Computer Interaction*, 7:91–139, 1992.

28. D. Navarre, P. Palanque, F. Paterno, C. Santoro, and R. Bastide. Tool suite for integrating task and system models through scenarios. In Johnson [25].

29. P. Palanque and R. Bastide. Synergistic modelling of tasks, users and systems using formal specification techniques. *Interacting with Computers*, 9:129–153, 1997.

30. J. Pearl. *Probabilistic Reasoning in Intelligent Systems: Networks of Plausible Inference*. San Mateo, CA: Morgan Kaufmann, 1988.

31. G. Salvendy, editor. *Handbook of Human Factors and Ergonomics*. Wiley-Interscience, 2nd edition, 1997.

32. R. Schäfer and Thomas Weyrath. Assessing temporally variable user properties with dynamic bayesian networks. In A. Jameson, C. Paris, and C. Tasso, editors, *User Modelling: Proceedings of the Sixth Internation Conference*. Springer Wien New York, 1997.

33. A.D. Swain and H.E. Guttmann. Handbook of human reliability analysis with emphasis on nuclear power plant applications - final report. Technical Report NRC FIN A 1188 NUREG/CR-1278 SAND80-0200, Prepared for Division of Facility Operations; Office of Nuclear Regulatory Research; US Nuclear Regulatory Commission; Washington, D.C. 20555, August 1983.

34. M.Q.V. Turnell, A. Scaico, M.R.F. de Sousa, and A. Perkusich. Industrial user interface evaluation based on coloured petri nets modelling and analysis. In Johnson [25].

35. C. Ware and R. Balakrishnan. Reaching for objects in VR displays: Lag and frame rate. *ACM Transactions on Human Computer Interaction*, 1(4):331–356, December 1994.

36. C.D. Wickens. *Engineering Psychology and Human Performance*. Charles E. Merrill Publishing Company, 1984.

Towards Uniformed Task Models in a Model-Based Approach

Quentin Limbourg[1], Costin Pribeanu[1,2], and Jean Vanderdonckt[1]

[1] Université catholique de Louvain, Institut d'Administration et de Gestion
Place des Doyens, 1 - B-1348 Louvain-la-Neuve, Belgium
{limbourg, vanderdonckt}@qant.ucl.ac.be
[2] National Institute for Research and Development in Informatics
Bd Averescu 8-10 - R-71316 Bucharest, Romania
pribeanu@acm.org

Abstract. Multiple versions and expressions of task models used in user interface design, specification, and verification of interactive systems have led to an ontological problem of identifying and understanding concepts which are similar or different across models. This variety raises a particular problem in model-based approaches for designing user interfaces as different task models, possibly with different vocabularies, different formalisms, different concepts are exploited: no software tool is able today to accommodate any task models as input for a user-centred design process. DOLPHIN is a software architecture that attempts to solve this problem by introducing uniform task models. A series of representative task models was first selected. The meta-models of these individual task models were then designed and merged into a uniformed task meta-model. Semantic mapping rules between individual task meta-models and the uniformed task meta-model allow DOLPHIN to read and understand any potential task model towards its exploitation in a model-based approach.

1 Introduction

Human-Centred Design (HCD) has yielded to many forms of design practices where information about the context of use is considered. Among these, task analysis is widely recognised as one fundamental way not only to ensure some HCD, but also to improve the understanding of how a user may interact with a user interface (UI) for accomplishing a given interactive task. For this purpose, many task analysis methods have been introduced from disciplines having different backgrounds, different concerns, and different focuses on task [14,17].

Task analysis typically results in a task model, which is a description of any interactive task to be accomplished by the user of an application through the application's UI. Individual elements in the task model represent specific actions that the user may undertake. Information regarding subtask ordering as well as conditions on task execution is also included in this model. A task model may be issued from [17]:

C. Johnson (Ed.): DSV-IS 2001, LNCS 2220, pp. 164–182, 2001.
© Springer-Verlag Berlin Heidelberg 2001

- *Cognitive psychology*, where it is aimed at improving the understanding of how users may interact with a given UI for carrying out a particular interactive task from a cognitive viewpoint. This model is considered useful for identifying cognitive processes and structures which are manipulated by a user when carrying out a task, for understanding how a user may dynamically change these processes and structures as the task is proceeding, and for predicting cognitive work load.
- *Task allocation*, where it is intended to plan and distribute working tasks in time and space among workers in a particular organisation.
- *Software engineering*, where it captures relevant task information in an operational form which is machine processable.
- *Ethnography*, where it focuses on how human users could behave with a particular UI in a given context of use, also possibly interacting with other users.

Many different task models, task analysis methods, and supporting tools have been introduced as reported in the CHI'98 workshop [3] on task modelling approaches. This situation leads to a series of important shortcomings, among them are:

- Lack of understanding the basic concepts: in each individual task model the rationale behind their method, their entities, their relationships, their vocabularies, the intellectual operations involved for task modelling.
- Heterogeneousness of these concepts as they were initiated by various methods issued from various disciplines.
- Difficulty to match concepts across two individual task models or more: it is even likely that sometimes no matching across these concepts can be established.
- Lack of software interoperability: since task modelling tools do not share a common format, they are only restricted to those task models that are expressed according to their accepted formats. For instance, a task model drawn in a graphical editor cannot be reused in a simulation tool.
- Reduced communication among task analysts: due to the lack of software interoperability, a task analyst may experience some trouble in communicating the results of a personal task analysis to another analyst or stakeholder of the UI development team. In addition, any transition between persons may generate inconsistencies, errors, misunderstandings, or inappropriate modelling.
- Duplication of research and development efforts: where teams conduct research and development on their own task models, it is likely that each research and development effort needs to be reproduced for their specific task models, instead of benefiting from each other. This shortcoming is particularly important for software development efforts which are resource-consuming.

To address the above shortcomings, three major goals were set:

1. To provide an improved conceptual and methodological understanding of each individual task model and their related concepts.

2. To establish semantic mappings between different individual task models so as to create a transversal understanding of their underlying concepts independently of their peculiarities. This goal involves many activities such as vocabulary translation, expressiveness analysis, identification of degree of details, identification of concepts, emergence of transversal concepts, and task structuring identification.

3. To rely on these semantic mappings to develop a User Interface Design Assistant (UIDA) which accommodates any type of individual task model as input. This UIDA should help designers and developers to derive presentation and dialog from any starting task model, whatever its model type. The ultimate goal of this UIDA is to capitalise design knowledge valid for each task model into a single tool and to avoid reproducing identical development effort for each individual task model.

The remainder of this paper is structured as follows: Section 2 summarises open questions regarding task modelling and reports on some previous work done regarding the question of understanding task models. Section 3 defines the differences between an individual task model and a uniformed task model and presents the hypotheses, the method followed towards uniforming task models. Section 4 applies this method to selected individual task models to come up with their corresponding meta-model. Section 5 sums up the results provided by the meta-models of individual task models into a uniformed task meta-model, along with semantic mappings between corresponding concepts. Section 6 outlines how the final meta-model and the semantic mappings are exploited in DOLPHIN, a UIDA that accommodates any individual task model as input.

2   Related Work in Task Modelling

In general, a task is understood as an activity performed by people to accomplish a certain goal. A task could be further decomposed resulting in smaller tasks corresponding to lower level goals. Task decomposition is usually represented as a tree. Inner tasks are said to be *composite* (or abstract, complex) while the leaves are *elementary tasks*, which in turn are decomposed in actions performed upon objects.

As pointed out by activity theory [13], tasks are goal driven, being performed consciously while actions depend on operational conditions of the task and become automatic by practice. However, this distinction is rarely used in the practice of task analysis for UI. In this respect, most task models do not make a clear distinction between task and actions but rather they decompose tasks up to the level that is relevant for the analysis. Goal hierarchies could be consequently seen as complementary to task hierarchies (that include both tasks and actions), each of them holding its role.

Recent approaches put an emphasis on the context of use, sometimes termed as the task world [23]. In this respect, user's characteristics, people and organisations, objects they manipulate and actions they undertake should be considered to develop a usable UI. As a consequence, most task models have a heterogeneous conceptual framework aiming to represent tasks, roles, task decomposition, data flows, goals, actions, objects, and events. The importance given to different models (e.g., environment, domain, and user) varies according to the application type.

Task analysis describes, represents, and analyses computer-supported work, i.e. tasks that are delegated (in part or in full) to the computer. Task analysis for UI should not be considered in isolation but as an activity in a UI development life cycle. When using task models as prerequisites for designing UI, compatibility between the domain-task world and design knowledge is needed. To this respect the following elements are important for a task model:

- Goal hierarchy, because it reflects the goal structure, not necessarily equal or similar to a task structure.
- Task decomposition, because it shows the task structure and the constraints in grouping related tasks in the interface.
- Temporal relationship between tasks, because they show constraints for placing interaction objects.

Other models of the context of use provide critical elements for modelling a task:

- Data flow diagram, as a complementary view that shows the functional requirements of the application in terms of information exchange.
- Command and interaction objects available, because it shows the possible ways to perform an elementary task.

Many of these aspects are considered in an ontology of task models designed by van Welie et al. [23]. Although this ontology was mainly intended to assess concepts in their Groupware Task Analysis (GTA) method [22], this pioneering work has the merit of identifying fundamental concepts of a task model. However, the method used for building this ontology is only partially described in the paper and does not provide any analysis of cross-task models concepts and matching. Dittmar [7] introduced a more general expression of task models where relationships between model elements are expressed as general equations between any level of the model. This generalisation extends the traditional way of characterising a task model as a hierarchy of concepts. But it was neither intended to analyse cross-task models concepts.

3   A Method for Uniforming Task Models

In this section, we present the steps of the method followed to build a uniformed task model from a number of existing individual task models. An individual task model is referred to as any model produced by a specific task analysis method. Uniforming an individual task model is the process of expressing an individual task model into a uniformed model in such a way that its concepts keep always the same form, manner, or degree, and present an unvaried appearance of concepts.

Our method for uniforming task models consists of four major steps: selection of individual task models, identification of the concepts within each model, representation of those concepts into a meta-model, and consolidation of these meta-models into one single meta-model, called *uniformed task meta-model*. Although these steps are presented sequentially, some feedback is still possible at some points.

Considering all existing task models is probably beyond our capabilities. Thus, a selection among task models was operated from the list of task models reported in the CHI'98 workshop on task models, which is supposed to be rather extensive and correct [3]. The following criteria were used:

- The task models should be integrated in a development methodology as a core (e.g., CTTE [17]) or side (e.g., HTA [1]) component and tool supported.
- The task models should be widespread and accepted within the Human-Computer Interaction (HCI) community (e.g., TKS [10]).
- The selected models should be supported by theoretical studies to assess their soundness and experimental studies for effective case studies (e.g., MUSE [15]).
- The selected set should cover the wide scope of disciplines that originated different models (e.g., as CPM-GOMS and NL-GOMS belong to the same family, only one representative member is kept [9]).
- The selected set should also reflect the geographical diversity of origin of different models.

After selecting individual task models, the foundation references of each chosen task model were analysed. Each model was then decomposed into constituting concepts using an entity-relationship method of analysis. The terminology used in original references to refer to concepts was preserved. A definition of each concept is then given. For the sake of concision, only relevant definitions of concepts were retained.

These concepts are then represented into an individual task meta-model, which is made up of entities and relationships expressed according to an entity-relationship-attribute methodology. To support this representation, facilities offered by the DB-MAIN CASE tool [8] have been exploited, as well as their organising rules to ensure a common representation scheme. The ERA formalism was chosen for a main reason: this semi-formal method is recognised for its expressiveness and widely used in both the computer science and the software engineering fields. Furthermore, it is understandable for a non-computer scientist. However, the ERA formalism does not allow the analyst to represent the concepts semantics, as it is more focusing on the information structure than its underlying semantics. For this purpose, a more formal approach would be helpful, for instance defining each concept with an abstract data type. But the analysis of the cost/benefit ratio of such an approach discouraged us to adopt it. Indeed, such a formal approach would force a formal definition of each concept for each individual task model, thus leading to a huge formalisation effort. In addition, this solving becomes even more compound when the originating documents did not formally define their concepts themselves.

Finally, a uniformed task meta-model is obtained from the individual task meta-models. To build this final meta-model, different intellectual operations were performed. Firstly, a syntactical uniforming was conducted to provide a single way of referring to different concepts where possible. This step implies that concepts having the same definition but different names were uniformed under a same label. For concepts having different definitions, even if they refer to a similar fundamental concept, a semantic uniforming was needed. This step implies the identification of semantic mappings between concepts having different aims and scopes. To maximise the semantic scope of the uniformed task meta-model, the union of the concepts present in each particular task meta-models was preferred rather than the intersection. Indeed, choosing the intersection would produce an "emergent kernel of concepts" common to all methods, but this set may be rather limited. Conversely, the union while keeping commonalities preserves specific contributions of individual models.

To avoid the problem of an all embracing model, some concepts (i.e., entities, relationships, or attributes) were withdrawn from this union for several reasons: the concept is semantically redundant with an already existing concept, the concept is not practically used by the methodology in which the particular task model is defined, the concept does not basically belong to the task model but rather to other models like user, organisation, domain, or presentation model [17]. This reason is motivated by the Separation of concern principle which assumes that only concepts relevant to a similar domain of discourse should be kept in a particular model, thus avoiding mixing different concepts into a single model.

4   Analysing Task Models

From task models reported in the CHI'98 workshop [3], criteria defined in Section 3 resulted in the selection of the following alphabetical list of individual task models: CTT [17], Diane+ [20], ETAG [21], GOMS [2,4,9], GTA [22], HTA [1], MAD [19], MUSE [15], TAKD [6], and TKS [11,12,10]. Various objectives underlie the elaboration of each individual task model, thus featuring a certain type of representation:

- To inform design about potential problems of usability like in HTA.
- To evaluate human performance like in GOMS.
- To aid design by providing a more detailed task model describing task hierarchy, object used and knowledge structures like in TKS, GTA or CTT.
- To generate a UI prototype like in Adept supporting TKS approach

Due to space constraints, the analysis of only a subset of these selected models is reproduced here. Details can be found in [16].

4.1   The GOMS Model

The Goals, Operators, Methods and Selection rules (GOMS) model was developed as a model for predicting human performance while interacting with a system. The original GOMS model, referred to as CMN-GOMS, is the ancestor [4] of a family of GOMS models that were refinements of the original model [2]. Among them are GOMS Language (GOMSL) [10] and Critical Path Method GOMS (CPM-GOMS) [9]. The first is using a mental programming language and is based on a parallel cognitive architecture, the latter is using a PERT chart to identify the critical path for computing the execution time.

GOMS is, at first, a cognitive model of the user that is used in task design. Therefore, task is not a central concept but rather the method that is describing how tasks are actually carried on. A meta-model describing GOMS concepts is given in Fig. 1.

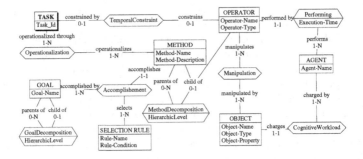

Fig. 1. GOMS task meta-model

A method is a sequence of operators that describes task performance. Tasks are triggered by goals and could be further decomposed into sub-tasks that correspond to intermediary goals. When several methods exist for the same goal, a selection rule, referring to the context of use, is used to choose the appropriate one.

Methods describe how goals are actually accomplished. Higher level methods are describing task performance in terms of lower level methods, operators and selection rules. The lowest level of a GOMS decomposition is the unit task defined as a task the user really wants to perform [9]. Higher level methods are using task flow operators that are acting as constructors that control task execution.

GOMS makes a clear distinction between tasks and actions. Firstly, task decomposition stops at unit tasks. Secondly, actions, termed as operators in GOMS, are specified by the methods associated to unit tasks. Action modelling is varying along different GOMS models and also methods specification.

Operators are cognitive and physical actions the user has to perform in order to accomplish the task goal. Since each operator has an associated execution time (determined on experimental basis), a GOMS model can serve for predicting the time needed to perform a task.

In GOMSL [9], the method is split into steps. Each step is assumed to be a production rule for the cognitive architecture of the user and is assigned 0.05 sec in the execution time estimation. This takes into account the decision time spent for loading a method or returning to the calling one and applies for such control statements as "Method for goal", "Accomplish goal" or "Return with goal accomplished" in the representation above. Therefore, the execution time is calculated as the sum of the statement time and the operator time.

Actions undertaken by the user are specified using external and mental operators. Some special mental operators are flow control operators which are used to constrain the execution flow. Although the granularity is varying according to the purpose of analysis, GOMS is mainly useful when decomposition is done at operational level, i.e. under the unit task level. GOMS cognitive analysis starts after task analysis and it is constrained by the technological options. It is aimed at improving task design with respect to human performance by enabling quantitative predictions like estimation of execution time, learning time, and memory workload.

4.2   The GTA Model

GroupWare Task Analysis (GTA) [22] was developed as a means to model the complexity of tasks in a co-operative environment. GTA takes its roots both from ethnography, as applied for the design of co-operative systems and from activity theory adopting a clear distinction between tasks and actions. An ontology describing the concepts and relations between them was developed in [23]. Fig. 2 graphically depicts five GTA fundamental concepts: task, role, object, agent, and event.

In GTA complex tasks are decomposed into unit tasks [4] and basic tasks [21]. However there is no indication about how this relates to UI design. More recent developments of GTA also include additional techniques like ETAG [21] for decomposition of basic tasks. An attractive feature of GTA relies in its capability of representing co-operative tasks (groupware) by integrating the role concept in the task world, thus enabling representations of task sets for which a role is responsible of and also of organisational aspects like how a role is assigned to different agents.

Although the GTA ontology improves the conceptualisation of the task world the representation it is not appropriately expressed for our purpose. For example, goals and actions are represented as task attributes and not as concepts. This is somewhat inconsistent with the fact that GTA allows a goal to be reached in many ways.

Also, since the same action could be used in many tasks, actions could be better represented as a concept. This way, object manipulation is represented as a relationship between actions and objects rather than between tasks and

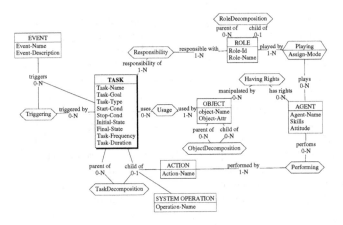

Fig. 2. GTA task meta-model

objects. Since actions are depending on operational conditions when using different objects different actions might be needed. Another remark concerning the GTA ontology is that constructors are not represented. However, the Euterpe tool used for a GTA task specification allows for specification of constructors in a similar way to MAD (see Section 4.4).

4.3   Concur Task Trees (CTT)

In Concurrent TaskTrees (CTT) [17], CTT constructors, termed operators, are used to link sibling tasks, on the same level of decomposition. This is different from previ-ously described notations where operators describe parent-children relationship thus ranging over all sub-tasks in a task.

CTT uses a tool for editing the task model used to specify tasks, roles, and objects as well as the task hierarchy with temporal operators (Fig. 3). Another feature of CTT is its graphical facility providing means to describe different task types like abstract, co-operative, user, interactive, and application.

CTT provides us with means to describe co-operative tasks: a task model will be composed of different task trees: one for the co-operative part and one for each role that is involved in the task. Tasks are further decomposed up to the level of basic tasks defined as tasks that could not be further decomposed. Actions and objects are specified for each basic task. Application objects are mapped onto perceivable objects in order to be presented to the user.

Another interesting feature of CTT is the specification of both input and output actions that are associated to an object. Object specification is mainly intended for the specification of UI interaction objects (interactors).

CTT modelling tool also provides useful support for task modelling like a model checker and a function to extract enabled task sets. Enabled task sets are consisting of tasks that are enabled in the same time and are produced on

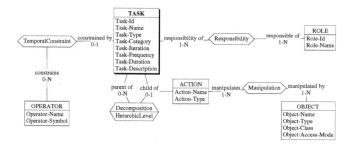

Fig. 3. CTT task meta-model

the basis of temporal dependencies. This feature is intended as a support for analysis of relationship between the task model and the presentation design.

4.4 The MAD Model

Méthode Analytique de Description de tâches (MAD) [19] aims to provide object-oriented task specifications to support design phases. Main concepts of MAD are: task, action, and structure (Fig. 4).

The structure concept is implicitly represented in the task decomposition relationship and the relationship with the constructor entity. As in GTA, the concept of task is divided into two broad categories: elementary tasks and composite tasks.

Elementary tasks are tasks that cannot be further decomposed. An elementary task contains direct reference to one or several action(s) performed on objects of the domain. The concept of action refers to procedures or methods performed by the system. Composite tasks are tasks that can be further decomposed. A composite task makes direct reference to a single constructor aimed at describing its relationships with its child tasks.

Either composite or elementary, the concept of task, in MAD, is characterised by several attributes. The initial state specifies a state of the world prior to the execution of the task. The final state specifies a state of the world after the task execution. The goal is the objects modifications which the agent want to reach. The goal is explicitly defined here as a subset of the final state.

Though the goal is attached to the task as an attribute, a same goal could be reached by accomplishing different tasks. This would have motivated to make the goal concept into an entity type. The precondition is a set of assertions constraining the initial state. Those assertions must be satisfied prior to the execution of the task. Preconditions are classified between sufficient conditions and necessary and sufficient conditions. The post-condition is a set of assertion constraining the final state. The post-condition must be satisfied after the execution of the task.

The last central concept of MAD is the structure: it includes the set of decomposition relationships within the task tree and the temporal relationship spec-

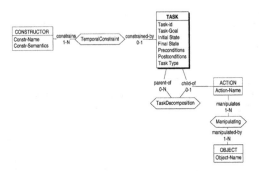

Fig. 4. MAD task meta-model

ification mechanism termed constructor. Constructors operate on all children of a same task. Constructors are classified into two categories: synchronisation operators (SEQ for sequential tasks, PAR for parallel tasks, SIM for simultaneous tasks) and ordering operators (ALT for alternative task, LOOP for iterative tasks, OP for optional task).

4.5   The TKS Model

Task Knowledge Structure (TKS) method [11,12,10] manipulates a TKS, which is a conceptual representation of the knowledge a person has stored in her memory about a particular task (Fig. 5).

A TKS is associated with each task that an agent (i.e. a person, a user) performs. Tasks which an agent is in charge of are determined by the role this person is pre-sumed to assume. A role is defined as the particular set of tasks an individual is responsible for performing as part of her duty in a particular social context. An agent can take on several roles. A role can be taken on by several persons.

Even if tasks or TKSs may seem similar across different roles (e.g., typing a letter for a secretary and a manager), they will be considered as different. The "similarity" relationship is aimed to represent this situation.

TKS holds information about the goal. A goal is the state of affairs a particular task can produce. A particular goal is accomplished by a particular task. A goal is decomposed into a goal substructure, which contains all intermediate sub-goals to achieve it.

Goal and task hierarchies have been represented in Fig. 5 as two overlapping substructures, the first decomposing the goal into sub-goals, the latter decomposing tasks into subtasks. Each sub-goal in the goal structure has a corresponding subtask in the task structure and vice versa. The structure is composed either by task decomposition mechanisms and temporal relationship mechanisms termed constructors. Constructors operate on tasks and by association on goals.

A same goal associated can be reached by different sub-goals sequencing. This leads to the concepts of plan. A plan is a particular setting of a set of sub-goals

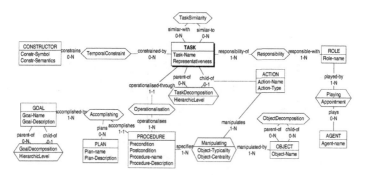

Fig. 5. TKS task meta-model

and procedure to achieve a particular goal. As in other models, actions and objects are found at the lowest level of the task analysis. They are the constituents of procedures which operationalise subtasks. One or several procedures can be linked to a same subtask. TKS proposes a production rule system to choose the appropriate procedures depending on the context of use.

Actions are directly related to task tree as they form its leaf level. Actions and objects hold properties of interest. They can be central to the execution of a task, they have typical instances: centrality and typicality of an object or action is always expressed with respect to a task or a procedure that operationalises it. Note that objects are structured into a decomposition hierarchy.

4.6   The DIANE+ Model

DIANE+ [20] formally models a task with three concepts (Fig. 6): operation, sequencing and decomposition.

The operations describe the characteristics specific to a particular task, apart from potential standard actions common to any task such as quit, cancel. This assumes that previously defined standard actions are really common to any task in a particular domain of discourse. Cases where they are not applicable are described.

The described operations, optional or mandatory, are the linked together with operation decomposition and a precedence mechanism. In this decomposition, the triggering condition of an operation is expressed on its sub-operations. Pre-condition and post-condition are expressed as either a logical formula on events or on data. Each operation is the property of an owner, which is similar to the agent concept. DIANE+ represents constraints on operation ordering through algorithmic structures resulting from the combination of the basic concepts. For example, an ordered sequence is represented by a simple precedence, an unordered sequence is represented by the required operations and by a lack of precedence. The loop is implicitly represented: an unconstrained user-triggered DIANE+ operation means that the user may execute it as often as she wants.

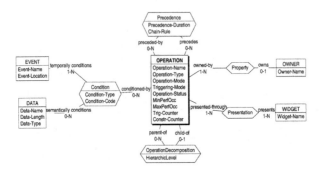

Fig. 6. DIANE+ task meta-model

The required choice is represented by an operation with constraint on its sub-operations whereas the free choice is represented by an operation without constraint on its sub-operations. The parallelism is represented through the triggers and a lack of constraint. The loops makes possible to perform the same operation many times in parallel, and several loops can be performed in parallel. The number of constrained sub-operations to perform is specified for each operation.

5 A Uniformed Task Model

Individual task models analysed in the previous section show a variety of concepts and relationships between these concepts. Differences between concepts are both syntactic and semantic. For example, constructors in GTA, MAD or TKS express temporal relationship between a task and its subtasks (although the set of constructors is not identical in all models) while operators in CTT are used between sibling tasks. However, operators used in GOMS have a double semantics. Firstly, they are specifying actions (cognitive and motor) performed by the user. Secondly, in GOMS some operators are also used as syntactic constructions of the language that control the task flow in a way that is similar to a programming language.

In order to access representations that are provided by different task models, a uniforming of concepts is needed. Fig. 7 illustrates common concepts that are used by most models and that are used to build a uniformed task model.

These concepts are believed critical for a task-based design of the UI. In this respect, goal hierarchies enable an identification of presentation units. Operators are expressing temporal constraints between tasks, which in turn impose visibility constraints for grouping the interaction objects. A minimal requirement for dealing with co-operative aspects is role specification, which is done in terms of tasks the user is responsible for. Objects and actions that are performed on them makes possible the detailed modelling of presentation and dialog.

A more detailed rationale for not including concepts of an individual task meta-model in the uniformed task meta-model is given below.

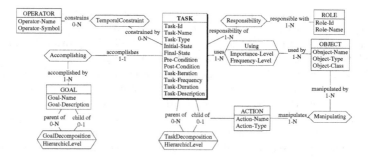

Fig. 7. Uniformed task meta-model

GOMS models assume the preexistence of a given UI. There is no explicit task decomposition but a hierarchic organisation of methods used to operationalise tasks. Cognitive analysis in GOMS is done at unit task level and it requires variable effort of specification which is depending on the level of detail envisioned by the analyst. GOMS is built for the lowest level of task decomposition thus giving no support for the user interface modelling. Rather, the objective is the optimisation of user performance and early evaluation of execution time, memory workload and learning time. Concepts are more related to user modelling than to task modelling.

Event concept is mentioned by few task models. Although GTA and DIANE+ include the event in the task world ontology, they do not model it. Therefore it was not included in the uniformed task meta-model.

GTA defines basic task as being composed of user actions and system operations. However, system operations are relevant for the user only if they are visible in the interface. In this case they are triggering user actions which are related to evaluation of the displayed information. Hence basic tasks are decomposed in actions and this is consistent with task specification from the user point of view. System operations are part of the application model (functional decomposition). Although they could be mentioned for documenting and explaining user actions, they are not part of the task model.

Role concept is used by GTA, CTT and TKS. A role is defined by the task a role is responsible for. Roles are useful to cope with co-operative aspects. Having a role specification and temporal constraints among tasks it is possible to refine task decomposition in several task trees that show both individual and co-operative aspects. Role decomposition is not relevant for the task model since roles are defined in terms of task sets.

Agent concept is used by GOMS, GTA and TKS although the semantics is differ-ent. As it could be observed from the GTA task meta-model, agent concept implies three relationships: performing actions to manipulate objects, having rights to use certain objects, and playing a role. While the first is drawing on cognitive aspects that could be analysed under the elementary task level, the last two are related to organ-isational aspects. Nor the concept itself neither its relationships to other concepts are useful to this level modelling.

TKS is using both plans and procedures in a similar way with HTA uses plans and GOMS uses selection rules and methods. Although plans are attractive and precise they are informal and could not be checked for proof. Moreover, plans are describing temporal constraints in a procedural way. Adding new tasks lead to rewrite plans that are associated to the next higher level task which may be laborious and error prone. Plans are suitable for early task analysis when information are elicited in an informal but unambiguous way. However they do not provide a representation able to support a (computer-aided) derivation of the UI model.

Table 1. Main features of task models

Features	GOMS	GTA	CTT	MAD	TKS	DIANE+
Task planning	Operator	Constructor (parent)	Operator (sibling)	Constructor (parent)	Plans/ constructor	Precedence/ attributes
Operationali-sation	Method		Scenario		Procedure	Operation attributes and constraints
Task tree leaves	Unit task	Basic task	Basic Task	Task	Action	Operations
Operational level	Operators	Actions/ system operations	Actions			
Specification of objects used	Cognitive objects	Object hierarchy	Objects	Objects	Object hierarchy	Data
Cognitive aspects	User performance	User performance/ user knowledge			Knowledge structures	
Co-operative aspects		Roles/agents	Roles co-operative task trees		Roles/ agents	Owners

Like methods, procedures are useful for a detailed specification of the elementary task when there is a need to describe actions performed upon object. However, models should be rather declarative than procedural in order to support successive transforms and to be suitable for using computer tools.

A matching table is presented in Table 1 to evaluate the degree to which task models that were analysed in previous sections fit the uniformed concepts of Fig. 7. The comparison is done on the basis of six features that characterise these task models: task planning, capabilities for operationalisation, lowest level in task decomposition, operational level, cognitive aspects, and co-operative aspects.Regarding the distinction between task and actions an observation should be made. While GOMS, GTA and CTT define an elementary task, other task models do not. For example, the ele-mentary task in MAD is an action. In a similar way, HTA uses the task concept but do not restrict actions to be represented in the task tree.

As it could be observed, none of them satisfies all requirements. On the other hand, optimisation of user performance through a cognitive analysis is not critical for a task-based design of the user interface. From this point of view, task models that are primarily intended as support for evaluation and user training like GOMS are not suitable to support the user interface modelling. Rather, they require an initial design of the interface that is intended to be improved with respect to usability criteria.

This uniformed task meta-model and its underlying semantic mappings will now enable a software tool to accommodate multiple individual task models.

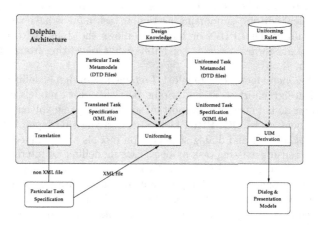

Fig. 8. DOLPHIN software architecture

6   A Software Architecture Based on Uniformed Task Models

Domain Ontologies Leading to the Production of Human-computer INterfaces (DOLPHIN) is a UIDA aimed at producing dialog and presentation models from various task models independently of their types. Its architecture is presented in Fig. 8. The input of the system is a task specification file in native format or in a XML-compliant language. If the file is not Extensible Markup Language (XML)-compliant, the file is transformed into an syntactically-equivalent XML-compliant file using the appropriate task meta-model, which has been transformed into a Document Type Definition (DTD) file. At this stage, the file containing the task model is not transformed: only a "XML"ification is generated.

XML-compliant files are directly sent to the uniformisation process which maps the concepts of individual task models to the concepts of the uniformed task model. Uniformisation rules, based on the semantic mappings, transform concepts of the individual task model into their uniformed equivalent. For this purpose, uniformisation rules are written as Extensible Stylesheet Language Transformations (XSLT) language [5]. XSLT (XSL Transformations) is a standard way to describe how to transform (change) the structure of an XML docu-ment into an XML document with a different structure. The output of uniformisation process is a uniformed task model expressed in a eXtensible user Interface Markup Language (XIML) file [18]. Design knowledge (e.g., design rules and formalised guidelines) are exploited to produce specification of the dialog and the presentation models. This process and the underlying technology is further detailed in [16].

Main benefits of this software architecture are:

- To allow reusing of existing task tools. Numerous tools (e.g., elicitation tools or graphical editors) supporting particular task models have already proven their qualities. DOLPHIN architecture allows the designer to use the tool that best fits to her needs or her habits while benefiting from a continuous approach.
- To enable incremental design effort. Incremental design is defined as the fact to lead design effort to its end. Some particular task models considered in this paper do not currently support all steps which are involved in a complete development cycle. DOLPHIN facilitates deriving this type of specification until presentation and dialog specification models are obtained.
- To allow reusing existing task models. Task modelling for interactive systems exists and is widespread for a few decades now. The diversity of models has enriched the panel of modelling concepts but it also prevented designers from reusing existing task specifications. Specifications were not accumulated and exploited at a global scale. DOLPHIN permits to consider such practice.
- To enable integration of other task model concepts that could arise in the future. Thanks to DOLPHIN openness, any integration of other task models should be achieved in a cost effective manner.

7   Conclusion

This paper presented a method to transform individual task models into their uniformed counterpart while minimising the loss of information. The stability of the uniformed task meta-model is guaranteed by a correct consolidation of individual task meta-models. If a new task meta-model needs to be consolidated, the uniformed task meta-model should not change, unless more elaborate task characteristics which were not present in the studied task models need to be modelled (Separation of concern).

In this study, only task models have been considered, leaving aside concept relevant to other models (e.g. user, domain). To take this information into account, a similar process may be applied to come up with a more expanded meta-model. In this case, it is no longer a task meta-model as it encompasses aspects of other models.

The main contribution of this paper is a partial solution. Firstly, only a part of the concepts are retained in the uniformed model. The union of the models concepts was chosen rather than the intersection and a selection on the concepts was applied. Secondly, concept semantics is only partially represented. A more formal approach would certainly produce a more reliable representation, but the cost of doing so for each concept for each individual model was judged too high with respect to the expected results. The original DOLPHIN feature described in this paper relates to its capability of accommodating several studied task models as input. For example, any task model stored in CTT's native format or converted into its XML equivalent can be used in DOLPHIN.

References

1. J. Annett and K. Duncan. Task analysis and training design. *Occupational Psychology*, 41:211–227, 1967.
2. L. K. Baumeister, B. E. John, and M. D. Byrne. A comparison of tools for building GOMS models tools for design. In *Proc. Of ACM Conf. On Human Factors in Computing Systems CHI'2000*, pages 502–509, New York, 2000. ACM Press.
3. B. Bomsdorf and G. Swillius. From task to dialogue: Task based user interface design. *SIGCHI Bulletin*, 30(4):40–42, 1998.
4. S.K. Card, T.P. Moran, and A. Newell. *The Psychology of Human-Computer Interaction*. Lawrence Erlbaum Associates, New York, 1983.
5. J. Clark. XSL: Transformations (XSLT). version 1.0 W3C recommendation. Technical report, W3C, 1999. http://www.w3.org/TR/xslt.
6. D. Diaper. Task analysis for knowledge descriptions (TAKD): The method and examples. In D. Diaper, editor, *Task Analysis for Human-Computer Interaction*, pages 108–159. Ellis-Horwood, 1990.
7. A. Dittmar. More precise descriptions of temporal relations within task models. In P. Pallanque and F. Paternó, editors, *Proc. of the 7th Int. Workshop on Design, Specification, and Verification of Interactive Systems DSV-IS'00 (Limerick, 5-6 June 2000)*, volume 1946 of *Lecture Notes in Computer Science*, pages 151–158, Berlin, 2000. Springer Verlag.
8. V. Englebert and J-L Hainaut. GRASYLA: Modelling case tools GUIs in meta-cases. In J. Vanderdonckt, editor, *Computer-Aided Design II. Proc. Of the 3rd Conference on Computer-Aided Design of User Interfaces. CADUI'99 (Louvain-la-Neuve, 21-23 October 1999)*, pages 217–244, Doordrecht, 1999. Kluwer Academics.
9. B. E. John and D. E. Kieras. The GOMS family of user interfaces analysis techniques: Comparison and contrasts. *ACM Transactions on Computer-Human Interaction*, 3(4):320–351, 1996.
10. P. Johnson. *Human-Computer Interaction: Psychology, Task Analysis and Software Engineering*. McGraw-Hill, Maidenhead, 1992.
11. P. Johnson and H. Johnson. Knowledge analysis of task: Task analysis and specification for human-computer systems. In A. Downton, editor, *Engineering the Human-Computer Interface*, pages 119–144. McGraw-Hill, Maidenhead, 1989.

12. P. Johnson, P. Markopoulos, and H. Johnson. Task knowledge structures: A specification of user task models and interaction dialogues. In *Proc. Of Task Analysis in Human-Computer Interaction, 11th Int. Workshop on Informatics and Psychology (Schraeding, Austria, June 9-11)*, 1992.

13. V. Kaptelinin and B. Nardi. Activity theory: Basic concepts and applications. ACM Press (New York), 2000. CHI'2000 Tutorial Notes vol. 5.

14. B. Kirwan and L. K. Ainsworth. *A Guide to Task Analysis*. Taylor and Francis, London, 2000.

15. K. Y. Lim and J. Long. *The MUSE Method Pfor Usability Engineering*. Cambridge Series on Human-Computer Interaction. Cambridge University Press, Cambridge (UK), 1994.

16. Q. Limbourg, C. Pribeanu, and J. Vanderdonckt. Uniforming of task models in a model-based approach. Technical Report BCHI-2001-4, Université Catholique de Louvain, 2001. Available on request.

17. F. Paternó. *Model-Based-Design and Evaluation of Interactive Applications*. Springer-Velag, 1999.

18. A. Puerta and J. Eisenstein. XIML: Towards a universal user interface markup language. Submitted for publication, 2001.

19. D. Scapin and C. Pierret-Golbreich. Towards a method for task description: MAD. In L. Berlinguet and D. Berthelette, editors, *Proc. Of the Conf. Work with Display Units WWU'89*, pages 27–34, Amsterdam, 1989. Elsevier Science Publishers.

20. J-C Tarby and M-F Barthet. The DIANE+ method. In J. Vanderdonckt, editor, *Computer-Aided Design of User Interfaces, Proc. of the 1st Int. Workshop on Computer-Aided Design of User Interfaces CADUI'96 (Namur, 5-7 June 1996)*, pages 95–119, Namur, 1996. Presses Universitaires de Namur.

21. M. J. Tauber. ETAG: Extended task action grammar. a language for the description of the user's task language. In D. Diaper, D. Gilmore, G. Cockton, and B. Shackel, editors, *Proc. of the 3rd IFIP TC 13 Conf. On Human Computer Interaction Interact '90 (Cambridge, 27-31 August 1990)*, pages 163–168, Amsterdam, 1990. Elsevier.

22. G. C. van der Veer, B. F. Van der Lenting, and B. A. J. Bergevoet. GTA: Groupware task analysis - modelling complexity. *Acta Psychologica*, 91:297–322, 1996.

23. M. van Welie, C.G. van der Veer, and A. Eliens. An ontology for task world models. In *Proc.of the 5th Int. Workshop on Design, Specification and Verification of Interactive Systems DSV-IS'98 (Abingdon, 3-5 June 1998)*, pages 57–70, Vienna, 1998. Springer Verlag.

Heuristic Evaluation of Website Attractiveness and Usability

Alistair Sutcliffe

Centre for HCI Design,
Department of Computation, UMIST, Manchester, UK.
a.g.sutcliffe@co.umist.ac.uk

Abstract. Web interfaces challenge traditional definitions of usability. A three phase model for website evaluation is proposed, based on initial attractiveness, exploration/navigation and transaction. Usability is redefined as trade-off between increasing the user's motivation to encourage exploration and purchasing in e-commerce, and the costs of usability errors. Heuristics for assessing the attractiveness of web user interfaces are proposed based on aesthetic design, general arousal created by content, corporate identity and brand, and the perceived utility matched to users' requirements. The heuristics are tested by evaluating three airline websites to demonstrate how different attractiveness and traditional usability trade-offs contribute to overall effectiveness.

1   Introduction

Traditional definitions of usability have emphasised utility and operational ease of use [4]. Usability evaluation methods concentrated on heuristics approaches to assessing design quality (e.g. Nielsen [11]) or observing user errors and inferring their causes in usability defects [16]. However, web interfaces are causing many to rethink such traditional definitions. Website designers are rightly concerned with aesthetic appeal and attracting users. If you cannot attract a user to stay on a website, it doesn't matter how well designed operational usability may be. In acknowledgement of these trends, variations of heuristic evaluation have appeared that assess 'minimal and aesthetic' design [12], or affinity, i.e. bringing objects to life through good visual design [2].

However, no revised definition of usability has been proposed that accounts for attractiveness and user satisfaction with an interface, beyond simple questionnaires to capture users' ratings of such variables. Furthermore, designers have little guidance for creating attractive user interfaces. Some advice can be found in the visual/graphics design community [10,6]; however, interaction designers give advice in the form of examples and scenarios, leaving the practitioner to abstract generalisable laws and interpret them in a design context.

This paper is motivated by two problems: firstly, how traditional definitions of usability need to be re-examined in light of experience of the web applications; and secondly, how attractiveness can be operationalised in terms of design guidance. The paper is structured in three sections. Firstly, the psychological

C. Johnson (Ed.): DSV-IS 2001, LNCS 2220, pp. 183–198, 2001.

background to attractiveness is reviewed and set in a model of usability proposed for websites and e-commerce in particular. This is followed by investigating how one component of the new usability, attractiveness, can be evaluated. The third section provides a case study evaluating the usability and attractiveness of web interfaces. The paper concludes with a brief discussion.

2   A Model of Effectiveness for Web User Interfaces

2.1   The Psychology of Attractiveness

Attractiveness is governed by design effects that direct our attention to a medium and the content contained therein. Attention is diverted by change, so dynamic media such as film, animation and sound dominate our attention over static media such as pictures and text. Attention to time varying media is determined by the medium itself, i.e. we have little choice but to listen to speech or to view animations in the order in which they are presented.

Attention is strongly influenced by content and by the psychology of motivation and arousal; it is also influenced by the difficulty of the task and by distraction in the environment. The recent interest in persuasive computing and captology [1] explores the boundaries of attention and motivation. The design issue is how to persuade people to take a decision or follow a course of action, i.e. the attention grabbing power of a computer interface to capture the user. The motivation for this interest is transparent in the growing e-commerce economy.

Motivation. Motivation, the internal will of an individual to do something, can be influenced by physiological factors (e.g. hunger), psychological factors (fear, sleepiness) and sociological matters such as companionship and responsibility. Motivation affects task performance, decision-making and attention. It can be decomposed into arousal, which tunes our senses to attend to certain stimuli; intrinsic motivation which reflects the individual's own will; and extrinsic motivation linked to properties of a particular resource. Of course these variables interact; for instance, if we are hungry (intrinsic) and smell cooking with garlic (extrinsic stimuli) and have had previous good experience of garlic-tasting food (arousal effect by priming) then our motivation to seek out the food will be increased.

Intrinsic motivations can be ranked in a series of satisfiability [8], from basic survival needs (food, shelter), to reproductive drives (sex, find a partner), curiosity (learning), individual self esteem (job satisfaction), societal influence (power, politics, possessions) and altruism (benefit for others). Once basic motivations (e.g. food) have been satisfied, motivations for self esteem, curiosity and power come into play in subtle combinations that marketing specialists are forever trying to guess.

Arousal. Arousal is poorly understood. Dynamic media (video, speech) are generally more arousing because we find these stimuli harder to ignore than static images; however, content plays a more important role. Arousal is bound up with our good/bad reaction to content, termed valence by psychologists. Dangerous, threatening (chased by a tiger), gory (mutilated body) and erotic content all increase arousal, more so than pleasant images (e.g. flowers, sunset) [14]. Arousal also affects memory. We remember events after unpleasant incidents more effectively than events beforehand (pro-active inhibition).

The relationship between arousal, motivation and attention is illustrated in Figure 1. The links and interactions are complex and each cognitive component has some influence on all the others. The nature and strength of these influences is still a subject of active research, so the following description is a brief summary.

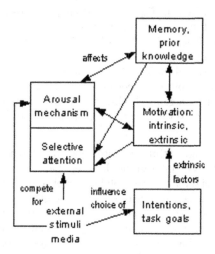

Fig. 1. Components of cognitive architecture associated with attention, motivation and arousal

Selective attention controls our response to external events. This is partly an automatic process but there is also conscious direction, which is under the control of our will. Arousal interacts with the attentional mechanism by tuning our responses to stimuli as well as making events more memorable (pro-active and retroactive inhibition) and increasing motivation to investigate information and take action. Motivation, in turn, is influenced by our intentions and the task. Goals also influence our attentional mechanism to search for particular information within perceived media input, and memory also influences the process of comprehension. Finally, motivation and prior knowledge affect our arousal and responsiveness to certain content; for instance, memory of a lover increases the probability of our attention to a photograph of him or her.

2.2   Designing to Attract Users

Control of attention has a complex cognitive mechanism. It is not surprising therefore that the connection to design can be mediated by many variables. The design stages that need guidance start with requirements and content selection, followed by selecting appropriate media to represent the content and design of the form of the media, and finally the design of representational detail. These design stages are associated with the second set of variables, starting with choice of material to inform or stimulate. Design of form involves creating media for aesthetic purposes as well as selecting appropriate media for the message and finally design of attention directing effects.

The model that anchors the design issues in a general process of interaction with websites is illustrated in Figure 2. Assuming a website of interest to the user has been found, the objective of the first phase is to get the user to stay on the website for sufficient time to explore it further. Attracting the user's attention is vital at this stage. Attention has two components: selection of media and salience effects, and judicious choice of content [15]. For content, visual style and presentation of brand or corporate image are important. Attractiveness can be measured by logging dwell-time on sites, as well as user ratings of sites in questionnaires; however, it is an external manifestation of three complex variables:

- Arousal: how exciting/restful a website appears to the user. Arousal is linked to the excitement and interest of the user. Generally, moderate states of arousal are beneficial for problem solving and encouraging exploration [3,13], both of which are necessary for the next phase of searching and navigation. Images of natural scenes, such as landscapes, tend to be restful and decrease arousal; in contrast, images of technology, unusual objects, sex, injury and violence are all arousing, although in different ways. Clearly sexually explicit material relates to sexual motivation; however, other arousing material has a more general effect of increasing excitement and attentiveness. Dynamic media, especially speech and video, also have a more arousing effect than static media, especially when they engage us in conversation.
- Motivation is reflected in our will to act or hold a belief, and has a complex literature in psychology [8]. Motivation is an under-researched area in HCI that concerns our attitudes and predispositions to act, depending on variables such as need for goods, power, self esteem and less powerful factors of curiosity, learning and altruism. Arousal interacts with motivation by tuning our awareness, e.g. arousal increases curiosity. Measuring motivation is a complex subject because it runs into the problem of individual differences. Assuming that a group level of motivation can be identified, some guess can be made about how the different facets of motivation will be served by content and design features of user interfaces.
- Perceived utility gain is influenced by our motivation for goods, services and wealth in a direct manner, and less directly for power, self-esteem and altruism. Utility requires a detailed model of the user to match the user's need with the product/service.

Key success criteria

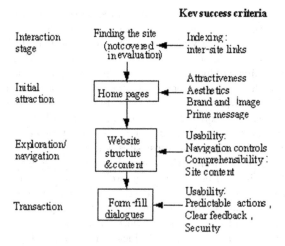

Interaction stage	Finding the site (not covered in evaluation)	Indexing: inter-site links
Initial attraction	Home pages	Attractiveness Aesthetics Brand and image Prime message
Exploration/ navigation	Website structure &content	Usability. Navigation controls Comprehensibility: Site content
Transaction	Form-fill dialogues	Usability. Predictable actions, Clear feedback, Security

Fig. 2. Attractiveness and usability criteria during the stages of interaction with e-commerce websites

The initial stage of attraction involves gaining the user's attention. Use of appropriate media is important, as are highlighting techniques. For instance, dynamic media (video and speech) are more attention directing than static media (text, still image) [15]. However, the effect can be overdone; for instance, too many animated banners compete with each other and rapidly become annoying, as many of us have experienced with search engines. Video, audio and change in image by highlighting all focus attention [15]. Once the user's eye has been drawn to the web page, content-based attraction takes over. Projection of brand and organisational identity that promote trust [5], and information that conveys the potential utility of the website to the user will also contribute to holding the user's attention. This implies user modelling to specify their knowledge of brands as well as requirements.

More general attraction can be fostered by aesthetic design and use of media for arousal. Aesthetic attractiveness is a complex variable that is subject to individual differences, as summarised in the saying 'beauty lies in the eye of the beholder'. Nevertheless, some general principles of aesthetic design can be described and their application should result in a longer dwell-time on the site.

Once the user has been attracted to the website home page and has been persuaded to stay, the next phase begins. In most cases, finding the goods, service or information the user requires necessitates navigation. In exploration and navigation, the conventional quality of usability is paramount. Clear prompts, consistent layout and controls and observable effects all promote ease of use, which can be assessed by standard evaluation methods [9]. However, on websites information plays a key role that goes beyond conventional usability. Early hints on direction to follow towards the search target are important.

Usability problems can terminate user interaction as this stage, so careful design is vital. Critical incidents in which users are confused but can eventually guess what to do may be survivable if their motivation is high; however, errors from which the user cannot recover must be eliminated. Misleading cues for information searching will have a deleterious effect on users' patience. Motivation will have to be high to continue searching after they have followed false cues. User motivation will be subject to the conflicting forces of the promise of perceived utility on the plus side, and the cost of errors on the other. Sites with a close match between their product offering and users' requirements may be able to get away with poor usability, but most sites will not.

The final stage is the transaction when the user purchases the goods/service. Operational usability will be important as well as motivation to counteract any usability difficulties. In information intensive applications, presentation in appropriate media with a well-structured layout will be a key usability requirement [4]. In e-commerce, information presentation has a key influence on purchasing behaviour; for instance, ranking product attributes (quality before cost) can sway users' choice [7]. Other techniques are use of speech and images of people to engender human response to computers by praising the user, being polite, showing interest and attention via gaze and posture, and use of authority figures or young women to persuade [14,1].

Design of successful websites therefore has to recruit different design guidelines to fulfil different needs at each stage. Initial attention is replaced by arousal and content related attraction. This raises the user's motivation by the promise of the utility reward to come. The motivational capital has to be maintained during the exploration/navigation stage to counteract any difficulties and disappointments when searches result in dead ends. Once the search target has been reached, user motivation needs to be encouraged and usability errors eliminated to engender successful interaction.

User costs are composed of interaction steps, which in websites tend to be simple, so the number is vital. Long winded multiple step dialogues incur more cost, a lesson not lost on amazon.com who implemented one click shopping. The other element of cost is error, caused by usability problems, misleading cues and failed searches. The phases of interaction can be evaluated by the following measures and techniques:

1. Finding the website: tests with different search engines using a selection of keywords. %age of searches that correctly identify the website, with a relevance ranking more than x%.
2. Initial attraction: dwell-time measured from user interaction logs, de-briefing interviews to investigate what features users noticed and what attracted or repelled them. Free recall memory tests to establish the topics and features users remembered about a site.
3. Exploration and navigation: usability measures such as errors (% of searches correct) and task completion times. Expert judgement about conformance to design guidelines and heuristics. Cognitive walkthroughs of interaction to identify design flaws [16].

4. Transaction: usability measures as above, plus de-briefing interviews to discover users' rating of website utility.

In the next section one aspect of the new usability, attractiveness, is investigated in more depth.

3   Evaluating Attractiveness

Matching content to users' requirements and motivation is already a complex topic; when judgement on aesthetic design is added, the source of variation from individual differences will become even greater. In spite of these problems, it is better for HCI to attempt to understand the quality of attractiveness rather than leave such issues to designers' craft skills.

Attractiveness can be divided into generic qualities of a user interface such as aesthetic design, use of media to direct attention, and content related issues of linking visual style, brand image and messages to users' knowledge of the organisation and their requirements. Heuristics are proposed for both generic and content related design issues. The following heuristics extend existing advice on website design (e.g. Nielsen's [12] heuristics, IBM's [2] design principles) and can be used either as design advice or evaluation criteria. Proposing principles for aesthetic design is contentious because the graphics/visual design community follows an experiential approach rather than an engineering design philosophy, so articulating design principles is not encouraged. Nevertheless some researchers have partially formalised good design qualities and the following heuristics are based on their recommendations [10,6].

The generic heuristics for attractiveness and aesthetic design are as follows:

- Judicious use of colour: colour use should be balanced and low saturation pastel colours should be used for backgrounds. Designs should not use more than 2-3 fully saturated intense colours.
- Symmetry and style: visual layout should be symmetrical, e.g. bilateral, radial organisation that can be folded over to show the symmetrical match. Use of curved shapes convey an attractive visual style when contrasted with rectangles
- Structured and consistent layout: use of grids to structure image components and portray a consistent order; grids need to be composed of rectangles which do not exceed a 5:3 height to width ratio.
- Depth of field: use of layers in an image stimulates interest and can be attractive by promoting a peaceful effect. Use of background image with low saturated colour provides depth for foreground components.
- Choice of media to attract attention: video, speech and audio all have an arousing effect and increase attention. Music can attract by setting the appropriate mood for a website.
- Use of personality in media to attract and persuade: this principle applies primarily to e-commerce websites when use of human image and speech can help to attract users and persuade them to buy goods by being polite and praising their choices [14].

– Design of unusual or challenging images that stimulate the users' imagination and increase attraction: unusual images often disobey normal laws of form and perspective.

Describing rules for each of these qualities is more difficult for some (unusual design) than others (structured layout). When used for design the heuristics are accompanied by examples to amplify their recommendations; in this paper they will be used for evaluation. Evaluators are requested to rate the interface on each heuristic using a 1 to 10 scale. As with general HCI heuristics, a greater number of evaluators will provide a more reliable opinion; however, experts may be unreliable in judging aesthetic qualities. Graphical design experts are prone to disagree about aesthetic qualities more than are ordinary users.

The content related heuristics are:

– Consistent visual style. This heuristic is on the borderline between the two sets. Visual style is generic in the sense that a website needs to be consistent in terms of layout and image, but the style also needs to reflect the corporate values. Hence a website targeted at the youth market should use arousing material, whereas a site targeted at older users may use more restful, natural images. For tranquillity, choosing natural world content is advisable; conversely the image of a modern, dynamic organisation is reinforced by technological subject matter (e.g. racing cars, jet aircraft, spacecraft) [14].
– Visibility of identity and brand. The effectiveness of this heuristic depends on the strength of the brand image and corporate identity. The design principle just recommends making the identity visible in a consistent manner.
– Matching arousal to user's mood and motivation. This heuristic focuses on the match between the user model and website content. Variations to be expected are between age and gender. Ultimately this is a complex topic dealt with in many books on marketing research.
– Stimulating users' interest by secondary motivation. Attractiveness can be increased by adding functionality that is not geared to the site's primary purpose, but may attract for another motivation. Some examples are placing games and simulations on e-commerce sites for users' amusement.
– Selecting content to suit users' requirements. This should result from a sound requirements analysis, but poor content display may confound a thorough requirements analysis. Content related to users' requirements should be clearly stated, in unambiguous language, with clear cues on how to find it.

These heuristics need to be combined with existing usability principles to give an overall usability/attractiveness assessment. The generic heuristics apply more strongly to the initial attraction phase of website interaction, while both sets apply to initial attraction, exploration and transaction stages. If the site is rated well on the above heuristics, user motivation will be maintained so some usability errors may be tolerated.

In the next section the heuristics and model of website interaction are used in a case study evaluation of three websites with similar business objectives.

4   Evaluation Case Study

Three airline websites are assessed: EasyJet (EJ), Virgin Atlantic (VA) and British Airways (BA). Nine undergraduate students (6 male, 3 female) from those who were taking the HCI module assessed the website after a tutorial lecture had introduced the heuristics. The subjects rated each site on a 1-5 scale for each heuristic and were asked to report the rationale for their decision and the ease with which each heuristics could be interpreted. The rating scores were converted into net positive values to reflect the range of the evaluators' assessments. A worked example of this analysis is given in Table 4. The frequency of the evaluators' ratings is multiplied by the +2 to -2 scale and the products summed to give a value for the heuristic.

Table 1. Worked example of the net positive value for the rating of website persuasiveness by the nine subjects

Rating	1	2	3	4	5
Scale	-2	-1	0	+1	+2
Rating Freq/subject	2	0	4	3	0
Product	-4	0	0	3	0
Total Net positive value					-1

All three sites aim to provide information about the airline as well as on-line sales of flight tickets. The companies concerned have different corporate images, which to a lay observer may be characterised as blue chip reliability and quality (British Airways), modern and exciting (Virgin) and cheap and cheerful (EasyJet). The ratings of each site are given following the model as a cognitive walkthrough with a common scenario of buying a flight ticket. The overall assessment of the sites is given in Table 4.

Table 2. Average scores for each site on attractiveness, persuasion and usability

	EJ	VA	BA
Overall attractiveness	-6	7	-2
Persuade to buy	1	0	1
Usability and Navigation	8	4	5
Total	3	11	4

Overall Virgin Atlantic received the higher scores, with EasyJet and British Airways being marginally more persuasive, even though two evaluators commented, that EasyJet's "buy now" message was obvious and on the home page.

All three sites were favourably rated for usability with EasyJet in the lead, while Virgin Atlantic was the leader in attractiveness.

Assessment on the design quality heuristics (32) tells a more complex story. Two used colour for projecting corporate identity (red for Virgin, orange for EasyJet); however, this led to a low rating for Virgin. Both organisations' colours are part of the corporate image, so judgement on this heuristic indicates a possible clash of aesthetic appeal and brand projection. Symmetry/style was judged to be below average in all sites; however, several evaluators reported that this heuristic was the most difficult one to interpret.

Table 3. Aesthetic design qualities of the websites judged from front pages, rated on 1 to 5 scale, where 5 = excellent

	EJ	VA	BA
Use of colour	3	-4	6
Symmetry/aesthetic style	-3	-5	-6
Structured layout	3	2	-2
Depth of field	-4	3	-3
Choice of media	-9	3	-11
People and personality	-8	-11	-10
Unusual images	-11	7	-14
Totals	-29	-5	-40

Virgin and EasyJet were rated more favourably than British Airways on well-structured and consistent pages, which seems to conflict with irregular appearance of the EasyJet's pages; see Figure 3.

EasyJet and British Airways scored poorly on depth of field and choice of media to attract interest, however, Virgin's use of the jet windows metaphor did show some innovation, which is reflected in higher scores. None of the sites scored well on use of personality and people to engage users. Virgin scored well on use of animated media to attract attention, and overall created more exciting content by use of animation and design layout, as illustrated in Figure 4.

The conclusions from the Stage 1 analysis rated Virgin highest in terms of aesthetic design; reflected in the evaluators' comments that its appearance was clearly different from the more traditional block structure layout of the other two websites. However the aesthetic qualities of all three sites were judged to be below average with British Airways being particularly bad.

The content assessment shows a less clear-cut picture, as summarised in Table 4. In this case, judgement is made by browsing throughout the website to assess visual style and brand visibility, while primary, secondary motivation and contents requirements match were judged on the first 2-3 web pages encountered when following the flight booking scenario.

Fig. 3. EasyJet web front page, which has a somewhat irregular layout but to its credit is good at presenting its basic message: cheap flights and the economic incentive for booking on the web

Table 4. Assessment using the content/attractiveness heuristics

	EJ	VA	BA
Visual style	11	8	-2
Brand visibility	12	9	6
Mood and first motivation	0	2	0
Secondary motivation	-3	2	-9
Content and requirements	5	2	5
Totals	25	23	0

Both EasyJet and Virgin Atlantic were rated well on a consistent visual style and good brand visibility. In contrast, British Airways was noted to be more discreet about their corporate identity; see Figure 5.

There was little to choose between the three sites in primary motivation, because all provided services for searching flight availability and booking, although EasyJet did make this functionality easier to access on the home page. Virgin scored slightly higher than British Airways and EasyJet by providing a clearer indication of secondary information on holidays, frequent flyer clubs, car rental, etc. on their front page. The match of content and requirements for flight information and booking was similar for all three sites. In the totals for content attractiveness British Airways came off worst, whereas the clear brand image and corporate visual style paid off for EasyJet and Virgin. Three evaluators commented that the chromatic identity of Virgin was striking even if they didn't like it (see colour rating in aesthetic heuristics)

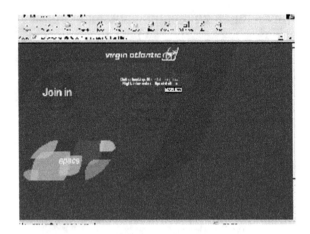

Fig. 4. Virgin website, illustrating the contrast in graphic design with Figure 3. The jet windows and keyhole metaphors contain animations to attract attention.

The final part of the assessment for Stage 2 (navigation) and Stage 3 (transaction) was judged by browsing extensively through the site and following a flight booking transaction. Heuristic evaluation criteria were used to judge the usability of navigation and transaction support. Space precludes reporting detailed results so a summary of the usability assessment for each site is given in Table 4.

In the latter phases of interaction, EasyJet does not compare so favourably. The navigation controls and support are weak because no site map is provided, navigation bars have overlapping content, the side bar animations contain link cues but change, making navigation confusing; no back to top commands are given on the bottom of long pages. Transaction controls also suffer from similar defects, e.g. no exit, long and cumbersome scroll boxes. Virgin Atlantic and British Airways do better by supplying the essentials of good navigation (site maps, consistent navigation menus, back to top and exit/home), although navigation controls are more consistent and visible in the Virgin site. Both Virgin and British Airways use a clear task step metaphor (1-2-3-4-5) to guide the user through flight reservation, booking and payment. EasyJet adopts the same metaphor, but implements it less clearly.

The evaluators' scores with Neilsen's heuristics (see Table 4) showed less variation and were more to neutral assessments apart from the high consistency score given to EasyJet. Easyjet and British Airways come out more favourably on these heuristics, however the high EasyJet rating on Consistency does not agree well with Structured Layout heuristic in the aesthetic set, demonstrating some inconsistency in evaluator judgement.

The summary picture is shown in Table 4. Overall, Virgin appears to be the best placed site with a first rank in the overall attractiveness, aesthetic

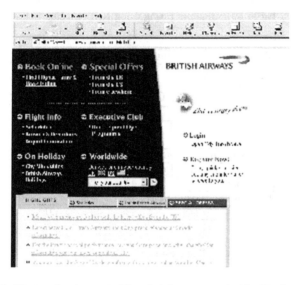

Fig. 5. British Airways front page, with a low-key corporate identity (compared with Figure 3), but the structure is well laid out and the content meets with users' requirements for flight browsing/booking.

Table 5. Usability assessment of the navigation and the transaction phase

Usability criterion	EJ	VA	BA
Navigation commands	1	3	2
Navigation support	2	3	2
Transaction prompts	3	4	5
Form fill layout	2	4	4
Transaction controls	1	4	5
Totals	9	18	18

heuristics and joint first on Usability/navigation. However, EasyJet ranked first on Neilsens' heuristics and Content related attractiveness.

The evaluation shows clear strengths and weaknesses of each site at each stage. Overall, Virgin wins on attractiveness and aesthetic design as well as having a well-designed transaction/navigation interface. EasyJet is strong on initial content-driven attraction but suffers from basic usability defects in the exploration and transaction phases, e.g. no escape route. Motivation created during the initial phase may encourage users to tolerate usability error costs in later phases; however, overall, the Virgin site is likely to be the more effective because it combines reasonable motivation with aesthetic attractiveness and sound usability engineering.

Table 6. Evaluators rating using Neilsen's Heuristics

	EJ	VA	BA
Visibility of system status	2	1	-1
System RW match	6	6	6
Control and freedom	-1	0	3
Consistency and standards	15	6	6
Error prevention	2	0	-4
Recognition opposed to re-call	8	-4	3
Flexibility and efficiency	1	-3	0
Aesthetic/minimalist design	3	6	4
Error handling	7	2	0
Help and documentation	-7	-8	4
Total	36	6	21

Table 7. Summary totals of all the evaluation heuristics and phases. * Denotes first ranking site

	EJ	VA	BA
Overall appeal	3	11*	4
Aesthetic attraction	-29	-5 *	-40
Content attraction	25 *	23	0
Usability/Navigate	9	18 *	18 *
Nielsen heuristic	36 *	6	21

Evaluators' Assessment. Overall the attractiveness heuristics were positively rated and judged to be easy to use (npv = 5 for design quality and 11 for the content heuristics) and fared slightly better than the Nielsen heuristics which were also used (npv 2). Only two heuristics attracted adverse comments: judgement of symmetry which 4 out 9 evaluators found difficult to interpret, and depth of field (2 evaluators). However, 3 or more evaluators commented that they felt their judgement was very subjective, in particular when judging motivation and visual content assessment, and usual/exciting content in the design heuristics. Two Nielsen heuristics (system match with real world and aesthetic/minimal design) were considered to be ambiguous by three of the evaluators. Flexibility and efficiency also required interpretation. The evaluators judged efficiency on response time and the ability to operate the interface quickly and with few errors, but the flexibility component was found to be difficult to judge. When inter-observer agreement was calculated by Kendall's coefficient of concordance only 3 of the heuristics gave significant agreement at the p=0.05 level-Depth of field, Use of Personality, and Unusual images. The lack of agreement is disappointing; however, Neilsen's heuristics fared no better with only two (Freedom and control, and Error prevention) passing at the p=0.05 level, so this may be a common problem with heuristic style evaluations. Since the evaluators did agree on the overall rating of attractiveness (P=0.05) and 3 of the general attractiveness heuristics with another 2 just missing significance, there seems a reasonable prospect for improving this evaluation approach.

5   Discussion

This study is a preliminary investigation into the role of aesthetic and other factors in re-defining website usability. However, it does demonstrate how explicit consideration of aesthetics and motivation factors can alter judgement of website quality. Heuristic evaluation [11] placed EasyJet first. In contrast, explicit consideration of attractiveness suggests the Virgin Atlantic design has many advantages. The influence of aesthetics in the overall effectiveness requires further research to investigate correlations between performance measures of visit frequency and durations, users' purchases and subjective assessment of web sites. The heuristics separate content from aesthetic based attraction so differences in their influence can be assessed i.e. aesthetics may play a more important role for initial visits but content issues may be dominant for repeat visits.

Clearly there are limitations in a subjective ratings style analysis of usability; however, quick and dirty approaches have become popular and do seem to improve designs. The new heuristics proposed in this study extend the range of evaluation from usability to more motivational aspects of design. It is difficult to reduce the subjectivity of assessment when considering aesthetic qualities of a design; however, the heuristics did show reasonable inter-observer reliability. The next step is to test and calibrate the judgements by further samples of evaluators: HCI experts, graphic designers, software engineers and users to see if each group produces different ratings. While some variance is to be expected, if the comparative judgement of each site is consistent then the extended evaluation heuristics will have demonstrated their reliability. The second validation is to check expert assessment against end-user judgement and purchasing behaviour of the test websites. However, this data may be difficult to interpret because other factors are involved. For instance, EasyJet advertises its Internet booking service extensively.

Attractiveness and aesthetic design are key factors in persuasive computing [1]; however, further research is required on articulating the design properties of attractiveness and aesthetics across different designs and user groups. Furthermore, we need to understand the interaction between user motivation and usability costs, the factors that augment motivation and the consequences for user interface effectiveness from motivation/cost trade-offs.

Acknowledgements. The author would like to thank Andreas Gregoriades for his help in preparing this paper.

References

1. Fogg, B.J.: Persuasive computer: perspectives and research directions. In Proceedings: Human Factors in Computing Systems: CHI'98, Los Angeles, 18-23 April 1998, 225-232. ACM Press, New York. (1998).

2. IBM: Ease of use: design principles.
   http://www.ibm.com/ibm/easy/eou_ext.nsf/Publish/6. Accessed 20 Nov (2000).

3. Isen, A.M.: "Positive affect and decision making". In Lewis, M. & Haviland, J. (Eds.), Handbook of emotions. Guilford Press, New York (2000).

4. ISO: ISO 9241: Ergonomic requirements for office systems with visual display terminals (VDTs) Part 10: Dialogue Principles. International Standards Organisation (1997).

5. Kollok, P.: "The production of trust in online markets". In Lawler, E.J., Macy, M., Thyne S., and Walker H.A. (Eds): Advances in group processes, Vol. 16. JAI Press, Greenwich CT (1999).

6. Kristof, R., & Satran, A.: *Interactivity by design: creating and communicating with new media*. Adobe Press, Mountain View CA (1995).

7. Lohse, G.L.: "Usability and profits in the digital economy". In Mc Donald S., Waern, Y. and Cockton G. (Eds), People and Computers XIV, Usability or Else! Proceedings BCS-HCI Conference. Springer, Berlin (2000) 3-16.

8. Maslow, A.H., Frager, R., McReynolds, C., Cox, R., & Fadiman, J.: *Motivation and personality* (3rd ed.). Addison Wesley-Longman, New York (1987).

9. Monk, A.G., & Wright, P.: *Improving your human-computer interface: a practical technique*. Prentice Hall, London (1993).

10. Mullet, K., & Sano, D.: *Designing visual interfaces: communication oriented techniques*. SunSoft Press, Englewood Cliffs NJ (1995).

11. Nielsen, J.: *Usability engineering*. Academic Press, New York (1993).

12. Nielsen, J.: *Designing Web usability: the practice of simplicity*. New Riders Publishing (1999).

13. Picard, R.W.: *Affective computing*. MIT Press, Cambridge MA (1997).

14. Reeves, B., & Nass, C.: *The media equation: how people treat computers, television and new media like real people and places*. CLSI/Cambridge University Press, Stanford CA/Cambridge (1996).

15. Sutcliffe, A.G.: "User-centred design for multimedia applications". Proceedings Vol. 1: IEEE Conference on Multimedia Computing and Systems, Florence. IEEE Computer Society Press, Alamitos CA (1999) 116-1123.

16. Sutcliffe, A.G., Ryan, M., Doubleday, A., & Springett, M.V.: Model mismatch analysis: towards a deeper explanation of users' usability problems. *Behaviour and Information Technology*, 19(1), (2000) 43-55.

Affordance and Symmetry

Harold Thimbleby

University College London
h.thimbleby@ucl.ac.uk

Abstract. Whilst it is generally accepted as a positive criterion, affordance only gives the weakest of hints for interactive systems designers. This paper shows how useful it is to consider affordance as generated by a correspondence between program symmetries and user interface symmetries. Symmetries in state spaces (for instance, as might be visualised in statecharts) can be carried through to user interfaces and into user manuals, with beneficial results. Exploiting affordances, understood in this way, in addition to their well known user interface benefits, makes programs simpler and more reliable, and makes user manuals shorter.

1 Introduction

Affordance was introduced by the influential ecological psychologist J. J. Gibson [4]. Gibson introduced affordance as a provocative yet quite vague concept, and this has led to subsequent research attempting to pin down the concept adequately to exploit it further. Norman's classic *Psychology of Everyday Things* [7] brought affordance to the attention of designers. Gaver [2] further widened the scope of affordance to the design of interactive computer systems, such as graphical user interfaces.

Gibson's view is that the environment is a surface that separates individuals from physical objects. The environment is perceived, which suggests that the values and meanings of objects can themselves be directly perceived. We say that an object may *afford* some or several sorts of action, and when it does so this is in some sense a set of natural or "easy" relations. The classic example is the door plate and door handle, which when used appropriately afford pushing and pulling the door. Occasionally one comes across doors with handles that can only be opened by pushing; occasionally one comes across doors with plates that cannot be opened by pushing. The lack of affordance in each case is frustrating.

Because affordance appears to be a simple idea and represents an unequivocably "good thing" it has become a very popular design concept. Yet in 1999 Norman wrote how designers had misunderstood affordance [8]. Norman now emphasises distinctions between the user's conceptual model, physical constraints, conventions (such as cultural conventions), and the difference between perceived and real affordances. These concrete distinctions are of less relevance to the more abstract discussion of this paper, because we are not concerned here with the mechanisms (physical, cultural or whatever) that bring about a relation between the properties of the environment and the cognitive models of the user, merely

C. Johnson (Ed.): DSV-IS 2001, LNCS 2220, pp. 199–217, 2001.
© Springer-Verlag Berlin Heidelberg 2001

that there can be, or may not be, a relation. It is beyond the scope of this paper to speculate about the cognitive processes — beyond pointing out that the experience of "bad affordance" is so common and widely appreciated that the relevance of affordance to good design is an uncontentious issue.

Many interactive systems are notorious for being difficult to use. Poor design, without any deeper analysis, is an easy scapegoat for interaction failures that result in varying degrees of loss to users, whether using video recorders or aircraft flight management systems. Can affordance be recruited more effectively to interactive systems design? Can the concept be tightened to have a more rigorous value in design? We believe so, and this paper describes how.

2   Symmetry

We are most familiar with the concept of symmetry in the spatial and visual domains, perhaps most especially as occurring in two dimensional pictures and patterns. For example, a reflection symmetry is a feature of an object that is unchanged when it is reflected, as in a mirror. Human faces have a vertical bilateral mirror symmetry, and more symmetric faces are more attractive, possibly because a symmetric face induces less cognitive load to memory. Facial asymmetries, which are not so attractive, arise mainly through imperfections. Imperfections to one's appearance may be caused by disease or trauma, and such accidents rarely have any cause to maintain symmetries. Indeed in the natural world, threats to survival are never specialised to the left or right: when one survives, say, a left-handed threat one's chances of survival are doubled by assuming the lesson learned should be symmetrical. To some extent, evidently, symmetry has evolutionary significance, which goes some way to explaining the widespread appeal of symmetry, including in more abstract domains such as in patterns and even rhythms. Culturally, symmetry has deep æsthetic significance, and of course is exploited in art in the widest sense, including visual arts, music and rhetoric. In the search for simplicity and power, symmetry is one of the best tools available [3].

As Hermann Weyl put it, symmetry occurs most generally when a property of an object is unchanged through a transformation of the object [17]. Of course, most transformations change objects in one way or another, but when they do not change some properties a symmetry is involved.

For example we can describe a picture of a face as a function $p(x, y)$, which tells us what colour to paint at coordinates (x, y). The face would be mirror symmetric about the line $x = 0$ if there was no change in the picture if we transformed x to $-x$. In other words, the transformation (x, y) to $(-x, y)$ leaves the property p (in this case, the face on the picture) unchanged. More specifically, the fact that $p(x, y) = p(-x, y)$ means p is symmetric in Weyl's precise sense, and of course also in the conventional mirror sense. This mathematical description of symmetry clearly captures the essence of the visual or physical symmetries of objects; it also shows how symmetry can be defined formally, just in terms of abstract transformations.

Very often we are interested in particular sorts of symmetry, and we define an S symmetry as arising when a property p of an object is unchanged through an S transformation. Mirror symmetries arise through mirror transformations, and so on. In the example above, the mirror symmetry was the S transformation (x, y) to $(-x, y)$, which is reflection about the line $x = 0$, and the property was the collection of graphical information in the picture p itself. Because of their importance, different words are used in different fields to describe the special properties involved in certain symmetries, *invariant* being a common term. We will see others below.

Physics might be called the science of natural symmetries,[1] and is concerned with many symmetries that are not visual at all. For example, special relativity arises when constant velocity transformations leave the property the speed of light unchanged.[2] Chemistry is the study of properties that are unchanged when objects (which chemists call atoms) are replaced with other objects of the same class (which chemists call elements). Chemistry makes a good example of how agreement on "better" symmetries advances reasoning: the conceptual move from heat, fire, water and air — through phlogiston and other conceptual models — enabled human reasoning to be more effective, reliable and indeed easier. Simply, in this paper, we want to use symmetry to help design, understand and use interactive systems, rather than chemical processes.

Mathematics has very general ideas of symmetry, expressed for instance in group theory. Felix Klein famously defined geometry in 1872 as the study of properties of figures that remain invariant under particular groups of transformation. In particular Euclid's geometry is the study of the so-called rigid transformations, such as rotation and reflection, that preserve area and distance. Interestingly, Euclid himself did not specify the essential symmetry axiom that geometrical properties are unchanged when a figure is moved about in space.

Symmetry represents key concepts. The laws of physics are invariant under translation (change of position): so we expect the laws of physics to be found unchanged if we did our experiments a million miles away. Yet the laws of physics are very different just a metre below where I am writing: few of the experiments I can perform on my desk work inside the concrete floor — for obvious reasons! Symmetries can be restored by translating more physical properties of my desk to the floor.

To a great extent, then, science advances by studying the ways in which symmetries are broken, and then finding newer more general symmetries to restore the elegance. Mathematics often advances by developing notations that are invariant under transformations; for example, vector algebra is a powerful tool (e.g., for physics) precisely because it is insensitive to rotation and translation of coordinate systems. Furthermore, because it is invariant vector notations

---

[1] Noether's Theorem shows a deep connection between symmetry, least action and conservation laws, and is one of the most profound theoretical results behind modern physics.

[2] Newton's laws of motions are invariant too, but they predict the speed of light varies with the observer's motion.

need not, and in fact generally do not, mention coordinates, and therefore become easier to use by removing irrelevant detail. In computing, symmetry arises in many areas, such as mobile computing (computing facilities are unchanged through transformation of place) and in declarative programming (which we discuss below).

Symmetry sounds ubiquitous, and if it was it would be a pretty vacuous concept. We are generally interested in things that change and how they change, and therefore by definition we are interested in broken symmetries, more than in the symmetries themselves, except in so far as they provide a "background" that highlights the changes. Certainly some symmetries seem trivial (for example, we are so familiar that movement in space leaves things unchanged that translation symmetry seems obvious). Other symmetries, though, seem more profound. Consider scale symmetry, where things are unchanged through a transformation in size. In the physical world, scale symmetry does not apply. Things are particular sizes, and they do not work or do not work well at other scales (though there are approximate scale invariants in fractals). Atoms are necessarily a certain size, and things therefore cannot be made too small; when things are made too large, their strength — which does not increase at the same rate as their mass — becomes insufficient to support them. Animals the size of insects can fly; we can't because we operate at a larger scale. And so on.

User interfaces for many applications, however, would be improved if they were scale symmetric (be the same even when you change their size), even though strictly speaking there is no corresponding physical symmetry to apply. People with limited visual acuity could "zoom in" without affecting any other aspect of the user interface. Images could be scaled so they could be read easily at any distance, or projected for an audience scaled to screens of any size. Unfortunately many auditorium projectors use digital display technology (e.g., LCD screens) and scaled images cause aliasing problems, often with the result that text becomes unreadable when projected at "the wrong resolution."

3   Affordance and Symmetry

Gibson wished to explain vision by positing some higher order features of vision that are invariant with motion and rotation and are "picked up" by the observer. He held the view that the function of the brain was to "detect invariants" despite changes in "sensations." With this conception he freed vision research of what computer scientists would call implementation bias — an idea later formalised by David Marr in his three-level model of visual processing into computational, representation/algorithm, and hardware implementation [6]. As Marr points out, whereas Gibson thought of the brain as "resonating" to the invariants, the detection of physical invariants is in fact an information processing task.

A typical wood pencil has two main symmetries. It has a hexagonal or sometimes circular symmetry along its long axis, and it has an approximate reflectional symmetry about its centre (strictly, about a plane through the centre and orthogonal to the major axis). Because of the rotational symmetry, it does not matter what angle a pencil is grabbed at. Because of the approximate reflectional symmetry, it is easy to make errors grabbing a pencil: it may be grabbed "up side down" and be unsuitable for writing — unless it really is symmetric, that is, sharpened at both ends. Clearly the symmetries provide freedoms in the way an object can be used, and any approximate symmetries provide opportunities for errors because users tend to expect the full symmetries to work.

There are many other pencil symmetries. For example, the property "pencilness" is unchanged when we swap one pencil for another made by a different manufacturer. The colour of the wood of a pencil is another symmetry, whereas changing the colour of the lead is (for most tasks) not a symmetry. We are disappointed in pencils made by cheap manufacturers because they persuade us that the pencil has symmetries that they fail to uphold. Conversely, we are pleased by pencils whose quality of symmetries exceeds our expectations: thus one that was indefinitely unchanged as one wrote with it would be very nice, as it would have an inexhaustible lead. More plausibly, a propelling pencil is "better" because it size and shape remains unchanged as it is transformed by use — it has an additional symmetry over conventional pencils, which get shorter as they are used. A pencil that was exceedingly smooth is merely one that feels invariant on any surface. And so on.

We could define a pencil (and everything equivalent to a pencil) by its full set of symmetries, namely the set of transformations that keep all "pencilness" properties invariant. *Affordance can then be defined as those symmetries that apply under the actions relevant to the activities or tasks that are performed with the object.* Rotating a pencil about its long axis makes no difference to how well it writes, and therefore an affordance of a pencil for writing is its rotational symmetry. However, if we had the unusual task to read the writing on the pencil shaft that says who manufactured the pencil or what its hardness was (H, HB, etc) then rotation does change the task, and it is therefore not an affordance for this task. In particular, we note that the visual properties of a pencil do not afford perceiving its hardness — suggesting (if this was a concern for some task) that a new perceptual representation of hardness (e.g., colour coded bands) that was invariant under a pencil's symmetries could be a practical benefit.

In summary, some pencil symmetries are interesting, others not; not all symmetries lead to useful affordances; enforcing some affordances leads to new designs, such as the propelling pencil. Clearly affordance raises design trade-offs: what is the cost of implementing a suitable symmetry against the benefit to the user, and how should this trade-off be accounted for (what are the manufacturing set-up costs; how many users are there; what are the risks of error; and so forth)?

Pencils are a very simple example, but for cultural and economic reasons do not pose interesting design problems for us here. (See Petroski [9] for a thorough discussion of pencil design.)

4   State Spaces

All digital computer systems implement state spaces, and with the exception of continuous systems (e.g., control systems), computer systems can be defined as state space automata. Even simple computer systems have enormous state spaces, so various means are used for describing the computer system without specifying the state space explicitly as such. Programming languages provide structures (most notably data types and procedure calls) that heavily disguise the underlying state machine, so that the programmer can concentrate at any moment on very simple components of the state machine (such as a single conditional). Provided we use reliable compilers, it is not necessary to distinguish between program source code and the compiled program itself (which is what actually creates the user interface and presents the interactive behaviour to the user). We won't emphasise this distinction in what follows.

Many states are closely related, and are considered simple variations of each other. For example, the state of a ticket vending machine strictly is dependent on the length of ticket roll available for printing, but for most purposes the length of tape is immaterial. One might wish to program a ticket machine abstracting away from the symmetries. Indeed, one imagines that many ticket machines have programs in them that do not explicitly mention remaining ticket roll length, and they are therefore much simpler and more likely to be correct — except in the circumstance that the ticket machine has actually run out of paper!

There are, then, large classes of state where if the computer system is transformed from one state to another within the class, its behaviour is practically unchanged. Thus the behaviour of a ticket machine is unchanged as the ticket roll is transformed into a shorter (but still non-empty) roll. Such symmetries are conventionally represented by abstractions in the program specifying the behaviour. For example, the program may have a function that prints tickets; this function will abstract away from many concrete details of printing tickets, and will be "the same" function regardless of the length of paper in the ticket roll. The program code that represents the function is much clearer, and therefore programmed much more reliably, because it does not mention any details whose changes should not affect the meaning of the function (everything else, all the other transformations, the machine is doing).

Conventional programs often go wrong when some of these unmentioned details somehow affect the meaning of an abstraction: in some sense the symmetry is betrayed. Functional programming, further, sets out to *guarantee* a precise correspondence between the abstractions and the symmetries. As there are no hidden state variables in functional programs, a function application has the same result everywhere, dependent only on its actual parameters. (Indeed, functional programming is promoted because, for many applications, it has a better affordance, in our sense, for the task of programming than imperative programming.)

Functional programming, and declarative programming more generally, avoids referential opacity: what expressions mean should not depend on how they are referred to. In other words, a transformation of context in a functional program leaves meaning unchanged: referential transparency is therefore a symmetry. In particular, referential transparency means parts of programs can be designed without regard for how they will be used, since their meaning is independent of their context of use. In imperative programming, in contrast, one often has to worry about concepts such as initialisation and global variables before some piece of code can be used — this makes imperative programming harder and less reliable. On the other hand, it is possible to program imperatively with any "degree" of referential transparency, and therefore the disciplined programmer can choose how to exploit the dependencies and so make the programming task easier in *other* ways.

These ideas of exploiting symmetry in programming are pursued thoroughly in [1], which, however, is concerned more with graphs and proof (i.e., logic programming). One point made is that programming is so flexible that determining simple patterns of symmetry is hard if not non-computable. Affordance, as understood in this paper, is concerned with the relation between program and user interface symmetries, rather than simply the symmetries within a program: therefore affordance is a much easier concept to apply than program symmetry without constraint.

Object oriented programming is a weakening of functional programming and has gained prominence for two main reasons:

First, there are objects in the real world (such as people) and objects can be created in programs whose behaviour, for the purposes of the program, are the same as the behaviour of the physical objects. In other words, as one transforms from the real world to the simulated world, the properties of concern (e.g., the person's salary) are unchanged. The wide range of such symmetries, and the notational support for preserving them, makes object oriented programming convenient for many sorts of programming task.

Secondly, graphical user interfaces draw images of things (also called objects) like windows and icons on computer screens and allow the user to interact with them. Object oriented programming provides a convenient notation where the visible screen objects are also objects within the program world. As one considers the transformation from the perspective of the user (figures on a screen, arrangements of pixels, etc) to the perspective of the programmer, many properties are unchanged — and thus symmetries are involved. Both the user and the programmer may agree on the "position" of a window, and they would agree that similar transformations of the position have the same effect. Furthermore the object oriented programming language provides a notation where the position and transformations of the position can be described without reference to all sorts of detail, such as how to redraw pixels, or how the size of the object affects (in immaterial ways) the positions of parts of the object.

In fact graphical user interfaces "go wrong" when the user thinks there are properties in objects but which the program has not implemented. The user assumes there are symmetries but which, unfortunately, the programmer has failed to provide. Often, an important symmetry the user believes in is that a program's behaviour is unchanged over time. If a window behaves like *this* now, it will — or should -behave like *this* later. A badly implemented object oriented system may have memory leaks or other problems, which are almost certainly never mentioned explicitly in the program because there were *supposed* to be symmetries. The consequence may be that a window can only be moved or resized so many times before the time symmetry fails.

Serious consideration of symmetries in the user interface may well improve programming standards: an example discussed in [14] is a mobile phone. The user might expect a symmetry in the user interface: specifically, the menu navigation system should be unchanged despite transforming the user's position in the menu hierarchy. The mobile phone examined in [14] makes various changes as the menu is navigated: evidently, it was implemented in an *ad hoc* fashion (there is no plausible rationale to explain deliberate variation!), and one has less assurance of its correctness than if user interface symmetries had been exploited by better programming. Furthermore, if this mobile phone's user manual accurately reflected the variations in the user interface, which it doesn't, it would have to be longer. *If affordance is the correspondence between state space and user interface symmetries, then the correspondence can be extended to user manuals and therefore be exploited to make the manuals shorter.*

5   Example: Pushbutton Devices

Interactive pushbutton devices are ubiquitous and one can argue that they are finite state machines [16]. There may be a huge number of states in their implementation (an astronomical number if the device is connected to the internet) but the user's explicit model cannot be so large.[3] The user must rely on symmetries, that certain transformations leave the user's model unchanged. To take a simple example, a digital clock works the same way whatever time it is, though obviously each individual time it can display must represent a different state. The user may rely for some purposes on the distinctions between the various states, but the way in which the clock can be used is *essentially* unchanged as states are transformed into other states in the same class through, in this case, the passage of time. Again, the way a video recorder is used depends only very weakly on the position of the video tape: having successfully done a fast forward so the tape is about midway, the transformation represented by [play] [stop] changes nothing in the way the user interface works that a user will notice.

The physical interface (whether knobs and switches in a strict physical sense, or their visual representation on a screen, as in an aircraft glass cockpit) may present symmetries to the user that the user will assume are implemented by the system.

Let us now consider a concrete example.

---

[3] The user has an implicit model, e.g., at the level of neuronal activity that involves a stochastic state machine with a vast number of states. For practical purposes this implementation model is inaccessible.

5.1   Affordance and Symmetry in a Digital Alarm Clock

A digital alarm clock has a large enough and complex enough state space to make its implementation a not completely trivial exercise. Moreover the user interfaces of real digital clocks come in a bewildering variety, and many are surprisingly difficult to use — so this is not altogether an academic example.

To make our discussion easier to handle, we will skip many interesting issues. For example, the clock should work the same regardless of what colour it is (a symmetry), so we do not need to worry about colour — except that we know that some users are colour blind and that for them colour choices can be crucial.

First consider a single digit display positioned above a press button. We will call this assembly a domino, here shown displaying the digit 8 (imagine it is warmly glowing in red so it can be read in the dark — perhaps the buttons glow too, so they can be found and pressed easily in the dark):

Pressing the button increases the digit by one, taking the display of 0 to 1, or from 1 to 2 ... and so on, and from 9 back to 0. The affordance is expressed in the correspondence between the physical symmetry (a vertical movement translates the position of the button to the position of the display) and the internal state system symmetry which is *also* cyclic.

Now take one domino and copy it right three times to get a row of four dominos. This makes a simple horizontal repeating pattern. In the picture below we have not required the specific state of each domino to be copied, and thus any particular time can be displayed. Of course the set of dominos would be easier to use (if not rather trivial) if they always showed the same number, but we have to make trade-offs if we want to deal with the complexity of the real world — in this case, that time is represented by four digit numbers not always all the same. It is a bit harder to use, but far more useful!

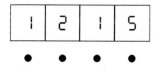

With this four-fold repetition, we can display times easily, for instance using a conventional 24 hour notation. But as the vertical translational symmetry is preserved, buttons still correspond with the digits immediately above them. The affordance of a single domino is retained, and thanks to using the same layout there is symmetry and the "ease of use" property of one domino transfers to any other domino (ignoring the user's cognitive resource limitations: if we had enough dominos, the usability would certainly decrease). We've got a user interface that controls a system that is four times more complex, yet is more-or-less as easy to use.

The statechart [5] representation of the state space, which is drawn below, has a corresponding symmetry. Each name in the statechart is the name of a process that implements the corresponding domino; the dashed vertical line is the statechart notation for allowing the processes to run in parallel. (The dominos can be represented in a statechart explicitly as simple transition diagrams, and they would then reveal their internal cyclic symmetry.)

Tens of hours domino	Hours domino	Tens of minutes domino	Minutes domino

An alarm clock not only displays the time but also has an alarm setting, which is also a time. The alarm setting mechanism is a reflection of the alarm time: the state spaces of the alarm and clock are identical except that the clock has an external "tick." Even the *"time = alarm"* detection is symmetric, and either or both alarm and time mechanisms could ring when the alarm goes off.

If we draw the obvious statechart for the complete alarm clock we would see translational symmetry in the state space (for clarity in the next statechart, below, we have not drawn the subsidiary statecharts for each component of the alarm clock, as they are just copies of the four-component statechart above):

In this statechart, there are two clusters of parallel states, meaning that actions can change the states either side of the dashed line independently. That's what we mean: on the time side, tick actions (caused internally by the clock) and user actions (button presses) change state, and on the alarm side, actions (again, button presses caused by the user) change the time the alarm is set to. Either side can be changed independently by the user, but the time side will continue ticking on its own.

Given the structure of the state space, then, our understanding of affordance therefore suggests the following physical layout for the alarm clock user interface:

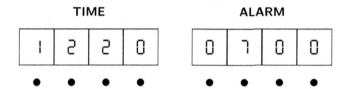

Here, by moving the alarm dominos left, they can be brought into coincidence with the time dominos: so there is a translation symmetry, just as there is in the statechart representation. As before, the physical symmetry is not just in how it looks, but is the same symmetry in how it is used. The time and the alarm buttons *all* look and work the same way. We've got a clock with a vertical symmetry (within dominos), and two sorts of horizontal symmetry (within and between blocks of four dominos).

If the classes of state are as closely symmetric as we say, why not make their representation in the user interface identical? If a manufacturer can halve the size of the gadget, and hence halve the number of buttons and digit displays yet retain functionality, there's going to be a powerful financial incentive to reduce the size of the interface. Yes, we can "fold" the user interface to take advantage of symmetry to make the alarm clock smaller:

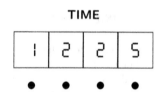

The messy overprinting of the **TIME** and **ALARM** words here shows that we have a broken symmetry. We don't know whether the display of 1225 is referring to the time or the alarm setting. (I think it's the time, as it was drawn five minutes after the last picture!) The appearance of broken symmetry is easy to fix: we put the words next to each other or erase them. We will choose to put them next to each other:

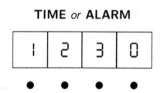

This design is obviously ambiguous, so perhaps we should have an action changing the mode of the alarm clock between showing its time or its alarm settings. (When the clock is in alarm mode, the buttons mean "change the alarm setting" and when the clock is in time mode, the buttons mean "change the time setting.") A single button can do this. To spell it out, in alarm mode, this button means get into time mode, and in time mode it means get into alarm mode. We might think of a layout like the following, which retains the vertical symmetry between a display and its controlling button:

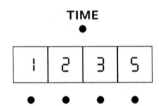

An alternative approach would be to replace the "or" with a physical knob or other control (such as a slider or rocker) to resolve the ambiguity. Here we try a small knob, and where the brightness of (in this case) ALARM has been reduced to confirm the knob is pointing away from it:

TIME ⊜ ALARM

By our definition of affordance, a knob that is intended to be rotated must have rotational symmetry, which is the case here. In general, of course, knobs need not have *visible* rotational symmetry, as is the case in the picture above, although if real knobs were to work mechanically by rotation there must be an internal rotational symmetry (else they would simply not rotate). Users learn when they come across various examples that "knobness" is preserved by rotation even when a knob may have no surface properties of rotational symmetry. One issue in user interface design is providing the contextual cues that, as the case may be, "knobness" applies particularly where no visible affordances are used. (In GUI user interfaces, knobness is problematic since mice, touch sensitive screens or equivalent introduce their own ambiguities when used to rotate controls — rotating a mouse, or rotating a finger pressing on a touch sensitive screen does not transfer rotation to the control.)

Most proprietary digital clocks throw affordance to the wind, and save manufacturing costs by having a minimum number of buttons. If we also abandoned affordance to make the correspondence of the button to the action more complex — so pressing buttons can do more complex things — then we can easily get down to two buttons, and discard the **TIME** and **ALARM** mode indicators:[4]

---

[4] It is theoretically possible to get down to just one button and retain all the required features, but we hope this reduction would make the alarm clock so obviously hard to use even very bad designers would not be so tempted.

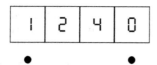

Of course there is a superficial physical symmetry (a mirror symmetry) but it relates to nothing about how to use the gadget, to nothing in the state space. *It is not an affordance.* Probably the buttons will be labeled, but there are so many ways to give them meanings that designers have almost got a free rein. As they can do what they like they do; and then we don't know and can't work out how it works. I guess in this case, it is likely that pressing the right-hand button increases the minute pair of digits, and pressing it for two seconds increases the hour pair of digits, and the button on the left does the same sort of thing for setting the alarm. Pressing both at once sets the alarm or unsets it. And perhaps we'll have a flashing colon in the middle of the four digits so we can tell if the clock is running or whether we are setting the alarm ... That's just one way of doing it! There are so many other ways of designing an alarm clock badly, without regard for affordance, that the user is at a loss to know how to use it. Learning one bad design is of little help for using the next, and users cannot transfer their skills.

5.2   Affordance and Symmetry in an Analogue Alarm Clock

The two digital clock digits on the left must not show a number exceeding 23, and the two on the right must not exceed 59, these being standard constraints on our notation for time. Life would be a lot easier (both for us as designers and for users) if there were 100 hours in a day, and 100 minutes in an hour: this would give us a much tighter symmetry for a digital clock! Unfortunately, our design brief is not to make time-telling *in general* easier to use, but to make clocks easier to use given long-standing cultural conventions that are immutable — we can't turn the clock back. These sorts of design constraints and tradeoffs are routine in any design process: should the designer improve the entire system and its basic assumptions, or should the designer provide the best possible user interface given that some parts of the system and some assumptions, attitudes and values are never going to be changed?

One might continue using symmetry to explore the best way of handling the different modulo arithmetic that is required for each domino. One possibility is to remove both "tens" buttons because the physical presence of these buttons suggests a state space symmetry that is not present, but the "units" buttons do work symmetrically so could be retained.

Alternatively, once might emphasise the cyclic state space symmetry: any setting plus 24 hours is the same time; and any setting plus 60 minutes is the same minute time. This state space symmetry can be carried into a physical rotational symmetry. Because there are several cyclic state space symmetries, the digital alarm clock should have several rotational affordances. Now, the only way several rotation symmetries can be maintained together is if their centres coincide. If further we require that an increase in time is in the same direction (clockwise, to follow convention) as an increase in alarm time, the rotations must be in the same plane. It is but a short step to designing a conventional analogue style clock face. The adjustment knobs could be concentric, perhaps with the alarm setting on the front and the time on the back.

Cyclic symmetry, then, gives us the conventional affordance for clock-based interfaces and avoids many of the potential confusions with a push button interface. A clock with such cyclic symmetry *cannot* be set to an invalid time (such as 26:78 hours) and this is manifestly obvious from its display behaviour. By exploiting affordance we eliminate possible user errors.

6   General Design Heuristics as Symmetries

Many existing design heuristics can be recast as symmetries. Here we give some brief examples; further details of the heuristics can be found in the references.

Modelessness means that the way a system is used does not change over time whatever we do; if I press a button, the system still behaves the same way. So modelessness is a time-translation symmetry: my machine will be the same in the future as it is now.

Almost every interactive system distinguishes between what humans can do and what computers can do. Hand held calculators make a good example [13]: although arithmetic itself makes no distinction, calculators want humans to press buttons to create a problem, then to press = before they give an answer that is only a number. The number a calculator displays is only correct immediately after = is pressed; other transformations (such as pressing +1) change the display so that it no longer shows a correct answer. There is a radical distinction, then, between the input, key pressing, and the display of the answer. Yet, with a different design, there could obviously be a symmetry. Why not ensure the display is correct at all times, so any input (transformation of the user's sum, even if partially completed) leaves the correctness of the display unchanged? How this is possible is fully shown in [12]; the method used brings referential transparency to user interfaces — which is a key symmetry of arithmetic and therefore a very appropriate affordance for calculators.

Equal opportunity [10,11] is the symmetry that input and output to a system are equivalent, and that they have equal status. Since most little gadgets have a few buttons and a very different sort of display (if at all), equal opportunity is a potential symmetry that is hard for the designer to apply, but in computer systems such as word processors it suggests many creative design ideas, including WYSIWYG as a special case.

It is simpler to build systems without equal opportunity, because there is no need to implement the other half of the relation. When equal opportunity is implied in the task domain but is not provided in the user interface, the results can be disastrous.

Systems typically, but restrictively, require the user to behave in particular ways, whereas the user does not distinguish between the different ways. For example, a ticket machine may require the user to choose the destination A before the discount B. To the user the transformation AB to BA leaves the world unchanged, and therefore an impermissive system that requires A first is hard to use for those users who try to do B first. The ticket machine may be designed to force A first, in the hope that the user will complete their task before applying any discount (which would lose the company money). *Permissiveness* [15] generalises these ideas, and also applies them to other non-temporal symmetries.

7   Passwords

Affordance, appropriate correspondences in symmetry makes user interfaces better. Can symmetry make user interfaces harder?

A secure system uses passwords. One password can be transformed into another and the behaviour of the system is almost always unchanged, namely it won't allow the user in unless the password happens to be exactly right. From the designer's point of view, it is very important to create a symmetry with exactly one exception, otherwise the user interface might provide clues (e.g., in the time it takes to process passwords) to a hacker. From the user's point of view there is no such symmetry because entering each password takes (say) ten seconds — and most secure systems significantly increase the time after a few attempts — and no user is prepared to consider transforming one password into another for very long.

For the authorised user their correct password is as good as any other they might have chosen — except in those infuriating systems that do not allow the user to use the password of their choice, because the system makes (no doubt well advised!) distinctions between valid and invalid passwords.

8   Affordance or Partial Affordance?

The opening example of this paper, of a door handle illustrates conventional affordance well, but it is not immediately apparent how, or even whether, this application of affordance relates to symmetry. We have left addressing this issue to last. The bulk of this paper showed that symmetry and some (possibly) restricted meaning of affordance are closely related. This still leaves open many questions. In particular: Aren't the broader ideas in affordance excluded by the symmetry formalism?

A physical object that has affordances has surface features that create (in some sense: physical, perceptual, cultural ...) the affordance. A simple pushbutton that affords being pressed by a finger tip probably has physical features, such as a dimple or dent in its surface (or it has a surface texture or image that suggests it is made out of a material that dents easily, or it is an on-screen picture of a button that creates the same or a similar retinal image as one that really does have the affordance). The surface of the dent matches or otherwise conforms to the surface of a finger tip. Metaphorically, if not quite exactly, the button and the finger reflect each other.

It seems in this way, then, that any affordance can be described as a correspondence with a symmetry. But this is a sort of "hand waving" approach to affordance and symmetry. That's a serious criticism, and one we must deal with.

We are very familiar with physical and mechanical devices, such as pushbuttons and door knobs, so it is quite hard to think of them being really badly designed. Everyone, even the very worst designers, have a good idea of the design requirements and trade-offs: every pushbutton is adequate, or it would not even be recognised as a pushbutton at all — it would be a block or a bump or a mere visual pattern. Egregiously designed pushbuttons would not sell, nobody would want them as pushbuttons. At best, a pushbutton without pushbutton affordance is a broken pushbutton.

Clearly affordance circumscribes an important property of design that pushbuttons (doorknobs, letterboxes and so forth) exemplify, but affordance does not constrain the design of pushbuttons when "common sense" does even better. Put the other way around: the conceptual constraints of symmetry as an interpretation of affordance appear almost completely trivial, and hardly a clarification, when applied to pushbuttons.

The main example of this paper was of the design of a digital clock. Unlike in the design of pushbuttons there are clearly very many ways of getting a digital clock's user interface wrong or inadequate but still more-or-less "clock like." Now symmetry appears, in this more complex design context, as a useful and powerful design constraint. We conclude that symmetry being a weak description of affordance in familiar contexts is not a problem.

It's rather like someone inventing numbers [symmetry] and saying counting is helpful with dealing with apples [design]. Some people might however say they can deal with apples perfectly well already without explicit numbers, because with familiar handfulls of apples explicit counting is unnecessary. This is certainly true of the apple tree in my garden, where "none," "one" and "amazing" are sufficient concepts to cover all eventualities. If we want to run an orchard growing apples, being able to count and understand numbers more generally (addition, percentage markup ...) would be essential to stay in business. Likewise with affordance: if we do trivial design, there is no pressing need to go deeper into the concepts. If we are designing complex devices, however, we need to understand affordance in a way that we can generalise to successfully constrain the design choices open to us. We need concepts that tend to make complex products easier to use.

Just as with counting apples where having "more apples" in itself is not sufficient to mean "more profitable," being "more symmetric" in itself is not sufficient to ensure "easier to use" without further design work, which will no doubt include careful evaluation to confirm whether and to what extent the design process is achieving its goals. But being clearer on the symmetries — just like counting apples — will give us good insights into good design.

9   Conclusions

Conventionally understood, affordance is an appealing design concept but suffers from vagueness, latterly recognised in the debate in the literature. Its combined vagueness and natural appeal has ensured its widespread recognition in the design community.

Symmetry is a familiar concept, with natural appeal, but unlike affordance is readily expressed formally. This paper argued that symmetry provides a very natural way of defining affordance as linking user interface symmetry to state space (implementation) symmetry. Moreover, once this abstract symmetry is recognised, it can be applied potentially in many other areas of interaction — being abstract it is not located in a physical place: relating to the user's conceptual model, to the user documentation, to interactive help, and so on. Of course, symmetries may be made evident in the visual representation of the user interface, or mathematically in the formal specification of the interface (e.g., as represented in statecharts), or in diagrams explaining the interface to users.

Preserving symmetries in the representation of an interactive system generates affordances. Norman [8] would regard real and perceived affordances as distinct; we note, however, that symmetry can apply to visual symmetry or to mechanical symmetry. It is important to emphasise that symmetries *generate* affordances, and thus that there may be affordances other than those generated by obvious symmetries.

Thus this paper proposed a new rigorous basis for affordance, and one that can be used constructively in a precise way in the design process, and obtains various advantages, such as better user manuals and reduced user error. Specifically:

- Something is symmetrical if you can do something to it so it is in some way the same afterwards. Moving something, rotating something or turning it over but leaving it looking the same lead to translational, rotational and mirror symmetries respectively.
- Affordance is a correspondence between symmetries in the user interface and in the state space of the system. If two buttons look the same, the buttons have (visual) translational symmetry; if the buttons control state machines that are the same, the state space has a translational symmetry; if both symmetries apply, then the symmetry in the user interface affords the corresponding symmetry of the state space. The symmetries may be stronger, applying to a row of buttons, perhaps, or applying to many classes of state, and the affordance will be stronger accordingly, provided the correspondence is maintained.
- Once an affordance exists, other structural correspondences follow that may be exploited, for instance in the user manuals and in the program implementing the system.
- The user activity and task allow a designer to select, out of all possible affordances, relevant affordances for a design to represent with appropriate state space and physical symmetries. Choosing a design that represents the

relevant abstract state space symmetries in physical symmetries (whether mechanical — in conventional knobs and switches, or visual figures) therefore creates a user interface that affords the user to infer the task-relevant actions. Affordance constrains the design options and makes both design and use easier.

Once such affordances are determined, in addition to the conventional benefits of affordance in terms of usability, both program and user manual can be simplified and made more reliable. In practice, a key contribution of this new understanding of affordance will be the reduction in user interface implementation bugs; perhaps, too, because affordance and symmetry is about fundamental interaction between users, user interfaces and implementations (a point Gaver *op. cit.* [2]) also alludes to), user interface designers and programmers will be able to work more constructively together. This paper alluded to the deeper symmetries available in programs which are explicitly exploited, for instance, in object oriented programming. A major area for future work will be to develop programming styles or paradigms that increase the correspondences between symmetries visible in source code and in user interface symmetries.

Acknowledgements. Ann Blandford, Paul Cairns, Matt Jones, Jef Raskin and Ian Witten made valuable comments on the ideas expressed here. Harold Thimbleby is a Royal Society-Wolfson Research Merit Award holder, and acknowledges that generous support.

References

1. Carbone, A., Semmes, S.: *A Graphic Apology for Symmetry and Implicitness*, Oxford: Oxford Science Publications, 2000.
2. Gaver, W.: "Technology Affordances," ACM CHI'91 Conference, 79–84, 1991.
3. Gelernter, D.: *The Aesthetics of Computing*, Phoenix, 1998.
4. Gibson, J. J.: *The Ecological Approach to Visual Perception*, Boston: Houghton Mifflin, 1979.
5. Harel, D., Politi, M.: *Modeling Reactive Systems with Statecharts: The Statemate Approach*, McGraw-Hill, 1988.
6. Marr, D.: *Vision*, New York: W. H. Freeman & Company, 1982.
7. Norman, D. A.: *The Psychology of Everyday Things*, New York: Basic Books, 1988.
8. Norman, D. A.: "Affordance, Conventions, and Design," *ACM Interactions*, **VI**(3):38–43, 1999.
9. Petroski, H.: *The Pencil: A History of Design and Circumstance*, New York: Alfred A. Knopf, 1990.
10. Runciman, C., Thimbleby, H.: "Equal Opportunity Interactive Systems," *International Journal of Man-Machine Studies*, **25**(4):439–451, 1986.
11. Thimbleby, H.: *User Interface Design*, Addison-Wesley, 1990,
12. Thimbleby, H.: "A New Calculator and Why it is Necessary," *Computer Journal*, **38**(6):418–433, 1996.
13. Thimbleby, H.: "Calculators are Needlessly Bad," *International Journal of HumanComputer Studies*, **52**(6):1031–1069, 2000.

14. Thimbleby, H.: "Analysis and Simulation of User Interfaces," Human Computer Interaction 2000, BCS Conference on Human-Computer Interaction, edited by McDonald, S, Waern, Y. & Cockton, G., XIV:221–237, 2000.
15. Thimbleby, H.: "Permissive User Interfaces," *International Journal of HumanComputer Studies*, **54**(3):333–350, 2001.
16. Thimbleby, H., Cairns, P., Jones, M.: "Usability Analysis with Markov Models," *ACM Transactions on Computer Human Interaction*, **8**(2):99–132, 2001.
17. Weyl, H.: *Symmetry*, Princeton University Press, 1952.

Author Index

Lecture Notes in Computer Science

For information about Vols. 1–2135
please contact your bookseller or Springer-Verlag